# WILLIAM S. BURROUGHS

## vs.

# THE QUR'AN

Other books by Michael Muhammad Knight

*The Taqwacores*
*Blue-Eyed Devil*
*The Five Percenters*
*Osama Van Halen*
*Impossible Man*
*Journey to the End of Islam*
*Why I Am a Five Percenter*

# WILLIAM S. BURROUGHS  VS. THE QUR'AN

MICHAEL MUHAMMAD KNIGHT

 Soft Skull Press

Library of Congress Cataloging-in-Publication Data is available.

ISBN: 978-1-59376-415-9

Cover design by Matt Dorfman
Interior design by Elyse Strongin, Neuwirth & Associates, Inc.

Printed in the United States of America

Soft Skull Press
New York, NY

www.softskull.com

for sons

"It is an established fact that one of the men of the Path has said: 'Whoever wishes to see three hundred men in one man has only to look at me, for I have followed three hundred teachers and from each of them I have derived a quality.'"
—Ibn 'Arabi

"So, is Mike Knight a follower of Louis Farrakhan?"
—Jello Biafra

# WILLIAM S. BURROUGHS

## vs.

# THE QUR'AN

Book 1

# VISIONS OF THE
# ANTI-CALIPH

# 1.

Anything can be an allegory for the path, even bestiality. Rumi, the greatest poet-saint of the Islamic tradition, the Sufi whose work gets called the "Qur'an in Persian," wrote about a slave girl who fucked a donkey. She placed a gourd on the donkey's penis to keep it from going in all the way. The slave girl's mistress, however, tried to take on the same donkey without using the gourd, and the donkey went balls-deep and killed her. Everyone loves Rumi today, but those parts of the *Mathnawi* get skipped. V:1333–1429, if you want to look it up.

You could interpret the verses as a warning against unrestrained sexual indulgence, but with these Sufi poets there's always a deeper meaning, and Rumi was on some real science. The donkey cock doesn't always have to be a donkey cock.

Sometimes at a reading, I'll pull out Rumi's donkey verses scribbled on a folded-up sheet of notebook paper.

"And now," I say, "a poem."

*Out of joy the woman's vagina became a nightingale restless and enflamed with lust for the donkey. . . . That woman closed the door and dragged in the donkey; happily, of necessity she tasted the punishment. . . . The donkey had become*

*well-trained; it pressed into the mistress up to the testicles, the*
*mistress died immediately. Her liver was torn from the injury*
*of the donkey's penis, the intestines were torn one from the*
*other.*

Assuming the words are mine, everyone gets awful looks on
their faces and they're easy enough to decode. Muslims who
don't like me have all the proof they need: to write such a poem
while claiming the blessed name Muhammad, they're sure, con-
stitutes an act of violence against Islam. Muslims who do like
me are disappointed, and women on both sides (and non-Muslims)
wonder what other porkshit's in my head if I've got creep style
like this. Across the board, the audience has tagged me as an immature scumbag trying to get a reaction.

Then I tell them who wrote it, the great master Jalal ad-Din
Muhammad Rumi, yes, *that* Rumi, and they don't know what
to do. They can't match it to the Rumi who wrote, "I am the
servant of the Qur'an as long as I have life; I am the dust on the
path of Muhammad, the Chosen One," nor can it work with
Rumi as non-Muslims read him, the New Age Rumi who plays
with energy crystals and dream catchers and chills with Buddha.
It certainly doesn't match anyone's idea of Islam, or what Islam
can be, how Muslims can look and sound.

There's always at least one Muslim kid who comes up after
my reading and thanks me for the Rumi, really thanks me like
I had gone to the bottom of the ocean and rescued this treasure
just for her. Not that these kids want to have sex with donkeys
or even write about sex with donkeys. In fact, that's the whole
point: these poor confused ones with their little transgressions
and doubts and strange ideas think that they're such failures
as Muslims and it breaks their hearts, but then immortal Rumi
shows up with farm porn and puts things in perspective. Rumi's
donkey show detonates the chart against which they've meas-
ured themselves. Sometimes it's the only thing that I can offer,
but I do think it helps.

# 2.

The old writer and the young writer, together in a car at night, the old writer going on about his travels. It's not like the 1960s, he mourns for the young writer's sake, no more of his golden day when you could just stumble across the Pakistan–Iran border with long matted hair and strung out on opium, declaring your intention to study Sufism.

The young writer glances over to catch a quick look before they pass the lights and it becomes dark again. The old writer's white beard reaches out in geometric sturdiness, but frays at the end as rebellious hairs escape its authority. The young writer can't remember how he imagined the old writer before meeting him. He expected the long white beard, and probably the red Tunisian skullcap too. Maybe not the knee-high rubber galoshes or the droopy eyes.

"Tell me about Libya," I ask, my eyes on the road.

"What do you want to know about Libya?"

"You went to a conference there in the nineties. You were presenting a paper on what you called the presence of 'neo-Sufism' in Qadhafi's *Green Book*."

"How'd you hear about that?" asks the old writer.

"Someone put your paper online." As soon as I let out the words, I know that it's bad news for him. Peter sighs.

"I wish I could just take a hammer and smash the Internet," he says. But he does tell me about Libya, and then our conversation goes back to the '60s. The emerging postcolonial world was crowded with American hippies blowing their trust funds on mystical quests, and of course he was one of them, but it couldn't be like that today.

We're heading out of the city, following I-87 into New York's vast wilderness called "upstate." It feels like I've rescued him. The old writer insists that his reading was a failure; sandbagged by obscure references and overdeveloped vocabulary, his poems couldn't fly. I try to reassure him: at least the room of white male anarchists and Islamophiles, the usual Peter Lamborn Wilson audience, took interest in his political thought. "What's your take on 9/11?" one had asked. While making it clear that he did not approve of mass murder, Peter called the attack a "brilliant piece of artwork." Another wanted to know what Peter thought of Islam as an alternative to capitalism. Peter snapped back, "What, you think Muslims don't like money?"

Just the two of us in my car, Peter laughs at that dumb whiteman dualism of Spiritual East vs. Material West, though we're both white men who have been guilty of it at some time. "It's a dangerous trip for the seeker," he warns; but he also advises me not to "throw out the Oriental baby with the Orientalist bathwater."

I have to remind myself that I'm not just another Peter Lamborn Wilson groupie. If I ever was, I'd like to think that my position has changed. I'm the one who helps him with his coat and drives him home, the one who gets to see his life outside the city. They all imagine him in a castle fortress like Alamut, but I've seen his home on the edge of a college town, just before the point at which Main Street becomes a dark country road.

He lives in a weathered house, maintained with family money that keeps him "independently poor." We arrive shortly after midnight, just as he's starting to tell me about Libya. The front yard is dead, buried under a permanent blanket of matted leaves. He opens the door and I take in the smells of stale marijuana smoke, stale body odor, stale masturbation, and stale books, crowded shelves of musty manuscripts with yellowing pages. The first thing I see is the flag on his wall, the pre-revolutionary American don't tread on me with the coiling snake. The flag overlooks a religious syncretist's trophy room: paintings of blue-skinned Hindu gods, statues of dog-headed Egyptian gods, Javanese shadow puppets, a leather-bound Qur'an, and a faded photograph of a black man in a turban and sash, his right hand on his heart. Standing up straight, his elbow perpendicular to his torso, his body forms the shape of a seven, but you'd only notice it if you already knew what he's doing and what it means. I'm one of the people who know.

In the kitchen upstairs, Peter opens his oven to warm us. We smoke pot from a corncob pipe, which grants me a lineage, since Peter used to get high with Allen Ginsberg when they both taught at Naropa Institute, a Buddhist college in Colorado. Peter takes off his red cap. Despite the long white ponytail in back, his hair has thinned on top. I ask him about drugs in Muslim countries; he tells me about braving the frozen Afghan steppes in the winter of 1968, riding with a bus of young Americans to Herat, which he was told hosted five hundred Sufi shrines. At a checkpoint they were menaced by a large Afghan officer, who jumped on board and screamed, "ANY YOU GOT HASH-ISH?" The hippies all blurted out their nervous denials until the officer whipped out a brick of hash the size of a loaf of bread: "So, you like to buy?"

Our conversation wanders: Afghan hash becomes a segue into Siberian shamanism, from which Peter manages a jump into the Rg Veda, which then leads to a challenge of Wasson's claim that the sacred Soma was a psychedelic mushroom; Peter's findings lean toward hash. Then we somehow turn to the Amish—"The Amish don't theorize," Peter insists; "they just have a fantastic instinct about what will ruin their lives"—and then the secessionist movement in Vermont. Peter had briefly hung out with the Second Vermont Republic crowd, but could tell that it wasn't going anywhere. "I don't know what anyone can do," he sighs at their lost cause, all the lost causes. With Peter's work and life as a living intersection of marginal Islam and underground American history, we naturally get into the Ben Ishmaels, a semi-mythical, tri-racial, crypto-Islamic tribe of Native Americans, runaway African slaves, and runaway white indentured servants. When it looked like the Ben Ishmaels' native Kentucky was soon to become a slavery state, they fled west of the Mississippi, to lands set aside by Native Americans for the remnants of near-extinguished tribes. They were accepted as a legitimate nation by the Native Americans, settling upon a semi-nomadic rotation between three towns on the Illinois–Indiana border: Mecca, Mahomet, and Morocco. The towns are still there; I had driven the migratory triangle on a fact-finding mission, but came back to Peter empty-handed.

The conversation comes full circle and lands us back at Libya and Qadhafi's Neo-Sufi revolution, which itself had overthrown a Sufi monarch. Peter imagines a politically radical Sufism as resistance against both modern Western globalization and modern Islamic fundamentalism. He's still waiting for his "Islamic Zapatismo" to emerge, but recognizes that any potential for a cool and creative jihad is fucked. When Peter talks politics, I detect the same sentiment from him as when he speaks about his overseas adventures—that his was the last generation with any real chance.

We build for a while on Ibn 'Arabi, the medieval Sufi who proclaimed himself Seal of the Muhammadan Saints, the culmination of Islam. His disciples called him Shaykh al-Akbar, the Greatest Shaykh, and opponents mocked him as Shaykh al-Akfar, the Most Blasphemous Shaykh. He was also known alternately by the honorific Muhyi ud-Din (Animator of Religion) or the pejorative Mahi ud-Din (Abolisher of Religion) or Mumit ud-Din (Destroyer of Religion). Around the time that Ibn 'Arabi made his journey to Mecca, he began to compose erotic poems about his teacher's fourteen-year-old daughter, Nizam. "The smooth surface of her legs is like the Torah in brightness," he wrote, "and I follow it and tread in its footsteps as though I were Moses." When the poems brought Ibn 'Arabi some trouble, he republished them with an added commentary full of disclaimers. Nizam, he explained, was only an allegory for the real beloved, Allah. According to the new commentary, "Arab girl" actually meant "one of the Muhammadan kinds of knowledge," and "virgins" symbolized "Divine sciences embodied in the world of similitude." Lest anyone get the wrong idea, Ibn 'Arabi pleaded, "'full-breasted damsels' and 'shy gazelles' refer to the abstruse sciences of pure unification."

Whatever he intended by writing about Nizam, Ibn 'Arabi's commentary sums up his argument: that Allah lives not only in mosques and sacred books, but in the world itself as a site of Allah's infinite self-disclosures. All things exist only as expressions of Allah's Names—whenever you see compassion or forgiveness or mercy, or power or punishment or lordship, it's only the divine Names revealed through cuddly kittens and poisonous snakes, sweet grandparents and brutal dictators or whatever. The entire universe is nothing but Allah revealing Allah-ness to you over and over. So when Ibn 'Arabi was struck by the beauty of this girl, he understood it as Allah's Beauty shining through her, manifesting the unknowable, unlimited Divine Beauty in a limited form that a human being would comprehend.

Peter makes the guest bed for me downstairs. I curl up under layers of blankets with the space heater up close, and feel the presence of his icons in the darkness—the Anubis, the Krishna, and the turbaned man in the photograph. Peter has supplied the tools to harmonize his idols with my idol-smashing Islam: if Ibn 'Arabi was right and everything is only an *ayat,* a sign of Allah, and you recognize it as such, what's an idol? As Peter explains in one of his books, to love and worship anything other than God is not so much wrong as "impossible."

Wrapped in Peter's blankets and their smell, which must be his smell, I fall asleep to the sounds of his movements upstairs. When the space heater fails, his smell and sounds are my warmth. Yes, I'm a groupie. We entered each other's lives through my fan letter to Autonomedia, the anarchist publisher that put out most of his books. I had wanted to send him my photocopied novel and interview him for an article. The first time that Peter invited me to his house, I hoped that I could impress him by showing up in costume: an old Shriner jacket punked out with spikes and pyramid studs, patches of Islamic calligraphy and Black Power fists, and a Shriner patch reading ISMA'ILIA LEGION OF HONOR—BUFFALO N.Y. with the image of a curved scimitar and crescent, like a character straight from his anarcho-Sufi dreams.

I remember that there had been an old writer in Peter's life. His name was William S. Burroughs, and he was thirty-one years older than Peter. Peter is thirty-two years older than me. Burroughs was obsessed with Hassan-i Sabbah, Old Man of the Mountain, leader of the allegedly drug-crazed medieval Nizari Isma'ili sect that became notorious in the West as the Assassins. Besides the fables of drug use and ritualized murder emanating from their mountain fortress of Alamut, the Assassins were famous for their doctrine of Qiyamat, in which Resurrection had already come and voided religious obligations; so the Assassins could neglect their prayers, eat and have sex during Ramadan, drink wine and smoke up ("Assassin" was derived from *hashishi*, a derogatory term used by the group's opponents). French scholar Henri Corbin would describe Qiyamat's promise as "nothing less than the coming of a pure spiritual Islam, freed from all spirit of legalism and of all enslavement to the law, a personal religion of the Resurrection which is spiritual birth." Burroughs learned about Sabbah from his friend Brion Gysin, who had been reading Corbin. Burroughs placed Corbin's image of Sabbah at the center of his own literary mythology, which Peter absorbed during a short stint at Columbia University. A few years later, Peter found himself in Iran with Corbin, translating classical Persian texts.

After ditching Iran in 1979, Peter lived in the same New York brownstone as Burroughs, and they bonded over their love for the Old Man of the Mountain and, as Peter put it, "other mutual interests." In the acknowledgments for his novel *The Western Lands*, Burroughs thanks Peter for providing material on Sabbah. Burroughs's back-cover blurb for Peter's *Scandal: Essays in Islamic Heresy* calls Sabbah "the only spiritual leader who has anything interesting to say in the Space Age."

Even if *The Western Lands* and *Scandal* were published in the mid-1980s, when I was in elementary school, and Burroughs died before I ever published a word, I get this strange thought that Burroughs's acknowledgments of Peter are also acknowledgments of me. My inheritance from Peter means that I have inherited his Burroughs, whatever he had with Burroughs, and whatever imagined connection they both had to Sabbah.

It's a Muslim thought, since the vocabulary of Islam consumes itself with genealogy. Shi'a Muslims hold a special respect for *sayyed*s, descendents of the Prophet, and the Imamate passed through the bloodline of his house, but our genealogies aren't strictly biological. The commander of the Sunni faithful, *the Khalifah*, was regarded as the Prophet's political successor. Stories of the Prophet's deeds and words must be authenticated with *isnad*s, chains of transmission. To teach what you know, you must have an *ijaza*, permission from a higher authority. A Sufi master demonstrates his or her spiritual legitimacy with a *silsila*, a lineage of teachers usually going all the way back to the Prophet, even if some of the teacher-student initiations took place only in dreams and visions. Ibn 'Arabi was taught by Muhammad centuries after Muhammad's death. The medieval philosopher Shihab ad-Din Yahya Suhrawardi received a vision in which Aristotle confessed to him the greatness of both Plato and martyred saint Mansur al-Hallaj over Aristotle's own heirs, the Peripatetics. Sunni Muslims of the Salafi persuasion strive to follow the example of their Pious Ancestors, believing that Islam has steadily decayed with each generation after them; I'm not a Salafi by any stretch, but I get the idea. Whoever you follow, there's always the question of where your man got what he has, who passed it down to him, who passed it to the one before him, and where that trail begins. Even the fabled Night Journey, in which Muhammad ascends to heaven and leads all of the previous prophets in prayer, is an act of genealogy. Muhammad needed Adam, Noah, Abraham, Moses, and Jesus to sign his permission slip.

Peter signed mine.

I wake up early and lie in bed for a long time, just recognizing the fact of where I am, the Catskills Alamut. And I stare at the ceiling and think of Ali, the Prophet's son-in-law, first Imam of Shi'ism. The Thousand Chapters of Knowledge were transmitted between them through the flow of perspiration, Muhammad's sweat and Ali's sweat mingling together, each chapter leading to a thousand more. There are also stories of Muhammad signing Ali's permission slip by putting his saliva in Ali's mouth. "Question me before you lose me," Ali told the people. "Here is the basket of knowledge! Here is the saliva of the Prophet, which he had me drink drop by drop!" Another narrative has the Prophet spitting into Ali's eyes, which gives Ali the power to see ultimate reality and know his companions' innermost thoughts with a mere glance.

Over green tea and a bagel, Peter asks how my books are selling. "They're doing good," I answer, and I have to thank him again. At the time of our first encounter and the spiked Shriner jacket, I was printing my novel on Xerox machines and handing it out from the trunk of my car; Peter's endorsement led to Autonomedia publishing it and my next book, bar codes and everything. In the second book, my nonfiction travelogue *Blue-Eyed Devil*, Peter appears as a character, my own personal Old Man of the Mountain. The book was hailed by Beat alum Andrei Codrescu as "today's *On the Road*," which is cool because of Codrescu's authority to say something like that.

The green tea's a bad idea because caffeine aggravates my prostate and I have to keep departing from our conversation to piss. Peter's bathroom is pretty grimy. His one towel looks hardened in spots. The bathtub has cobwebs around the faucet. Before I leave, Peter looks over his shelves and pulls out some books, mostly products from his decade in Iran: *Nasir-i Khusraw: Forty Poems from the Divan,* his co-translation with Gholam-Reza Aavani; *Kings of Love,* his study of the Nimatullahi Sufi order; *The Drunken Universe: An Anthology of Persian Sufi Poetry;* and a hardcover edition of the book that nuked my old Sunni life, *Scandal: Essays in Islamic Heresy.* I gladly accept them, shake his hand, trade farewells of *salam*s, and walk out to my car.

Stopped at a red light on the edge of town, I glance over at the pile of Peter's books in my passenger seat, where Peter had been. The cover of *Scandal* uses the same famous painting as the new edition of Edward Said's *Orientalism:* Jean-Léon Gérôme's *Snake Charmer,* in which a huddle of black and brown men sit in a mosque, the walls ornamented with Allah's Name in Arabic calligraphy. The men are enthralled by the naked white boy putting on a show with a long python coiled around his body. I don't know why the boy has to be naked, or pale, or standing on a prayer rug, or possessing such a tight ass. On Said's book cover, the image is an indictment of the colonialist ideologies that gave Gérôme his juice. Not sure what it means on Peter's book cover. Don't throw out the Oriental baby with the Orientalist bathwater, I guess.

Peter had signed this book to Douglas Emory Wilson, his father. Douglas was an editor at Harvard University Press and one of the world's eminent Ralph Waldo Emerson scholars. The signature is dated 1988. Opening *Scandal* to its middle, I put it close to my face and inhale from the crevice between pages, where I again find the trapped stale smell of Peter's house, almost sour.

It is at this moment, sitting at the red light with his book in my hands, that I decide to write a book about him, *the* book about him. Not only to write—writing's just a byproduct of the real work, the spiritual part of it—but to get lost in Peter, spend hundreds of hours at his kitchen table smoking bowls and listening to stories, read every word that he has ever put down, sift through thirty years' worth of academic journals and radical zines and all of his books, and *inherit* him, get the *ijaza* to properly explain his thought to the world. It will be an act of love and religion, ensuring that people finally recognize this man's importance, and also the forging of myself as a link in his chain.

# 3.

Sitting at my desk with open Beat histories everywhere, I start to put together my first chapter on Peter, his pious ancestors:

There is an end-of-the-world feeling in Tangiers.
—William S. Burroughs to Allen Ginsberg

After World War I, Tangiers was made an "international zone," to be shared by France, Spain, Britain, and later Italy. What resulted was a uniquely autonomous city-state, home to colliding cultures, an expatriate art scene, drug smugglers, and spies, that fascinated Burroughs and inspired the "Interzone" of his novel *Naked Lunch*. Burroughs arrived in 1954 and wrote Ginsberg with the good news that marijuana was "absolutely legal, and you can smoke it anywhere." He also found that for a little money, he could get his fill of local adolescents.

Kerouac joined Burroughs in Tangiers in February 1957 to smoke opium and *kief*, hang out in queer bars, and help with the assembly of *Naked Lunch*. Describing the Tangiers scene, Kerouac wrote of an "absolutely cool bunch of hipsters and urchins probably of a new 'beat' east . . . gangs of bluejeaned Arab teenagers playing rock n roll records" who would flee from a stern glare by one of the "Old mournful Holy Men of the Mohammedan world . . . who walked the streets in white robes and long beards."

It was in Tangiers that Burroughs first encountered his longtime collaborator, Brion Gysin, who had arrived with Paul Bowles. Through Bowles, Gysin met an eighteen-year-old aspiring painter and alleged smuggler named Mohamed Hamri, whom Gysin would call his "little back door to Islam." The two shared a room in Bowles's house. Hamri's uncle in Jajouka was the leader of the Master Musicians. Gysin took interest in their Islamicized celebration of the Rites of Pan, which took place after one of the Eid holidays. In the Jajouka version of the rites, Bou Jeloud (Pan) marries "Crazy Aisha" (based on Aisha Qandisha, a jinn girl of Moroccan legend); but since Arab women did not dance in public, the role of Crazy Aisha was played by little boys dressed as girls.

The Master Musicians called Brion "Brahim" and convinced him to open up a café to showcase their music and dancing boys. The establishment, named the 1001 Nights by Gysin, became popular with expatriates until falling victim to evil magic. In one of the ventilators Gysin found a curse made with seven seeds, seven pebbles, seven shards of a mirror, menstrual blood, pubic hair, and other items, wrapped in a note for the Jinn of Smoke imploring that Brion "leave this house as the smoke leaves this fire, never to return." Gysin lost his restaurant within days, though this could perhaps be better explained with the economic effects of the International Zone of Tangiers returning to the newly independent Morocco. Gysin would later return to Tangiers and reopen the restaurant, but it wasn't the same; Burroughs complained to Ginsberg of Gysin's new "sorry" dancing boys, "all with ferret faces and narrow shoulders and bad teeth, looking rather like a bowling team from Newark."

In Paris, Burroughs brought Gysin to a cheap rooming house famously known as the Beat Hotel, where Burroughs finished *Naked Lunch* and Ginsberg wrote "Kaddish." When the American living in Ginsberg's former room refused to let Gysin have it, Gysin put himself in a hashish-induced state and performed magical spells that he had learned in Morocco until the American left.

"Prisoner, Come Out!"
See the Silent Writing of Brion Gysin, Hassan-i Sabbah, across all skies!
          —William S. Burroughs

I am not Hassan-i Sabbah nor was meant to be. And you . . . William?
          —Brion Gysin

Sabbah and his Assassins had teased the Western imagination since Marco Polo. The myth of Sabbah's drug-addled, sword-swinging Isma'ili ninjas would be employed by Harry Anslinger, America's first "drug czar," to build power for the Federal Bureau of Narcotics in the 1930s, '40s, '50s, and early '60s. The Assassins were also mentioned in a CIA manual on assassination, and modern Orientalists such as Bernard Lewis would even attempt to link Sabbah with modern jihadism.

Though giving a cynical response to canonical Islam ("Mohammed? Are you kidding? He was dreamed up by the Mecca Chamber of Commerce"), Burroughs readily bought

into the vision of Alamut as a den of heresy, hedo-
nism, mind control, and mystically motivated violence.
Whether this depiction of Alamut was historically ac-
curate did not seem to matter; Burroughs wrote that
since Sabbah had left behind no books or record of his
teachings, "any thought system that derives from the
Old Man must be made up of suppositions." "Over the
years," writes Beat historian Barry Miles, Burroughs
"evolved an elaborate cosmology around Hassan, which
bore little relationship to actual fact."

Burroughs discovered his revelatory truth of Sabbah
through "cut-up" writing, a Gysin-influenced literary
mysticism in which new meanings were found by the random
cutting and rearranging of texts. According to Gysin,
Sabbah himself had been the victim of a cut-up when
one of his speeches was sliced into pieces and rear-
ranged by a political opponent. The concept spoke to
Burroughs's fascination with the Isma'ilis, who emphasized the Qur'an's inner meaning *(batin)* as opposed to
its outer, literal meaning *(zahir)*. For Burroughs, every
text had its own *batin* that could be revealed with a pair
of scissors. Through one cut-up experiment, Burroughs
arrived at "'Nothing is true—everything is permitted.'
Last words of Hassan Sabbah. The Old Man of the Mountain quoted from *The Master of the Assassins* by Betty
Bouthoul." The phrase "Nothing is true—everything is
permitted" had been a chapter heading in Bouthoul's book.

"Everything is permitted *because* nothing is true,"
he explained to Tennessee Williams. When Williams ques-
tioned Sabbah's amoralism, Burroughs answered, "It's
obvious that what you want to do is, of course, eventually what you *will* do, anyway. Sooner or later."

Appropriate soundtrack for this writing session: Jim Carroll's
"Nothing Is True" on loop, allowing me to trance out on the refrain,

"She said, 'Nothing is true—everything's permitted.'" Burroughs, the real godfather of punk, had successfully smuggled a piece of fringe Islam into the American subconscious—which would also make him the real godfather of *Muslim* punk. Underground producer Bill Laswell had built a whole album around the concept of Sabbah, *Hashisheen: The End of Law*, featuring Burroughs, Patti Smith, and Iggy Pop reading pieces about Sabbah. Peter's on there too, but it's not as fun as Jim Carroll.

My new project will argue that we cannot tell the story of American Islam and its endless variety of strange new mutations without proper reflection on the life and writings of Peter Lamborn Wilson. Peter has cred with the larger tradition, traveling across what we call the Muslim world and building with the greatest Sufi scholars of his generation, but he's also grounded in America, even against his wishes. He grew up on Ralph Waldo Emerson and later discovered the Beats, and he cherry-picked the parts of Islam that would mesh with his American-ness. Peter would have been barking up the wrong tree to search for God and religion in William S. Burroughs, so Burroughs's Sabbah must have given him something else.

Anyway, for as much as Peter's quest might have been about God, it's not such a big leap from Emerson to Ibn 'Arabi, if you look at the various New Thought movements that Emerson and the transcendentalists influenced—which in turn influenced patriarchs of American Islam such as Noble Drew Ali, the black man in the turban from Peter's old framed photograph. Noble Drew Ali's scripture, the *Circle Seven Koran*, was itself a cut-up of a New Thought book, *The Aquarian Gospel of Jesus the Christ*. Noble Drew Ali pasted the word "Allah" into the text in place of "God," and now it reads like Sufism.

But is Peter a Muslim?

I'm not sure that the question even applies to him; when someone at the reading asked, Peter answered only, "I never quit anything." He's Muslim on some level, but he's lots of other things; the best answer might come from that famous Ibn

'Arabi line about his heart being a Ka'ba for Muslims, a church for Christians, an idol for idol-worshipers, and a pasture for gazelles. It explains his guest room, at least.

Even so, there was a time when the old writer—like this young writer thirty years after him—chose Islam as his means of cutting up whiteness and America and the modern world, hoping that he could come up with something better. He started out as one of Norman Mailer's "white negroes," smoking reefer and listening to jazz, which back then was filled with Muslims; Dizzy Gillespie's band alone boasted five converts. In "Fantasy: The Early History of Bop," Jack Kerouac dreamed of Dizzy explaining:

> the importance of becoming Muslims in order to give a solid basis of race to their ceremony . . . When you say "race," bow your head and close your eyes and give them a religion—no Uncle Tom Baptist—make them wearers of skullcaps of respectable minarets in actual New York, picking hashi dates from their teeth. Give them new names with zonga sounds, make it weird!

*Zonga sounds.* The word "zonga" is itself zonga, possibly a meaningless Kerouac scat word, but it could mean more than what it says, I know, and Peter knows. You only know the electricity of zonga sounds and what they can do if you've already gone and *made it weird.* You have to come up with your own zonga and walk the earth wearing it. Peter and I love the feeling so much, we both have multiple zonga names, to switch up whenever one loses its zap.

Young Peter at Columbia wanted zonga sounds, he wanted to make it weird, and he wasn't alone. At his particular moment in the twentieth century, the right ingredients came together in the right ways for a whole mess of white boys to get zonga:

The Sultan grew up in Baltimore. In the 1950s, before he became the Sultan, he was just a white bebop kid hanging out in mosques and going by his convert name, Yahya Sharif. His birth certificate said "Yale Jean Singer." That was before his run-in with a local faction of the Moorish Science Temple of America (MSTA), a politico-religious movement founded in 1920s Chicago by Noble Drew Ali. For his declaration of prophethood and authoring of his own *Circle Seven Koran,* scholars at Cairo's Al-Azhar University issued a fatwa branding Noble Drew Ali a heretic who had transgressed the limits of Islam. By the time the fatwa came out, however, Noble Drew Ali had already died while in the custody of Chicago police. Either way, it does not appear that his followers lost much sleep over the judgments of Egyptian religious scholars.

After Noble Drew Ali's presumed martyrdom, his Moorish Science movement underwent the expected schisms and civil wars as varying parties claimed his authority. The Moors in Baltimore were led by the Dingle El brothers, each of whom made alternating claims to be Noble Drew Ali's reincarnation. The Dingle Els weren't into white people so much, but this Yahya/Yale kid apparently had something special. They allowed him to read their prophet's *Circle Seven Koran,* containing the secret doctrines about God and the Devil being our higher and lower selves and each of us being our own priest, and blessed him with a fez and even another zonga name, J.J. Noble Bey. Most importantly, the Dingle Els gave him an *ijaza* (authorization) to spread Moorish Science among Caucasians. On the mathematically significant date of July 7, 1957 (7/7/57), J.J. Noble Bey and three friends started their own officially sanctioned MSTA branch, the Noble Order of Moorish Sufis. They attracted a handful of white jazzheads, who carried gold membership cards ("Moorish passports") and hailed J.J. Noble Bey as the Sultan.

Peter was among the white hipsters who would find Islam through this strange new portal; unfortunately, he's such a technophobe that when major figures in his life pass away, he doesn't get the news. When the Sultan dies, I'm the one who has to tell him.

"Where'd you hear about it?" Peter asks.

"The Internet," I answer.

Among the Sultan's early disciples was a teen saxophone player, aspiring poet, and opium smoker named Warren Tartaglia. The Sultan keyed Warren into Moorish Science teachings, added some material on Hassan-i Sabbah and the Assassins, and then initiated him with the name Walid al-Taha. In 1962, Warren/Walid moved north to start his first year at New York University, where he introduced Moorish Science to the white jazz-heads, coffee-shop poets, and recreational drug users. He renamed New York State the Orissa Province and declared himself its Moorish governor; his friend Greg Foster became Ghulam El Fatah, Governor of Behar (New Jersey). The two collaborated on prose poems using William S. Burroughs's cut-up method and performed their works on Walid's WBAI radio program.

The Noble Moors became known among the anarchists, Marxists, and syndicalists at NYU and Columbia, and Walid played his alto sax around town, performing with Muslim jazz greats such as Yusef Lateef. Drug connections introduced him to a Columbia classics major named Peter Lamborn Wilson, who accepted initiation into the Noble Order and took Ustad Selim for his name. Peter/ Ustad then joined with four other Noble Moors—Ghulam Fatah El, Sasha Zill El, Mike Majiid Bey, and Stephen Scully, a Columbia psychology dropout who called himself Ali Yazid El—in starting their own extension of the Noble Order, the Moorish Orthodox Church. The group's catechism consisted merely of the Five Pillars of Moorish Science (Love, Truth, Peace, Freedom, and Justice) with an added sixth: Beauty. Through Walid, the church befriended members of the legit Moorish Science Temple in Brooklyn, who provided copies of the *Circle Seven Koran.*

The Moorish Orthodox Church, in Peter's imagination, was only the newest revival of a psychic war dating back to the beginnings of colonial life in North America—a "hidden and secret struggle," he would write decades later, "for the future becoming of the New World." In these tensions, pitting the imperialists, Anglican aristocrats, and Puritans against the Native Americans, African slaves, and "dregs of European society," which included witches, criminals, indentured servants, and the Irish, we all know which side won, but there has always been resistance. The anthology *Gone to Croatan,* MOC member James Koehnline's effort to "recover and untangle the spiritual roots of the Moorish Orthodox Church," recounts acts of spiritual anarchists, mystical extremists, and white people disowning their whiteness in early American history. Peter contributes two articles to the volume. In colonial New England, he writes, some Puritans who were captured by Native Americans refused to be rescued, instead choosing to be adopted into the tribes. Such race traitors were considered to be possessed by demons and often burned at the stake. Understanding the American marriage of race treason to religious heresy—exemplified by figures such as Thomas Morton of Merry Mount, who in 1627 organized the first interracial neo-pagan gathering in North America—the Moorish Orthodox Church would count itself as the tradition's rightful heir. As the great traitors of their own time, these racially heretical and theologically miscegenated white Moors were doing their part to destroy the devil's kingdom through jazz, drugs, and Islam.

# 4.

I followed their path without even knowing it; in the early 1990s, I was a teen extremist with my own zonga name (Mikail Muhammad), powered by late nights taping *Yo! MTV Raps* to rewind and replay Public Enemy telling me, *Farrakhan's a prophet and I think you oughta listen to what he can say to you.* I would utter his name and feel the power. *FARRAKHAN.* Brand Nubian put out "Allah U Akbar" with a video that portrayed them rolling through the white suburbs, faces covered in stockings like they were going to take the devils off the planet. Rakim the god-MC said that he was "in control of many, like Ayatollah Khomeini." In my sophomore year of high school, I drew Khomeini's face on my bedroom wall. I'm afraid of what Peter would say to that, since it was Khomeini who drove him out of Iran.

Brand Nubian, Rakim, and most of my 1980s and '90s hip-hop heroes came out of Five Percenter culture: Big Daddy Kane, Busta Rhymes, Erykah Badu, the Wu-Tang Clan, Nas, King Sun, Poor Righteous Teachers. Back when New York ruled hip-hop, you couldn't hear a song without some veiled Five Percenter reference: "dropping science," "dropping knowledge," "word is bond," "ciphers," and calling things "the bomb" all began as Five Percent lingo. There's such a wealth of vaguely Islamic mystico-political subversion in these songs, it seems like something that

Peter could get into. I've tried, but none of the names or lingo means anything to him, and he despises contemporary music. At least he can give grudging respect for the content if not the form, since historically it's all family: the Five Percenters came out of the Nation of Islam, which appears to have come out of the Moorish Science Temple.

The Five Percenters were born as a third party during the schism between Malcolm X and Elijah Muhammad, when a man named Clarence 13X left the Harlem mosque and gave himself the ultimate zonga name, Allah. Clarence/Allah went among the throwaway kids, teaching the Nation's lessons while he smoked weed, drank wine, did coke, rolled dice, and played numbers— he always used to bet on combinations of three, seven, and nine, because the Nation's lessons said that black people had been waiting 379 years for the white devil's destruction. Islam is mathematics, he said. And Allah told the kids that they were gods too, honoring them with their own zonga names like Black Messiah. This was the same time period of and just ten or so blocks away from Peter's founding of the Moorish Orthodox Church at Columbia. It seems like the two movements should have encountered each other, but Peter hadn't even heard of the Five Percenters until the 1980s.

I don't care much for conferences, since I'm not a scholar or an activist and writing for me is just a matter of spilling guts. Scholars can find value in your work only by relating it to things that have already happened: "Oh, you live your Islam like a heretic? You must be heir to the Qalandars and Hassan-i Sabbah." Activists only read in search of a manifesto, and oppose honest art as much as organized religion does.

But at the 2005 National Conference on Organized Resistance in D.C., there's a panel for scholars and activists, "Islamic Anarchism: Pipedream or Reality," and for some reason they want me on it. The panel is arranged and moderated by a white Muslim convert. The rest of the group consists of some professor, a guy from reformist scholar Farid Esack's clique, a South Asian girl who organized something somewhere, and me. We sit together at a table in front of these anarcho-punk kids who are all sitting on the floor. I have no vocabulary for these things and can't follow what anyone says. When my turn comes, I speak about the Five Percenters as a movement against the use of religion for power and exploitation. It sounds like something that Bakunin readers can get into. Because the Five Percenters at least have a vaguely quasi-Islamic aesthetic, using Allah for their names and wearing a crescent and star, you can manipulate them into an Islamically rooted anarchist critique of religion. That's the best I've got for this mess, because I don't know shit about real anarchism. During the question-and-answer period, a young white woman stands up and warns me about the dangers of a white man appropriating "Five Percenterism," apparently because I am missing some important facet of it.

After the panel, I drive from D.C. to West Virginia, running over her comments in my head and returning to the same question I've been asked enough times by Muslims, non-Muslims: How'd you get into this white-devil trip? Why do you wear that pin with a black man's face and the word ALLAH?

"It's an appropriate response to American history" is the easy answer, but I don't have to go back four hundred years for the proof.

My dad's house sits atop a wooded mountain, just beyond a gas station that sells pickled pig knuckles. It's dark, so I end up passing the mountain a few times before finding his hidden driveway. My car would never make it up this incline, and I leave it by the road. I can barely handle it on foot. Catching my breath at the top, I survey his territory: piles of garbage, trash bags, stacks of firewood, a shed with the Lord's Prayer carved into its door, and a row of buckets along the side to catch the rainwater. Two pickup trucks, one black and one white. Oil drums, piles of metal sheets and pipes and things for salvage. Ancient-looking equipment, the purposes of which I could never guess. A trail of particleboard planks leading to his house.

*You won't like my house,* he told me the first time I saw this place, *and you won't like my lifestyle.*

He seems glad enough to see me. Turns out he has a TV now and we're in the third quarter of the Super Bowl. Apart from the new TV, the house is Unabomber-style, like he has bunkered himself in there for years with all the necessary survival items (I notice his stacks of Campbell's soups and three dozen gallon jugs of water, and I know that he has guns) excluding cleaning supplies. His life and everything in it wears a blanket of dust.

"They have to stop McNabb," he says with a cough. Then he asks me what I'm doing in the area.

"I was in D.C.," I tell him, "talking about the Five Percenters."

"Are they like the One Percenters?" He confuses my black supremacy with his biker-speak. In his younger years, my father used to ride with the Hells Angels. Biker gangs called themselves "One Percenters" as a response to the American Motorcycle Association's claim that 99 percent of all motorcyclists were law-abiding citizens.

"Five Percenters say that eighty-five percent of the people are blind to the truth, because there's a wicked ten percent that conceals the truth from them. That leaves just five percent who really get it."

"Get what?"

"The black man is God."

"That," he says, leaning forward, trying to get professorial on me, "is a cultural lunacy." He says it again. "A *cultural* lunacy. You understand?"

"Yeah."

He turns to his little television filled with black men running and tackling.

"They have black skin because of cannibalism," he adds.

"Really?"

"This is their project, their *ancestral* project. Their ancestral project is the eating of human flesh."

"Really?" All I can ever say to him. If our dialogues are at all compelling, it's not from my contribution.

"Listen to this," he says. "If you have sex with a white woman on a freshly covered grave, her skin will turn black too."

"Okay." I nod my head.

"You are a transformational agent in the life of this girl." Which girl, I don't know—the hypothetical white girl that fucks on graves. "This is your power. You can have sex with her on a freshly covered grave, and there is a change. You understand? You reimagine this girl as a nigger and that becomes her condition."

"Okay," I say again.

"That's what it actually means when they say, 'Once you go black, you never go back.' Got it?" He has this crazy grimace on his old face as though he had been laughing really hard and his face had froze in the middle of it, and he sticks his hand out for me to slap. "Give me some skin!" he says, and I do and then he stands up and says, "It was good seeing you," meaning *Leave.*

That's my dad, the white devil. So my answer is no, White Girl at the Anarchist Conference, I'm pretty sure that I get the point of the Five Percenters.

A few days later I'm in Pittsburgh, which the Five Percenters call Power Born, for their monthly parliament. It's a decent cipher of gods. My Power Born connection, a god named I Majestic Allah, is respected as one of the more prolific teachers in the region and maybe the Five Percent Nation as a whole. The parliament is held at the home of Zyhier, one of the earliest gods to teach in Pittsburgh.

Zyhier's house is decorated with Five Percenter emblems everywhere, framed paintings of the Universal Flag:

The Universal Flag was designed in 1967 by a kid in Brooklyn named Universal Shaamgaudd Allah, who had apparently combined the Nation of Islam's flag with the compass-rose emblem of his gang, the Cross Park Chaplains.

Drawing from the doctrines of the Nation of Islam, Five Percenters believe that white people are the result of experiments in selective breeding led by a rogue scientist, Dr. Yakub. The story goes that Yakub preached among the dissatisfied citizens of an ancient black civilization, convincing them to join him on the Aegean island of Patmos (also called Pelan in the lessons), where he bred all the blackness and righteousness out of them. I can get into this stuff, but Peter prefers the less hostile Noble Drew Ali. William S. Burroughs had no problem with calling the devil on his shit, denouncing the white race as a "perfect curse on the planet . . . conditioned by their cave experience, by their living in caves. And they may actually have contracted some form of virus there, which has made them what they've been, a real menace to life on the planet." The Burroughs novel *Cities of the Red Night,* set one hundred thousand years ago in a fictitious civilization in the Gobi Desert, would imply at least a casual exposure to Yakub mythology: the all-black nation is enslaved after a meteor causes "mutations" resulting in brown, red, and white people. In *Place of Dead Roads,* his description of Alamut—a "mutation center" where "free from harassment, the human artifact can evolve into an organism suited for space conditions and space travel"—reads like a more optimistic version of Yakub's island regime.

Naturally, the gods want to know what brought a devil among them.

"I've been building with Azreal," I tell a young god when he asks.

"That's peace," he says; dropping Azreal's name justifies my presence. Azreal's the Five Percenter equivalent of the Sultan, an exceptional devil who found his way into the secret lessons and became something other than white. Before getting the zonga name, he was John Michael Kennedy. He was just seventeen years old when he met Allah at Matteawan State Hospital for the Criminally Insane.

The god asks how Azreal's doing.

"Last time I was at the Allah School, they said he hadn't been around for a while," I tell him. That's what you always hear when it comes to Azreal, who has been alternating between homelessness and institutionalization since 1965.

"Wait, are you Michael Muhammad Knight?" the god asks.

"I am."

"I hear that you're a Sufi."

"I wouldn't call myself a Sufi, exactly, but I study some things."

"That's peace," he says again. "Now let me ask you this: is it true that somewhere in the Muslim world, they stand in a circle and say that man is God?"

I've observed this kind of discussion among the Five Percenters. It's a paradox at the heart of their tradition. While rejecting identification with "mainstream" Islam, even taking offense if you call them Muslims, some Five Percenters will also insist that their understanding reflects the truest reading of the Qur'an. It makes the culture's exact relationship to Islam that much harder for outsiders to comprehend.

I get it, though. So-called "orthodox" and "mainstream" Muslims will happily shit on Five Percenters all day. It makes no sense for Five Percenters to seek acceptance from communities that will never treat them as anything but a corruption of the Prophet's Islam; Sufism, on the other hand, potentially allows a way around the assholes, a means by which Five Percenters can stake their claim on Islam without having to deal with the guards at the front gate—and a way to have Islam without calling yourself a Muslim. Sufi history tells a few stories of Muslims getting killed by the protectors of institutional Islam for saying Five Percenter-ish things.

"Sufism is full of people finding the Divine in the human form," I tell the god. "There was a tremendously important saint named Ibn 'Arabi who taught that everything in the universe manifests God, with man as the highest and most perfect manifestation." He nods. "Allah creates all things with either one hand or the other, Beauty or Majesty," I add. "Only man is created with both hands."

"But you're still talking about Allah as an abstract thing that creates us," he says.

"It's more like the Black Mind," I answer. "You know, the universe and everything in it emanates from the Black Mind, and the Black Mind manifested itself as man—and Imam Ali said, 'I do not adore a god I cannot see.'" Using Peter's *Scandal: Essays in Islamic Heresy,* I could go further, but it might get awkward with what Peter calls "sacred pedophilia." *Scandal* discusses medieval Persian Sufis who, inspired by Ibn 'Arabi's theophany through his teacher's daughter, would experience God's Beauty through contemplating beautiful young boys. They called it *shahed bazi,* "witness play." As one might expect, orthodox Muslims and most Sufis objected to the practice, on the grounds of both sexual inappropriateness and *shirk,* the sin of worshiping created beings as divine. The real threat posed by sacred pedophilia to orthodox Islam, according to Peter, was merely that "human beings can realize themselves in love more perfectly than in religious practice."

I don't go there. It's easier to skip theology and turn to the issue of religious authority, building on the Nizari Isma'ili fortress at Alamut. Hassan II's declaration of *Qiyamat* meant that all religious laws were canceled, which Peter reads as a call for each Muslim to realize the "Imam of his own being." "It's more or less saying that you're your own god," I tell the god.

He shakes my hand. It's peace, as he says.

The "Imam of one's own being" interpretation is a bit problematic (and the sacred pedophilia stuff isn't Peter's shining moment), but Peter's work at least proves that we can't depict Islam—as both Muslims and non-Muslims like to do—as unified and beyond compromise. Despite what Peter calls the "monochromatic bigotry" of modern interpretations, he writes that Islam remains as "fragmented, divisive, polyvalent, varied, [and] subtle" as any world religion.

I can't overstate what his books did for me; coming off a failed stint as a hardcore Wahhabi teenager, wondering if I could ever squeeze myself into such impossible definitions of Islam, I saw my religion rescued by Peter. Reimagining Islam as a *disorganized* religion, his work gives me a usable history of characters outside the regular structures: figures like Hassan-i Sabbah and Hassan II, Ibn 'Arabi, Lal Shabazz Qalandar ("shaykh of the lawless dervishes"), and Hafez Shirazi, who said to "stain our prayer carpets with wine." Even accepted voices in so-called mainstream Islam were often renegades in their day, only to have the tradition swallow up their dangerous words, like Rumi's verses about a girl copulating with a donkey. In *Sacred Drift: Essays on the Margins of Islam*, Peter describes this outlaw heritage as the Anti-Caliph. The Anti-Caliph comprises not only a precedent for our own creativity and rebellion, he argues, but our crucial genealogy, an authentic Islamic lineage to be invoked for its *baraka* (blessings). We make pilgrimage to their tombs, but also to their books, and possibly to their spirits in dreams. The Five Percenters are my Anti-Caliphs. In a nasty piece published online, "A Refutation of the 5%er Cult in America," Aboo Sumayyah Anwar Dupuis al-Anishnaabiyee charges that record companies are using the Five Percenters to alienate white people from authentic Islam. These corporations fear Islam, he argues, because Islam's *shari'a* law and prohibition of interest banking threaten America's democratic and capitalist foundations. For their assertion that black people are the fathers and mothers of civilization, al-Anishnaabiyee refers to the tradition of the Prophet:

And in a narration collected by Imaam al-Bukhaaree in his book of *adab* (manners), he reported that the Messenger of Allaah said, "Whoever calls to the affairs of the *Jaahiliyyah* (ignorance, tribalism, and racism), tell him to bite on the head of his father's penis and do not sugar coat it" (meaning don't sugar coat the statement). Based upon these proofs and the above statements we would like to advise the followers of the Nation of Islam the 5%ers and all the other racist and ignorant groups to do exactly that.

For Peter, terming a fringe sect "heresy" by no means carries a negative value judgment; heretics and their "fortuitous or even deliberate mistranslations of texts" become an ideal method of "cultural transfer," allowing for communities to more easily share philosophical systems and art forms. Iran, Peter insists, "could not have become Islamic, despite its military conquest by the Arabs, were it not for the heterodoxies of Shi'ism and Sufism, or outright heresies such as Nizari Isma'ilism, Hurufism and the Ghulat." His defense of Iranian Islam changed the way that I looked at our American Islam—our Noble Drew Ali claiming initiations at the Pyramid of Cheops, our Elijah Muhammad raving about spaceships that will first drop leaflets and then bombs, our Clarence 13X renaming himself Allah and shooting dice to reveal the inner mechanics of the universe. It's our own beautiful mistranslation, may our sisters and brothers love us. Thanks to Peter, I can be a Shi'a Five Percenter and whatever else I want, a white black supremacist, sure, and for Peter I can get into all the Azreals and rest on the unknowable border between Muslim and non-Muslim.

Pittsburgh's special in the Five Percent universe, because in walks the elder Abu Shahid, the last of the movement's original gods—he knew Allah back in the '60s, when Allah was just Clarence 13X in Harlem's Mosque No. 7. Back then, Abu Shahid was John 37X. I can't help but pester the god and ask him the same questions that he's been hearing for the last forty years. He answers them patiently and introduces me to his seven-year-old daughter, Princess Jhonazyia Mother Nature Mother Earth, who already knows the lessons. When she recites the earth's distance from the sun, she watches me write it down to make sure I have it right.

The gods assemble in a circle and have parliament, each one taking turns building on how he sees the day's mathematics. I stand outside the cipher and watch, sometimes pulling out my pad to take notes. Even with the precedent of Azreal, I'm not sure of my proper position. According to I Majestic, "colored men" (Caucasians) who study with the gods often fall into one of two categories: either they're suffering from racial guilt and want to repent for their ancestors, or they want to be gods themselves. The exact place that a colored man can find with Five Percenters has not yet been defined. The gods haven't seen enough white converts to make it an urgent issue, but there have been a few. I Majestic had told me about one named Gadreel whose father had actually tried to join the Nation of Islam before him, even writing a letter to Elijah Muhammad, and he knew of one god who had corresponded with a young John Walker Lindh online, years before the kid became famous as the "American Taliban."

After the parliament breaks up, I thank Zyhier for having

me in his home, and I Majestic for opening this particular gate, and Abu Shahid for building on his forty years in the desert. The elder wishes me a safe trip as I head back to my car full of Peter's books and Elijah Muhammad books. First stop at a gas station, I whip out a pad and scribble, merging my flag with the flag of my father:

They look close, but it's ninety-three million miles from a jagged sun to a quarter moon. Just so happens that we're in the first ten days of Muharram, Shi'ism's time of mourning for the Prophet's butchered grandson, Husayn, when people beat themselves with grief, so I drive to a Shi'a mosque in Monroeville with plans to slap a dent in my chest.

# 5.

Next time I'm smoking weed in Peter's kitchen:

"You know what the Five Percenters call pot?" I ask him.

"No, what?"

"They call it 'equality.'"

He does a snort-laugh out of his nose.

"How'd they come up with that?" he asks.

"I'm not sure. There are a few theories."

"It sounds right," he says.

"The Five Percenters in Harlem have parliament on the last Sunday of the month," I tell him, "if you ever want to check it out." But I know that he's not taking any unnecessary trips into town.

"What are their teachings, exactly?"

"The black man is God. They came out of the Nation of Islam, you know, so they're on a little bit of the white-devil thing—"

"How do they respond to you?"

"They've been completely cool," I say, while Peter finishes off the bowl. "They interpret the word 'Allah' as 'Arm Leg Leg Arm Head,' showing God as man. It reminds me of your work on traditional Islamic calligraphy, Muslims writing Allah's Names in such ways that they formed human figures. And the Five Percenters break down 'Islam' as meaning 'I Self Lord And Master,' which resonates with the 'Imam of one's own being' concept that you write about in *Scandal*. When you equate the family of Ali with 'perfect consciousness,' and write on self-perfection as making you a descendent of Ali on some level, it actually creates a shared space between these traditions. I was building on your stuff at the parliament in Power Born."

"Power *what*?"

"Power Born. That's their name for Pittsburgh."

"The Five Percenters also have some numerology, from what I understand."

"They call it Supreme Mathematics and the Supreme Alphabets," I explain. "Each number and letter has its own attribute, and they combine these meanings based on the date or whatever. That's how they came up with 'Power Born' for Pittsburgh. It's a pretty deep system."

"It sounds like the Hurufis," he says. The Hurufis were another fifteenth-century Iranian sect in Peter's deep reserve of sources.

"And Ibn 'Arabi got into numbers and letters too, right?" Sometimes I like to throw Peter softballs. Yes, Ibn 'Arabi got into numbers and letters. When Ibn 'Arabi wrote his commentary on the poems about his teacher's daughter, he explained that "maid of fourteen" expressed the perfection of the soul, because four is "the most perfect number" and 14=4+10 and ten consists of four numbers since 1+2+3+4=10. And then there was his mystical experience in the month of Ramadan, *hijri* year 597 (1201 CE):

I saw myself having carnal union with every single star in the sky, and deriving immense pleasure from it. When I had finished, the letters were presented to me and I had union with all of them individually and collectively.

From Ibn 'Arabi's orgy with the alphabet, our conversation moves to Master Fard Muhammad, the Nation of Islam's missing god-man with no known origin or final fate, perhaps still planning the devil's destruction in a mystical *ghaybat* somewhere. It has been suggested that Fard was a disciple of Noble Drew Ali and went into business for himself after Drew's martyrdom by Chicago cops. There's a text from the Nuwaubians, another sectarian branch from Fard's tree, claiming that Fard was actually from the planet Venus. Peter can get into that for its own value, but suggests that empirical evidence points to Fard as an Isma'ili, which would connect him to Hassan-i Sabbah and thus weave Iran back into the story. For Peter it always goes back to Iran.

Peter has built enough bridges for me within Islam, so here's one that I can build for him. For Peter to smoke with me means that he has smoked with Azreal, who was taught to smoke by none other than the man he called Allah, the former Clarence 13X. Connect the lineages of Peter and Azreal, and you end up with Allen Ginsberg and Allah getting high together, which just sounds awesome. "You could read Azreal as a genuine Sufi saint," I tell Peter.

"How so?"

"Well, within the logic of the Five Percenter culture, you could say that he had a theophanic experience of Allah, and loved that man all his life and became self-annihilated, totally lost to the world, no room in his heart for anything but Allah as he knew him. So he became a holy crazy person for God, a *majnun.*"

It works for Peter. I tell him that Allah regarded Azreal as his adopted son, and the night before the assassination, Azreal played "Color Him Father" for Allah on the jukebox. "Azreal gave me a righteous name," I add. "He named me Azreal Wisdom, which in the Supreme Mathematics means 'Azreal 2.'" Azreal's the kind of *majnun* character that you'd find in Peter's books, but he's *mine,* I'm the one who found him, he goes on *my* pages.

"What are you working on these days?" Peter asks. The answer, of course, is him. I don't know how to say it, and the equality is slowing my brain.

"I've been thinking about a project on you," I blurt out. "A book on your life and work." Then I get scared. In the brief silence after I say it, droopy old Peter suddenly seems huge to me—like he's two feet taller and all muscle and massive hands and so alive, so strong, and I'm a child who just ran his mouth and I'm about to get laughed down.

"You'd primarily be interested in my Islamic thought," he says. "Yeah, I guess so." I forget that Peter's body of work reaches into everything. He's a poet, countercultural critic, neo-Luddite philosopher, drug guru, and perhaps, at least for a time, the world's foremost anarchist thinker. He also wrote a book about pirates that does well. He can build on Žižek with the same level of comfort that he'd have for Ibn 'Arabi. Sometimes I get jealous of his other readerships, fans who might bond with Peter in areas that I'm not even qualified to discuss; but they couldn't get into Persian Sufism or black supremacist Islamic heterodoxies with him, so I suppose we're even. "The Moorish Orthodox Church," I insist, "has never received any academic attention, but it should. It deserves to be considered as an important part of American Islamic history, or the history of 1960s American counterculture, or whiteness studies, religious anarchism, whatever. People should be writing papers about Walid al-Taha."

Peter doesn't believe that anyone would read a book about him or Walid or their sect, but he still humors me, answering my questions and suggesting further reading. It's not long before I have enough on the early years of the Moorish Orthodox Church to start writing:

"Consider Sufism," writes Beat poet Lawrence Ferlinghetti, "especially its tantric ecstasy in which poetry on the tongue leads to the heart and so to the soul." Warren and Peter supplemented Noble Drew Ali's Moorish Science and Hassan-i Sabbah's Isma'ilism with the "Universal Sufism" of Hazrat Inayat Khan, discovered through Khan's popular series of orange-covered books. Aspiring to bring Sufism to the West but acutely aware of anti-Islamic prejudice, Inayat Khan had delivered a more open-ended vision that embraced all religions as

equal expressions of the Divine. Universal Sufism hon-
ored not only prophets, such as Muhammad and Abraham
along with Sufi saints, but also personages from outside the Islamic tradition, such as Zoroaster, Krishna,
Nanak, and Kabir, embraced under Inayat Khan's big tent
of Ten Sufi Thoughts:

1. There is one God, the Eternal, the Only Being.
   None exists save God.
2. There is one Master, the Guiding Spirit of all
   souls Who constantly leads all followers toward
   the Light.
3. There is one Holy Book, the Sacred Manuscript of Nature,
   the only Scripture that can enlighten the reader.
4. There is one Religion, the unswerving progress
   in the right direction toward the Ideal, which
   fulfills the life's purpose of every soul.
5. There is one Law, the Law of Reciprocity, which
   can be observed by a selfless conscience together
   with a sense of awakened justice.
6. There is one human Brotherhood, the Brotherhood
   and Sisterhood which unites the children of earth
   indiscriminately in the Fatherhood of God.
7. There is one Moral Principle, the Love which
   springs forth from a willing heart, surrendered
   in service to God and Humanity, and which blooms
   in deeds of beneficence.
8. There is one Object of Praise, the Beauty which
   uplifts the heart of its worshipper through all
   aspects, from the seen to the unseen.
9. There is one Truth, the true knowledge of our being,
   within and without, which is the essence of Wisdom.
10. There is one Path, the effacement of the limited
    self in the Unlimited which raises the mortal to
    immortality, in which resides all Perfection.

The Moorish Orthodox Church incorporated as its symbol the "Flying Heart" of Inayat Khan's order, the Islamic star and crescent in a heart with outspread wings:

In November 1965, Warren Tartaglia/Walid al-Taha was admitted into Mount Vernon Hospital for treatment of hepatitis. While there he called Stephen Scully/Ali Yazid El with a request for heroin. Scully was later found with a dead Warren on the hospital's third-floor bathroom, a needle hole in Warren's arm, at his side a book of matches, a piece of aluminum foil, a wad of cotton, a hypodermic needle, and a cooker made from a bottle cap and hairpin. He was twenty-one years old. The Moorish Orthodox Church carried on, naming an imaginary temple in Warren's honor, publishing a collection of his poems (*The Hundred Seeds of Beirut: The Neglected Poetic Utterances of Warren Tartaglia/Walid al-Taha*) and continuing to evolve alongside alternative spirituality movements of the 1960s.

The LSD gnosis of rogue Harvard psychologist Timothy Leary awaited them just ninety miles upstate at his new temple, a sixty-three-room Victorian mansion in Millbrook supplied by Billy Hitchcock, an heir to the Mellon fortune who had seen God after taking acid. Leary populated the estate with Nepalese dancers and counterculture figures such as Ken Kesey's Merry Pranksters—who showed up in a bus driven by immortal Beat hero Neal Cassady and lobbed green smoke bombs at the mansion. "On this space colony," Leary later wrote, "we were attempting to create a new paganism and a new dedication to life as art."

In the spirit of the "new paganism," Leary founded the League for Spiritual Discovery. He limited its membership to 360 people but encouraged others to form new sects, even publishing a pamphlet on the subject, "Start Your Own Religion." The "motley crew" of Bill Haines's Sri Ram Ashram claimed the main house's second floor but coexisted with the "mad monk," Art Kleps, self-declared Chief Boo Hoo of the Neo-American Church (which he bragged was the world's first "acid religion"). The Moorish Orthodox Church maintained a presence at the mansion, and Peter Lamborn Wilson/Ustad Selim made frequent visits for acid, at least until round-the-clock police surveillance and legal troubles caused the scene to break down. Billy Hitchcock evicted all the new religions, gave Leary a $14,000 parting check, and retreated to California. Leary headed for Algiers, where Eldridge Cleaver had set up a Black Panther government-in-exile.

"Panthers are the hope of the world," Leary told Allen Ginsberg. He brought with him twenty thousand hits of LSD and a scheme to "turn on" the entire continent of Africa. Cleaver gave Leary asylum until growing tired of his antics, declaring that "his mind has been blown by acid."

Leary's Millbrook experiment died during a time of natural transition for the Moorish Orthodox Church. The movement was no longer a college party scene; members had all either dropped out or graduated, and many left New York. Some journeyed abroad, such as Greg Foster/Ghulam El Fatah, who moved to Greece. Disgusted with the social and political climate, and fearing the draft, Peter left too. "America was finished," he recalls, "and I was planning to exile myself from it permanently. While I was at it, I would go on a mission for the Moors, to send back reports about whether Sufism still existed or not." Shortly after the assassination of Martin Luther King, Jr., he boarded a plane for Lebanon.

# 6.

For a chance to pick his brain and get the next chapter of his story, I agree to serve as Peter's driver and personal assistant for a two-day seminar with the Sufi Order International, in the small town of New Lebanon, near the New York–Vermont border. The order's "Abode" complex stands on the grounds of an old Shaker community. It is generally accepted that the Shakers died out because they were celibate, but Peter offers a thesis that they at least engaged in oral sex.

Sufi Order International is a Hazrat Inayat Khan group. It was Inayat Khan's orange-covered books that provided source material for the Moorish Orthodox Church, and also Peter's inspiration to seek a more traditionally grounded Sufism than what the Moors could offer. Peter tells me that he pursued the Inayat Khan group while in India, but it's a long story that begins after his six-month stint of braving "adventures and diseases" in Kathmandu's monsoon season of 1969. Upon making his way to Delhi, he met a Sufi Hindu named Raihana Tyabji.

"A Sufi *Hindu*?" I ask.

"They're harder to come by now," he replies. "That's the tragedy of the partition: they've taken the Hinduism out of Islam." He tells the story, some of which I already have from his scattered accounts, but he fills in the gaps. I keep my eyes to the road and consider how I'll retell it in the new book:

Though Peter's mission in India had been to study Sufism, he soon became distracted by Tantra, traveling to Bengal and finding Ganesh Baba long before Baba became a famous *High Times* drug guru in the West. Peter remembers Baba as a "fat white-bearded saddhu with overly impeccable Oxford accent" who smoked more ganja than anyone Peter had seen in his life, "chillam after chillam full." Ganesh Baba taught Peter two roles for elevating:

1. Whether cross-legged or sitting in a chair, when smoking one should sit up straight, backbone perfectly aligned.
2. One should dedicate one's smoking to Lord Shiva.

Baba also taught Peter "how to adopt a proper Indian dress as a white guy" and avoid clothing associated with any particular caste. The two of them would then wander the Darjeeling streets, Baba taking part in alley football games with children or threatening clerks with his umbrella. Baba introduced Peter to Sri Kamanaransan Biswas, described by Peter as a "tiny wispy middle-aged Bengali government clerk in a shabby suit" who lived in a "tiny bungalow perched on a steep pine-tree misty hillside." According to Peter, Biswas had belonged to the "Bengali Terrorist Party," whose diverse ranks included devotees of Kali, Islamic anarchists, and extreme leftists. Biswas became Peter's tantric instructor and encouraged him to smoke during lessons, since the cult of Kali considered ganja sacred. Around the time that Peter's border area permit expired, Biswas took him on a jeep

trek through the Himalayas to his ancestral city of
Siliguri and its Kali temple, a "modest half-ruined
little roadside shrine." Amidst chanting and drums in
a graveyard, feeling the effects of alcohol and ganja
while only feet away from a half-burnt corpse, Peter
was initiated into Tara Tantra. The following day,
"feverish and spaced out," he left Siliguri for Assam,
hoping to reach the temple of Shakti's *yoni* in Gauhati
for an annual festival. Assam was forbidden territory,
however, and Peter had no permit. After midnight he
snuck off his train and ran through the mud and darkness to reach the city and find an infested hotel. That
morning, "sick as a dog," he rode a bus up a nearby
mountain to the temple. After making it through the
ritual, he would spend a month in Kathmandu's German
missionary hospital for hepatitis.

Peter practiced meditation techniques he had picked
up from Ganesh Baba and Sri Kamanaransan Biswas while
living in a cave loaned to him and Moorish Orthodox
friend Mahmud/James Irsay by a local yogi, in the hills
of Rishikesh above the east bank of the Ganges. After
running out of ganja, Peter and Mahmud left the cave to
find more. Unfortunately, according to Peter, "Rishikesh
is Vishnu's city, not Shiva's, and Vishnu doesn't much
approve of grass." The owner of a teahouse told them
about a nearby field supposedly overgrown with ganja,
which Peter discovered was actually ropelike ditchweed
("better than nothing"). Peter and Mahmud's "pure yogi
lives" had rendered their bodies especially vulnerable
to the ditchweed's effects, leading them to agree that
there was "no such thing as bad cannabis."

Raihana the Sufi Hindu had told Peter to seek Pir
Vilayat Inayat Khan, son of Hazrat Inayat Khan and head
of Sufi Order International, in the Delhi neighborhood
of Nizamuddin West, home to the tomb of Chisti shaykh

Nizam al-Din Awliya. Peter tracked down Vilayat at the home of Hayat Bouman, an elderly Dutch woman who had been a disciple of Inayat. At their first meeting, Vilayat immediately spotted Peter's Flying Heart pin. After Peter explained the concept of the Moorish Orthodox Church, Vilayat offered his retroactive consent for the group to use the Heart. Vilayat and Peter had tea and then made *ziyarat* to Inayat's tomb, a modest enclosure in a back alley, but found the gate locked by a rival Inayat Khan sect: the Sufi Movement, led by Vilayat's nephew Fazal Inayat Khan, who had sued Vilayat over control of the tomb. It was Fazal's group that printed the orange books.

Despite their growing friendship, Peter and Vilayat mutually agreed that they were not meant to be *murshid* (teacher) and *murid* (student). Vilayat felt that Peter, the former classics major at Columbia, was "too intellectual" for Indian Sufism; Peter needed a philosophized, systematized Sufism, the tradition of *'irfan* (literally "knowledge" but also loosely, perhaps badly, translated as "theosophy") tracing back through Shihab ad-Din Yahya Suhrawardi and Ibn 'Arabi. Vilayat gave Peter the contact information for Sufis in Iran, advised him to seek out a master named Javad Nurbakhsh, and sent him on his way.

The new book, I am certain, will be hailed forever as the essential work on Peter Lamborn Wilson and, most important, the proof that Peter Lamborn Wilson is a figure deserving of an essential work on him. But since I haven't come up with a title, the book still lacks a full self. It has no soul or personality and doesn't seem real yet.

*Anti-Caliph,* by Michael Muhammad Knight.

*Anti-Caliph: The Life and Work of Peter Lamborn Wilson,* by Michael Muhammad Knight.

*Anti-Caliph: The Anarcho-Sufism of Peter Lamborn Wilson,* by Michael Muhammad Knight.

*Anarcho-Sufism: The Life and Work of Peter Lamborn Wilson,* by Michael Muhammad Knight.

*Anti-Caliphs and Anarcho-Sufis: The Political and Religious Worlds of Peter Lamborn Wilson,* by Michael Muhammad Knight.

*Imaginal Islam: Peter Lamborn Wilson, His Life and Thought,* by Michael Muhammad Knight.

*Visions of the Anti-Caliph: Peter Lamborn Wilson and the Margins of Islam,* by Michael Muhammad Knight—which would be cool since it refers to Peter's work and makes a subtle Beat reference.

Or maybe just plain *Peter Lamborn Wilson,* since it will be the first and definitive treatment. *Peter Lamborn Wilson,* by Michael Muhammad Knight. I want to write it all over my notebooks, his name and mine together a thousand times, like the project has married us.

In my book about Peter, which of us would be the main character?

We leave Peter's biography as he glances out the window and remarks that right in Greene County where he lives, one could obtain an acre of land for only $11,000. "I'd like to set up a Moorish Science Ashram," he says. "It could just be a campsite, or an Amish-built barn with a lockbox for camping supplies. My dream would be a log-cabin pyramid. There are ways to do it." He then illustrates with his hands the means of stacking logs into a pyramid.

I ask him about an article our mutual friend wants him to write for a popular anarchist magazine. Peter dismisses the publication as "vaporous diatribe bullshit about how the world will be a better place if there are no more borders."

"A lot of anarchism seems like that," I say. "It just doesn't appear to be very realistic or applicable."

"Well, whether or not you believe you're going to save the

world, you have to act like you believe it or your life will be crap." He then explains the Sufi Order seminar, titled "Green Hermeticism," as approaching ecological activism with magical principles—fighting pollution with spagyrics (plant alchemy). Alchemy has all kinds of meanings and applications, he tells me; the transformation of raw food into cooked is alchemical "if you let the food touch your soul and not just your digestive tract." When Peter was in Iran, an alchemist told him that small quantities of gold could be scraped from the teeth of sheep, so "there's either gold in the grass, or sheep are performing transmutation." There's also evil alchemy, like Hiroshima as a dark transmutation fantasy or 9/11 as a fantasy of flight, and the alchemy of technocracy, which "turns gold into shit."

When we arrive in New Lebanon and pass the Abode's welcome sign with wood-carved Flying Heart, Peter takes off his straw hat and puts on the red Tunisian cap. I unload the car, carrying Peter's duffel bag and large cardboard box full of books to his room in Mughni Hall while he goes for a stroll with Zia Inayat Khan, son of Vilayat, grandson of Inayat, and current head of the order. The Green Hermeticism project was spawned from dialogue between Peter and Zia at a Sacred Theory of the Earth event during the 2003 autumn equinox.

Peter later declines his room, deciding instead on one of the scattered retreat huts up in the wooded hills. I walk behind him, carrying his things. Children from the Sufi Order's Mountain Road School are playing nearby. They're all white. The Order has gradually washed away its connections to brown Islam, even genetically: Inayat married a white woman, and their son Vilayat married a white woman. In Five Percenter language, that would make Zia "quarter original."

I watch as two boys, probably second-graders, venture beyond their allowed perimeter and cross Peter's path. The old man and the children share introductions, and then the teacher calls them back. Peter continues on his way and I follow.

The retreat hut is small but serves its purpose; Peter's only

complaint is that he can still hear the sounds of a nearby highway. "There's no escape," he moans. I take the room that had
been offered to him. Hazrat Inayat Khan stares at me from the
black-and-white framed portrait on the wall. Peter had told me
that when he was walking with Zia, they were speculating that
perhaps Hazrat Inayat Khan had been an influence on Noble
Drew Ali. It was even possible that the two saints had met, Zia
agreed, most likely in New York, before Noble Drew took his
mission to Chicago.

We're at a Sufi order, yes, but I still don't know if Peter is a
Sufi, or if anyone can call *me* Sufi. I'm not even sure of what the
word means or what qualifies one to claim it. Sufism is usually,
and perhaps badly, defined as "Islamic mysticism." I don't know
if that works, because what's mysticism? The label of Sufism
gets tagged onto all kinds of Islamically contextualized acts that
don't generally result in hallucinations: music, poetry, and devotional practices that are done by regular Muslims without
any special "mystical" quality, like repeating Allah's Names. If
you're a Muslim man but you have long hair and own a guitar,
someone will say dumb porkshit like, "He's Muslim, but *cool,*
like a Sufi."  Some would call Peter a Sufi just because he's a drug
guru who writes about Muslim things, and some would call me
a Sufi just for being a white Muslim convert who's doctrinally
and ritually slack.

I've seen scholars define Sufism as an Islamic spiritual life
with the direct guidance of a personal *master,* whether the
master is a living person or appears in dreams and visions, like
past prophets or saints. Peter has written a book about initiatic
dreams in Sufi and Taoist tradition. I once brought it to a saint's
tomb with hopes of falling asleep and getting a visit, but the
shrine's groundskeeper woke me up and said that I was being
inappropriate.

I sit on the bed and open my backpack full of Peter books
to flip through his words, sometimes shooting up a glance at
Inayat Khan's dark eyes. I haven't done a full investigation, but

it seems reasonable to guess that every room at the Abode contains a picture of the man. What does he mean to the people here, the followers of his grandson? In North American Sufism, the lineage might have a special meaning, because we're so far from the root.

But there's more, I know, because I feel traces of something when I look at him. I don't feel what they must feel for this man, but I get it.

> If you find one of noble lineage and high aspiration who directs you on the road of worship and protects you from pitfalls, you have found red sulphur—cling to him.
>
> —Ibn 'Abbad

I love Peter and I love Azreal. Before them I've loved and found Islam in other men, but I've never had a formal master. The idea sketches me out a little. It's scary like romantic love can be, giving your life and heart to someone in a way that seems fundamentally irrational. If the person deserves what you give them, your gift becomes something better. If not, they poison it and you. Azreal gave it to his Allah at Matteawan State Hospital for the Criminally Insane and has loved him faithfully in the forty years since Allah's martyrdom in a project elevator. Contemplating Hazrat Inayat Khan's long-lashed gaze makes me lonely for a master wish that a ghost would snuggle me.

People need this kind of thing, and I don't understand why, even though I need it too. "Our real Spiritual Father," wrote Malik al-Akram, "is Master Fard Muhammad who spiritually impregnated our Spiritual Mother, the Honorable Elijah Muhammad, who gave birth to the Body Christ in the person of the Muslim believers." One Nation of Islam offshoot taught that Elijah Muhammad had been "impregnated" with Master Fard Muhammad's wisdom, and I've heard Five Percenters refer to Elijah's mosque as the "womb" from which their own Father would emerge to make the nineteen (Knowledge Born). Elijah

Muhammad said that Allah and the Apostle were so wrapped up in each other that "when you look at one, you see both," and Allah discloses his Attributes to each person in forms that she will recognize, but Hazrat Inayat Khan's portrait escapes me. In fact, he looks a bit creepy, too explicitly cultic. I like the portrait of the former Clarence 13X at the Allah School in Harlem, and I like the Nation of Islam's portrait of Master Fard Muhammad holding an open Qur'an. In both of those pictures, you can't see their eyes. Allah's eyes are obscured by the shadows, and Fard is looking down at his book. Hazrat Inayat Khan just stares right at the camera, burning through it and into you.

Coming from a Roman Catholic family, I initially saw Islam as above this kind of thing. No popes, no Christ, and, for the

Sunnism of my teen years, no saints. We had Muhammad, but the absence of pictures kept him distant, almost an abstract concept. It makes sense that the Muslims who cry and beat themselves with grief for the Prophet's family are the Shi'as, who have also been friendlier to religious art. They have the emotional intimacy that comes only with seeing a face. If there were portraits of Peter for sale, I might buy one, even if he looks at the camera. Peter's kind of anticharismatic, though, and his sleepy eyes couldn't pull off the hard Inayat Khan stare. Not everyone can. My father used to practice in the mirror, but he called it "Charlie Manson eyes." Growing up on stories of my dad's Manson eyes, I became so fascinated with Charlie that as a teenager, I wrote him a letter and signed it with Dad's last name. Charlie sent it back with his comments.

The Green Hermeticism program spans the entire weekend, and when I grow tired of all their Masonic symbolism and alchemy lessons I hide in Peter's room with his books. At night I return to the main hall for what one of the teachers, an old white man with long silver ponytail and blue denim shirt, calls "Dances of Universal Peace." He explains the background behind a song (always something about Rumi), shows us our positions and movements, and then sings and strums his guitar. Peter sits in a corner, beating a large drum and wearing his red cap, not saying anything, just thumping his hand on the drum like he must have in similar ciphers from Java to Herat to Shiraz.

Picturing Islam as something native to America, I usually see it as black and militant and spawned from the oppressed inner hearts of New York, Philadelphia, Detroit, and Chicago. The Abode's white dervishes twirling around and beating drums provide my first real experience of the other side—which, some would argue, is more naturally *my* side. The Dances of Universal Peace originated with Samuel L. Lewis, aka Sufi Ahmed Murad Chisti (1896–1971). His father, Jacob Lewis, was vice president of the Levi Strauss jean manufacturer; his mother, Harriet Rosenthal, came from the Rothschild banking family.

In 1919 Samuel joined a community of Hazrat Inayat Khan's disciples in Fairfax, California, and a year later dove into Zen Buddhism. Though he took part in the opening of San Francisco's first Zen school, Samuel remained a student of Sufism. In 1967 he suffered a heart attack; while Samuel was recovering in the hospital, Allah spoke to him directly, saying, "I make you spiritual leader of the hippies." Samuel, soon to be known as Sufi Sam, developed the Dances of Universal Peace and taught them to followers until his death. Through Hazrat Inayat Khan, Sufi Sam boasted a legitimate Sufi lineage through the Chisti order, but I can't get into it. I'm a product of the '90s, not the '60s; my protest music was Public Enemy, not Bob Dylan. And the Islam here feels too soft and easy, like someone shoved the religion into a juicer and got rid of all the stuff that required chewing, leaving only water. This kind of liberal Sufism comes from a certain Western history, building on the ways in which anti-Semitic European writers had defined Christianity in opposition to Judaism, constructing a battle between "internal" and "external" forms of religion. Any appearance of love or beauty within the Islamic tradition is thus treated as anti-Islamic: "orthodox" Muslims are dismissed as hard-hearted slaves to law and ritual, but Sufis are imagined as all peaceful, tolerant, and philosophically advanced, the Christs of Islam.

Sometimes I pop in on Peter at his hut. He tells me of debate among the Abode's administrators over the name of its school, the Suluk Academy: *suluk* is an Arabic word meaning "path," and some in the Sufi Order International consider it "too Islamic," preferring a Greek word like *sophia*. We laugh at them together. Though a survivor of 1960s spirituality with an affinity for so-called Goofy Sufis—he's mentioned in an academic article on the New Age–style "Rumi for the American market" of white men like Coleman Barks turning serious Sufism into flake-out pop wisdom from a vaguely mystical "East" somewhere—Peter still isn't completely on the same page as the Abode dervishes. Perhaps it's for his early encounter of Islam through Noble Drew Ali's use of Islam as social resistance, or his more rigorous engagement of Sufism in South Asia and Iran. Three decades ago, after all, the current master's father had told Peter that he was too intellectual for this order. At least he could translate Persian for himself, unlike Barks. Sometimes Peter appears more "Muslim" than the Abode scene, whatever that means, but sometimes less. Growing tired of the Abode's vegetarian meals, he sends me on a mission off the grounds to bring back a ham on rye.

# 7.

At the start of the 1970s, after being "sort of thrown out of India," Peter arrived in Pakistan and bummed with the gutter Sufis. In Lahore, he visited the shrine of Shah Husayn to celebrate his 'urs (death anniversary) among a faithful throng of "intoxicated fakirs and transvestite dancers." Shah Husayn was a Sufi saint of the lawless Qalandars and a notorious boy-lover; he had loved a Hindu boy, no less, and named himself Mahdo Lal after him, and the two were entombed at the same shrine. In Baluchistan, Peter helped to prepare *bhang* (crushed cannabis), taking his turns on the mortar and pestle while others chanted, adding poppy seeds to the paste. Peter theorizes that Sufism of "the wild Qalandari variety" preserved pre-Islamic traditions, "harking back to an Indo-Iranian antiquity or even a common shamanistic culture traceable in the earliest Indian and Iranian scriptures." These traditions were all but stamped out by state-sponsored orthodoxies: first Brahmanism, then Zoroastrianism, then Islam.

From Peshawar, Peter went to Quetta, which he describes as a "cosmopolitan smugglers' paradise." Among the "wild-looking, long-haired types with crossed bandoliers and rifles" he found a "total disregard of all government." People lived in what could be called anarchy, but not the self-centered variant of Western intellectuals; "the unit of freedom," Peter suggests, was not the individual, but "the coherent group— family, clan, tribe," practicing "tribal anarchy." Peter drifted between a *saki-khaneh* (teahouse) where he smoked hash with "ne'er-do-well Brahui 'princes'" and a *teriak-khaneh* (opium den) lorded over by an Uzbek named Khan Baba. The *saki-khaneh* was run by a "witty, disreputable" *sayyed*, an alleged direct descendant of the Prophet Muhammad. Peter remembers the *sayyed* often giving up his seat of honor for a disheveled, drooling madman who would wander in at random times. When Peter asked why this maniac was so respected, the *sayyed* replied that if you upset the Madman of Quetta, he would predict your future. "It was always bad news," Peter recalls, "and it always came true."

It was after months of heavy opium and hash indulgence and a "severe and hallucinatory bout of intestinal malaria" that Peter headed for the Iranian consulate, his brain fried, his hair long and matted, perhaps resembling the Madman of Quetta. In this condition he approached the consul, a "small sour man," and requested a three-month visa. The consul looked Peter up and down and took him for a bum or a maniac.

"Why shouldn't I just issue you a fourteen-day transit visa?" the consul asked.

"Well," Peter answered, "you see, I'm interested in Sufism."

"Sufism? Do you know what is Sufism?"

"I know enough to know that I want to know more. Some Sufis I met in India told me to go to Iran. So—"

"This is fantastic!" exclaimed the consul. Going through his stamps and seals, he offered Peter a full

year in Iran with extensions. "You must remain in my
country until you have learned everything," he said.
"Please, promise me!" Peter stayed at the consulate
for the rest of the afternoon, sipping tea and talking
Sufism. The consul explained that his job was specifically to handle "suspicious-looking cases" or "important travelers"; once revealed to be an aspiring Sufi,
Peter morphed from one into the other.

Following Vilayat Inayat Khan's suggestion, Peter
sought out and found Javad Nurbakhsh, master of a
branch of the Nimatullahi order. Vilayat, regarding
Peter as "too intellectual" for Indian Sufism, had advised him to head for Iran. In Iran, however, Peter
sought extreme sciences—i.e., dervishes who would show
their spiritual power by eating lightbulbs—that had
no place in the Sufism practiced by Nurbakhsh. While
forbidding such things in his own lodge *(khaniqah)*,
Nurbakhsh provided Peter with a connection in Sanan-
daj, an eighty-year-old former soldier near the Qadiri
*khaniqah*.

The old soldier took Peter into his home for tea,
where he proudly displayed a photo of himself as a
young man in military uniform, a gigantic live snake
on his shoulders. "You came to see us eat glass?" he
asked. "Ah, that's nothing. One need not even enter
the trance state for such tricks. I'll show you." He
snapped his fingers, prompting his young grandson to
fetch a lightbulb and bring it into the room on a
silver tray. The old man broke the lightbulb with his
bare fingers, said Allah's Name and then took hand-
fuls of glass into his mouth, chewing and swallowing.
Later that night he brought them to the *khaniqah*, where
dervishes handled scorpions, punctured their cheeks
with skewers, and ate electricity, none of which left
a mark. The old man topped them all when, chanting

himself into an ecstatic state, he ran as fast as he could across the room and leaped headfirst into the wall, only to land on his feet and resume whirling and singing unaffected.

It was there that Peter heard that the Grand Shaykh of the Qadiriyas in Baghdad could decapitate his disciples without killing them, merely reattaching the heads as if nothing had ever happened.

The glass-eaters were entertaining, but Peter remained mindful of his mission to find a master. While considering initiation into Nurbakhsh's Nimatullahis, he encountered followers of a Swiss convert named Frithjof Schuon, who claimed his *silsila* from the Algerian Alawiyya order through another convert, René Guénon. Like Guénon, Schuon held that all religious traditions sprang forth from the same *Sophia perennis*, the "perennial wisdom," thus sharing an essential and transhistorical unity beneath their external forms and cultural contexts; he even claimed to feel Allah's Name vibrating through him as he read the Bhagavad Gita. Guénon, however, remained a firmly committed Alawiyya and accused Schuon of stripping all traces of Islam from his order. In contrast with Guénon's Islamic orthodoxy, Schuon accepted Christian rites such as baptism and confirmation as valid initiations, and was accused of reducing the requirements of *wudhu* (ablution), waiving the pillar of fasting in Ramadan and allegedly allowing disciples to drink beer when in mixed company. Schuon and Guénon parted ways, and Schuon named his new order the Maryamiyya, inspired by a vision in which his statuette of the Virgin Mary came alive. He began to paint depictions of her naked, her genitalia explicitly drawn and her exposed breasts symbolizing "the unveiling of truth in the sense of gnosis."

Schuon's Maryamis won the war against Guénon, cultivating an all-star roster of contemporary thinkers as
disciples, counting Huston Smith, Martin Lings, Titus
Burckhardt, and Henri Corbin, the star French Orientalist who moved to Iran in the 1940s. Between Corbin
and another disciple, Seyyed Hossein Nasr, Schuon's
teachings were finding an audience among Iran's political elites. Nasr maintained close ties to the ruling
Shah, which would manifest in his scholarly work: in
his English translation of Muhammad Husayn Tabataba'i's
*Shi'ite Islam*, Nasr cut out Tabataba'i's entire anti-
monarchy critique. Nasr would eventually be appointed
personal secretary to the Shahbanou (Empress), with
the official title of Head of the Empress's Private
Bureau.

In 1974, the Shahbanou commissioned Nasr to start a
philosophical institute in Tehran, the Anjuman-i Sha-
hanshahi-i Falsafah-i Iran (Imperial Iranian Academy
of Philosophy). The name was Corbin's idea, inspired
by the Imperial Academy in pre-WWI Germany. The school
was endowed with a gorgeous house and two adjacent
buildings on Avenue France, just down the street from
the French embassy, decorated with blue motifs (blue
being the "color of eternity") and furnished with commissioned items from Isfahan. Corbin, who had formally
retired from teaching, would continue to live in Iran,
courtesy of the Academy.

As first president of the institution, Nasr would describe the Academy's mission as a presentation of the
"intellectual treasures . . . in the fields of philosophy, mysticism, and the like" found in both Islamic
and pre-Islamic Persia. He also declared his intention
for "encouraging intellectual confrontation with the
modern world" and "discussing from the point of view
of tradition various problems facing modern man." Nasr

would boast that during its short life, the Imperial
Iranian Academy of Philosophy published "some fifty important titles"; the opening pages of these books bore
the inscription UNDER THE ROYAL PATRONAGE OF HER IMPERIAL
MAJESTY FARAH PAHLAVI THE SHAHBANOU OF IRAN. The Academy's
catalog included Nasr's own works, such as *Sadr al-Din
Shirazi and His Transcendent Theosophy*, and his edited
volume *Isma'ili Contributions to Islamic Culture*. The
Academy also published *Toward a Philosophy of Zen Buddhism* by Toshihiko Izutsu, who had produced the first
translation of the Qur'an into Japanese.

Peter, who would be described by Nasr as a "gifted
American poet," first encountered the Academy while
working as a journalist at the *Tehran Journal*. Nasr
offered him a position as director of English-lan-
guage publications and editor of the Academy's journal, *Sophia Perennis*. Peter had some reservations, as
accepting the offer would more or less mean a full
immersion into the Maryamiyya scene. A Sufi Muslim who
accepted Hindu initiations, Peter was fine with the
concept of a "perennial wisdom" uniting all religions,
but the Maryamis still retained their own sense of
proper orthodoxy. After several years collecting religious affiliations like baseball cards, joining the
Maryamiyya required dropping everything else. But he
did, for the better part of the 1970s.

As the sect came to revolve less around Mary than Schuon's
own charisma, legends circulated of elephants and lions
recognizing his holy station and enemies freezing as if turned
to stone. Schuon played it up, claiming to be the spiritual
pole of the age, a living manifestation of the *Sophia perennis*,
sometimes a returned prophet Elijah or the goddess Kali. In
1980, Schuon would establish a community in Bloomington,
Indiana, where he'd take to wearing feather headdresses and

Viking helmets, painting graphic depictions of himself and the shaved Virgin Mary, and treating women as, in his own words, "a throne made of human substance." It was reported that Schuon, unable in his old age to obtain an erection, became preoccupied with ritually rubbing himself against half-naked women at "primordial gatherings." Three Maryamiyya girls, ages thirteen to fifteen, would charge him with molestation in 1991, but the case against the "summit of the human species" was eventually dropped.

It's a reminder that even cool Sufism can have ugly consequences. Frithjof Schuon strikes me as the Sufi equivalent of Anakin Skywalker: he showed exceptional gifts early on, advanced too soon, rebelled against his teacher, and finally turned into a dark-sided megalomaniac. Or he took the path of the mad scientist Yakub, who discovered that one piece of steel had the magnetic power to attract others—and with this knowledge set out to employ his own *magnetic* for some sinister world-conquering shit. Both Frithjof Schuon and Elijah Muhammad, who had impregnated several of his teen secretaries and rationalized it with scripture, accidentally made parables of their lives, demonstrating the danger of believing your own hype.

Given the anarcho-Sufi sensibilities of the Moorish Orthodox Church, I have to wonder about Peter's choice to align with the monarcho-Sufism of the Maryamis.

"Why'd you go with Nasr over Nurbakhsh?" I ask while Peter's eating his ham on rye.

"Nasr taught a more pure Sufism."

I sit with those words, *"pure Sufism"*; at this point, I have no idea what they mean.

The Pahlavi dynasty, a line that would span two monarchs and rule Iran from 1925 to 1979, faced the task of reconstructing Iran's sense of itself in the modern age of secular nation-states. As contemporary Western theories of "race" entered into Iran's public discourse, the

government crafted a myth of "Iranians" as a racially
and linguistically unified people; the myth helped in
the building of a national identity independent of the
throne's most threatening opposition, clerical Shi'ism.
Emphasis on Iran as a racial-spiritual reality over and
above its connection to Islam went so far that Islam's
*hijri* calendar would ultimately be replaced with one
starting at the 559 BC crowning of Cyrus.

As this racial mythmaking first took shape in the
1930s, it happened to lean on an Aryanist ideology that
linked Iran to its most significant economic partner:
Germany. The monarchy made an aesthetic embrace of
the swastika and sponsored Nazi lecturers to educate
its people on matters of race, while promoting "Iran"
(a cognate of "Aryan") over "Persia" as the country's
proper name. In 1936, as high-class Iranians came to
believe in their own Aryan supremacy, and Adolf Hitler
himself was praised in Iranian journals as "one of the
greatest men in the world," Germany's Reich cabinet
found Iranians to be "pure-blooded Aryans" and thus
exempt from the Nuremberg racial laws.

Iran's Aryanism persisted even after the 1941 abdica-
tion (under Allied pressure) of Reza Shah to his son,
Mohammad Reza Shah Pahlavi, and the later fall of Nazi
Germany. Henri Corbin, who arrived in Iran in 1945, found
resonance between the royal racialism and his own thought.
Corbin integrated the Shah's self-image as Aryamehr
("Light of the Aryans") into the "Prusso-Persian" spiri-
tual synthesis (described by scholar Steven Wasserstrom
as an "unreconstructed Aryan triumphalism") that drove
his work. As Corbin imagined it, the "great drama of the
Aryan nation" unfolded on a north-south axis, connecting
the heritage of Iran to that of Germany and hailing the
Shah and Zarathustra ("Prophet of the Aryans") alongside
Hegel, Schelling, Boehme, Wagner, and Swedenborg.

Corbin's work was sponsored by the Bollingen Foundation of Paul Mellon, whose vast oil interests in the
country were facilitated by the Shah. In turn, Corbin
crafted an image of the Shah as a living embodiment
of the *sophia perennis*. In Corbin's view, the Shah
achieved nothing less than the ultimate fulfillment of
Iran's spiritual evolution, a process spanning thousands of years from Zoroaster to gnostic prophet Mani
to medieval Islamic philosophers Shihab ad-Din Yahya
Suhrawardi and Mulla Sadra. Iranian spirituality was
shown to transcend Islam, while fully realizing itself
in the throne.

Corbin's most significant ideological support for
the Shah came in his work to depoliticize Islam.
Corbin located the essence of not only Sufism but
Shi'ism beyond time and space and thus outside of
human history, far removed from petty concerns of
social equality or economic justice. Worldly matters would only distract the seeker from Islamic eso-
tericism's most crucial project, the journey of the
self to God. Therefore, writes scholar Matthijs van
den Bos, "one would search in vain for statements by
Corbin on the *coup d'état* in Iran in 1953 or the student revolt in Paris in 1969, both of which influenced
Iranian Shi'ism."

Nasr and Corbin were just bloodsucking, slavemaking Ten
Percenters, court philosophers hired to do a job. If your intention
is to write a sympathetic—dare I say glowing—biography of your
anarcho-Sufi hero, his affiliation with a politically ambitious
mystico-fascist cult presents a real problem.

It's possible that I can get around Peter's time in Iran. He
bet on the wrong horse with Nasr, Corbin, and their Shah, but
people go through things and they change. I've been through
things too.

During our ride back to his house, I try to get some more out of him. He gives short answers, but I do my homework. A few weeks after our visit to the Sufi Order International, I search eBay and blow my last $200 on a complete 1975–1978 set of the Academy's Peter-edited journal, *Sophia Perennis*. The full run consists of seven biannual issues, spring and autumn. With Khomeini knocking on the Shah's door, the journal closed before completing its autumn 1978 issue.

The set includes a special supplement, a September 1975 report on the "Philosophy, Science, and Religion, East and West" conference in Mashhad that was visited by the Shahbanou. In the photos I see William Chittick, now the untouchable king of Ibn 'Arabi scholarship, bowing as he takes the Shahbanou's hand, with Nasr looking on. There's also a big group picture with Nasr seated in the center, smug as always, and on his right are two crusty old white men, one of whom might be Corbin. There's a row of guys in front of Nasr, sitting on the floor, and on the far end I see Peter. It's him, I know that it's him, but he's so insanely young—thirty years old in 1975, my age as I'm holding the book. His goatee and full head of hair are dark, and I wonder if they put him off to the side because he's not wearing a tie or even a proper shirt. He's slouching and smirking and looks like a stoner who just fell out of his dorm bed to make a noon class, but he's also happy, not tired like the only Peter I've known, the bitter Peter who pines for an Iran that no longer exists. I wonder how 1975 Peter sees himself, or how Peter at the Imperial Iranian Academy of Philosophy sees the 1965 Peter, the Columbia University radical getting all the campus Marxists and anarchists into Moorish Science—what does he say to that kid, or even the poppy-head who staggered into Iran just a few years before? By 1975, Peter has put in the work and matured into a serious scholar, at home with the Corbins and Chitticks even if he doesn't dress the part; 1975 Peter is living the dream, and he can't see the Ayatollah coming.

In 1975, Peter served as a consultant in both London and Tehran for the World of Islam Festival, which would be called "one of the most successful public relations exercises for Islam ever held in the West," even courting involvement from the Queen of England. For Peter, it was "an event of major significance for the whole history of the West's meeting with the East." In a review of the festival for *Sophia Perennis,* Peter writes that while acknowledging the "transcendent unity of religions," Islam stands alone in having produced "not only the most penetrating critique of our modernised-secularised-industrialized paradigm of reality, but also the most comprehensive outline of a possible plan of action in response to it." He finds this best expressed in Nasr's *Islam and the Plight of Modern Man,* which he praises for shaping his own argument, but affirms that the true heart of the festival would be found in Schuon's *Islam and the Perennial Philosophy.*

Peter returned to Shiraz for the Festival of Arts, a government-sponsored event and brainchild of the Shahbanou. According to Peter, she wept during performances of the previously banned *ta'zieh,* Shi'a passion-play reenactment of the martyrdom of the Prophet's grandson Husayn. The festival was widely boycotted to call attention to the torture of political prisoners by SAVAK, the Shah's secret police, and numerous artists who participated used their performances to voice dissent against the regime. They failed to move Peter, who wrote in the government's *Festival of Arts Bulletin* that an anti-Shah piece only rehashed "the same old problems: ugliness, insanity, loss of centre." Defending his royal sponsors, Peter dismissed art as a means of political resistance, lamenting that "the avantgarde never offers any beauty, any peace of mind."

During Peter's second year at the Academy, the Shah

abolished all political parties other than his own Rastakhiz (Resurrection) Party, which required membership from every Iranian citizen. While Peter worked on translations of classical Persian poetry, SAVAK pumped hot water into the anuses of political prisoners, and the Shah's soldiers shot at protesters from helicopters.

In 1978, its final year, the Academy published *Kings of Love,* Peter's history of the Nimatullahi Sufi order, coauthored with scholar (and Nimatullahi dervish) Nasrollah Pourjavady. It also includes a preface by Nasr. In their treatment of contemporary Iran, the authors praise the Shah for his tolerant attitude toward Sufism. Despite his policies of Westernization and the marginalization of Shi'a clerics, *Kings of Love* positions the Shah as a defender of Islamic tradition through contrast with the ultra-modernist Atatürk's persecution of Sufis in Turkey.

"The enemies of Sufism are no longer the exoteric mullahs," *Kings of Love* argues, "but rather the intangible though very real forces of secularization and modernization which threaten tradition, *the* Tradition, everywhere in the world." Sufism, as opposed to the form of Islam espoused by "Doctors of the Law," will therefore provide Islam's greatest response to the problems of modernism; Sufis are "the guardians of the heart of Islam, just as the saints in any religion contain the essence of that religion." Ironically, while this universalizing within "*the* Tradition" sabotages religious exclusivism, it feeds into nationalist chauvinism; Iranian Sufism is relocated as just one expression of Persia's timeless and immeasurable contribution to the *Sophia perennis.* An elitist philosophers' Sufism becomes the state-sponsored Islam, while the dissent of Muslims—as members of a distinct religious body with its own social and political concerns—is silenced.

Ayatollah Khomeini himself had been a Sufi; using the pen name "the Indian," he composed poems that bore the undeniable influence of Ibn 'Arabi, and he even taught private lessons in the mystical science of *'irfan*. Nevertheless, when the throne was toppled in Janauary 1979, Khomeini's assumption of power left the fate of Sufi orders uncertain. Javad Nurbakhsh, when invited to pledge his (and his order's) allegiance to Khomeini, chose instead to flee Iran. It was reported that following the Revolution, twenty-five of Iran's Nimatullahi lodges were closed.

When the Shah fell, Peter was vacationing in Spain. While he waited for news three thousand miles away, his world in Tehran disintegrated. Just a few months earlier, Corbin had died in his hometown of Paris. Nasr was already overseas and not coming back. Most of Peter's remaining colleagues either left the country or joined institutions of the new regime, such as the Shura-ye ali-ye Enqalab-e Farhangi (Council for the Cultural Revolution), an Islamist thought-police for Iran's universities. As with the Shah's secret police, the Imperial Iranian Academy of Philosophy would inevitably be taken over and assigned a new name and mission. With nothing left for Peter in Iran, he returned to the United States for the first time in a decade.

"Clearly in retrospect," he once told an interviewer, "the Shah was a violent son of a bitch who probably didn't deserve to survive. But I would make an exception for Mrs. Shah. She's a very sweet lady and I owe her a lot of fun in my life, so it would be churlish to make any remarks about her."

# 8.

There's not a whole lot of self-disclosure in Peter's work, even when he's telling travel stories, and I've found no meaningful reflection on his experience at the Imperial Academy. Even when I'm crashing at his house, it doesn't feel like his universe really allows visitors. He's a competent writer, so why am I the one putting together his life? Reading him while also knowing him makes his pages feel like veils.

I drive him to the Abode again for another Green Hermeticism weekend. On the way to New Lebanon, it gets crazy hot, but Peter refuses to roll down his window, even though my AC's busted. I try to sneak mine open a crack, but Peter always notices and asks me to roll it up. I've heard somewhere that it's a quirk going back to his Iran years, as Iranians supposedly believe that the wind from car windows would make you sick.

During one of the Abode's communal dinners, a middle-aged white dervish in T-shirt and blue jeans and dumb fisherman's hat takes a seat next to me, asking me where I'm from and how I found my way here.

"I'm Peter's assistant," I tell him, my eyes gesturing toward Peter at the other end of the room.

"Peter's great," he says with a huge smile, like he's about to tell a joke and can't wait to get it out.

"Yeah, he is."

"He's much more preferable than Hakim Bey."

"I'd bet."

"Oh yeah." He wipes his hands and then pivots to face me better. "You know, Hakim Bey came around here a while ago with a bunch of militant young guys."

"How'd that go?"

"They had a different energy than what most of us are used to— you know what I mean?" He looks me in the eyes and we share a terse moment, as though he's waiting for me to get the joke.

Hakim Bey had come onto the anarchist scene like a Master Fard Muhammad, with no traces anywhere on the grid and no real backstory, no known whereabouts, everyone guessing about him. In a piece for the *Village Voice Literary Supplement,* Erik Davis refers to Bey as Peter's "intimate colleague" who had "served as the court poet in a small sultanate in western Pakistan until an anarchist bombing incident forced him to flee to the U.S." Internet newsgroups spread rumors of Hakim Bey's pledging allegiance to a "semi-religious, semi-ethnic, semi-nationalist, semi-militia-type movement," getting arrested for child pornography, or committing ritual suicide. Fans debated his ethnic background, with theories pinning him as Turkish, Arab, Persian, South Asian, a white convert to Islam, or African American (there *is* a black Hakim Bey who's well known among the Moorish Science crowd in Brooklyn, and people often speak of the "black Hakim Bey" and "white Hakim Bey" as though they're oppositional twins in some cosmic dualism). When a Hakim Bey reading was released on VHS, the producers used psychedelic effects to distort his image.

Hakim Bey's politico-spiritual platform consists of a "revolutionary and esoteric Islam" in which the Prophet Muhammad's quote "I come for the black and red" refers to the colors of anarcho-syndicalism. While Peter assures his audience that Muslims like money, Hakim Bey insists that "Islam possesses a far deeper and more sophisticated critique of 'the modern world' than that proposed by the 'Islamists.'" Like Peter's Anti-Caliph, Bey digs up his own lineage, starting with the Prophet himself ("professional revolutionary, guerilla leader, returned from exile to establish an egalitarian iconoclastic mystical/militant regime in Mecca") and including figures such as "anti-colonialist Sufi" Emir Abdel Kader; the Chechen Naqshbandi who fought Russian imperialism; and Ali Shariati, the Iranian dissident. Shariati had been inspired to construct a revolutionary Shi'ism by his teacher, Louis Massignon (who, interestingly, also happened to be Corbin's teacher). Shariati's reading of Shi'ism as an urgent call for justice reveals a potential divide between Hakim Bey and Peter. Bey exalts Shariati's "Shi'ite socialism," in which the Prophet's family is reimagined as a clan of class-war heroes who fought for the oppressed proletariat; but while Shariati was imprisoned in Tehran and protests by Shariati's supporters resulted in bloodbaths with the police, Peter hung out with Corbin and the Shah.

Hakim Bey became famous in 1980s zine culture for his cryptic documents drafted on a manual typewriter and ornamented with various random images and Sufi calligraphy, printed on color paper with a Gestetner stencil duplicator and sent through the mail as psychedelic *fatwas*. "They smelt of fresh ink," remembers one recipient, "over which cannabis smoke had wafted. . . . They reminded me of a dodgy schoolteacher's handouts, which of course is a comparison that would have appealed to him."

Bey describes his missives as "Communiques of the Association for Ontological Anarchism (AOA)," the AOA being an imaginary group that assembled in "black turbans and shimmering robes, sprawled on Shirazi carpets sipping bitter coffee, smoking long chibouk and sibsi." Ontological Anarchism reads less as a political movement than as an "understanding of reality, ontology, the nature of being." Its model is the Assassins' compound at Alamut, where disciples climbed rock-cut steps to the fort and learned that "the Day of Resurrection [had] already come and gone." With all chains of law broken, Ontological Anarchism proclaims that nothing is true, everything permitted. Along with concepts like "art sabotage" and a masturbating-boy motif, Bey's use of Sabbah puts Burroughs in action. Hakim Bey himself seems like a character that Burroughs would have created, a thought of Burroughs's made flesh and now writing his own books.

Ontological Anarchism seeks to restore art in America to its former outlaw status. Bey muses that "in the East, poets are sometimes thrown in prison—a sort of compliment, since it suggests the author has done something at least as real as theft or rape or revolution." In the West, however, poets have free rein to write and publish whatever they want—"a sort of punishment in effect." Robbed of its power to threaten and scare, poetry lies dead and useless: "America has freedom of speech because all words are considered equally vapid." According to Bey, "if rulers refuse to consider poems as crimes, then someone must commit crimes that serve the function of poetry, or texts that possess the resonance of terrorism." Poetry's role as a radical opponent of "deadly and suffocating" ideas is now claimed by pornography, which is still banned in many places and continues to affect its readers physically and measurably, even changing lives. With words dead, only images matter, and porn—especially the most illegal and condemned varieties—rules over all: "the censors love snaps of death & mutilation but recoil in horror at the sight of a child masturbating." In the image of a child masturbating, Bey claims, one finds "the image . . . of the crumbling of the State."

In 1985 the Communiques were collected and published in book form as *Chaos: The Broadsheets of Ontological Anarchism.* Allen Ginsberg hailed *Chaos* as "exquisite porn." The *New York Native* raved, "It's like sending away Kix boxtops and getting back real bazookas by mistake. It's the long-lost chapter of Genesis." Bey's "about the author" bio provided only enough information to hype up the myth:

Hakim Bey lives in a seedy Chinese hotel where the proprietor nods out over newspaper & scratchy broadcasts of Peking Opera. The ceiling fan turns like a sluggish dervish—sweat falls on the page—the poet's kaftan is rusty, his ovals spill ash on the rug—his monologues seem disjointed & slightly sinister— outside shuttered windows the barrio fades into palmtrees, the naive blue ocean, the philosophy of tropicalismo.

Along a highway somewhere east of Baltimore you pass an Airstream trailer with a big sign on the lawn SPIRITUAL READ- INGS & the image of a crude black hand on a red background. Inside you notice a display of dream-books, numbers-books, pamphlets on HooDoo and Santeria, dusty old nudist maga- zines, a pile of *Boy's Life*, treatises on fighting-cocks . . . & this book, *Chaos*. Like words spoken in a dream, portentous, eva- nescent, changing into perfumes, birds, colors, forgotten music.

In 1991, as cultural critics and political theorists were hailing Hakim Bey as an "urban prophet" and shaman of the coming millenium, he released what would become his defining work, *T.A.Z.: The Temporary Autonomous Zone.* Bey's concept of the Temporary Autonomous Zone reads as an attempt to mani- fest anarchist principles after admitting that serious anarchism has no chance: the State's not going anywhere, so we should cultivate and celebrate freedom in fleeting moments whenever we can find it. "To say that 'I will not be free till all humans (or all sentient creatures) are free,'" he writes, "is simply to cave in to a kind of nirvana-stupor, to abdicate our humanity, to define ourselves as losers." Hakim Bey's solution is to have a party, or walk into a bank and have a bowel movement on the floor. May not sound like much, but he dressed it up in such cool materials—references to Burroughs, cyberpunk, Shi'ism, Sabbah's Assassins, pirates, magic, zine culture, European an- archists, thinkers like Foucault and Baudrillard and Deleuze and Guattari, and amazing terms like "psychic nomadism"— that its argument wielded an irresistible charisma. A group of

culture jammers known as the Cacophany Society, inspired by
the book, began organizing "Trips to the Zone," which evolved
into the Burning Man festival.

*T.A.Z.*'s charisma was helped by Bey's own mystique, with no
author photos on his books, no one seeing his face or knowing
how he lived beyond the back-cover scraps about Chinatown
hotels and trailers in the Pine Barrens. Timothy Leary pestered
Peter for information: "Who is this Hakim Bey? I love him!"

In a diner off I-87, about to pay for our pancakes and drop
Peter off after another weekend with the Sufis, I tell him about
that Abode hippie who brought up Hakim Bey. Peter just laughs
and shakes his head.

"Hakim Bey's more popular than I am," he moans. But that's
the same joke that the hippie pulled, and Peter knows that I get
it. If you're sufficiently initiated into these books, the new shaman's name is easy enough to unpack: Peter named him after
al-Hakim, the sixth Fatimid caliph, the Isma'ili alchemist-king
who allegedly ordered that day and night be reversed in Cairo.
"Bey" is a nod to Moorish Science, as Noble Drew Ali named
each of his followers either Bey or El.

The perception of Peter and Hakim as separate individuals
has been corroborated by Peter's friends in the underground
press: City Lights credits Wilson and Bey as distinct contributors
with separate author bios, even when they appear in the same
publication. On the acknowledgments page of *Gone to Croatan:
The Origins of North American Drop-Out Culture,* the editors
thank Peter "for the original idea for the book and his continu-
ously nurturing energy towards it" but also give "a final tip of
the fez to the ubiquitous Hakim Bey, wherever you are."

As Peter's official biographer, how do I handle Hakim Bey?
I'm pretty sure that Peter wouldn't be ready to drop the joke;
when I write about his colleague, I might have to play along.
I also think about my own secret zonga-zonga name, Azreal
Wisdom, and what kind of book he would write.

# 9.

To the sound of a flute
I move my hands
till the lid of the lake's eye
trembles
and the last cloud
like a sprinkling of iron filings
falls away from the sky's
azure face.
The eye opens
and perceives upon the cheek of heaven
not a single hair.
                    —Peter Lamborn Wilson,
                        "Contemplation of the Unbearded"

Peter/Hakim still has his apartment in the building once inhabited by William S. Burroughs, but he almost never uses it. The only time I ever see the place, I'm visiting Peter's friend and editor, and Peter's not there. While searching the crowded floor-to-ceiling bookshelves, I find another paperback anthology listing both Peter Lamborn Wilson and Hakim Bey as contributors: *Semiotext(e) SF,* a collection of radical science fiction published with financial support from Peter's family.

As in the City Lights publications, the two personas receive separate author bios. Peter's bio puts him over as a legitimate poet-scholar who taught at the Jack Kerouac School of Disembodied Poetics, but adds that he's a fan of "literary hoaxes and forgeries." Hakim's bio casually mentions that he has written for the *NAMBLA Bulletin*—

NAMBLA, as in North American Man-Boy Love Association, the social network and activist organization for pedophiles.

While making small talk with Peter's editor, I sneak discreet glances at the book in my hands, double- and triple-checking the bio as though the acronym's just a mistake of my eyes and the letters might rearrange and correct themselves.

They don't.

NAMBLA changes everything, makes it all read differently: Peter's scholarship on "sacred pederasty" in Persian Sufism, the stack of *Boy's Life* in Hakim's trailer, the rebellions against both Islamic *shari'a* and the secular police state, the friendships with Burroughs and Ginsberg—I guess it wasn't just weed and Sabbah. NAMBLA's most public advocate, Ginsberg, even self-identified as a member and spoke at the group's conferences.

It feels like I always knew. Peter left hints lying scattered throughout his books—I would have guessed that the man had some strangeness buried deep that he wasn't even aware of—but no smoking gun like his affiliation with a civil rights group for child molesters. Those letters aren't going anywhere; they've found a place in my brain and settled. My next time sleeping over at Peter's house, I dream that I'm at a Five Percenter parliament and pick up a plush doll of Ernie from *Sesame Street,* finding NAMBLA stitched across his forehead.

It's not a hard dream to break down: Peter's my foundation, the father of my second conversion to Islam. Peter's the one who empowered me to strip away all the laws and orthodoxies and search for the real heart of my religion—and by "my religion," I mean literally *my* religion, Islam as I choose to manufacture it with whatever sources and tools that I like. Tradition holds that every century will see the appearance of a *mujaddid*, a figure who restores or renews Islam. A mini-messiah. In my own life, Peter has been the guy. He's still right—I Self Lord And Master—but what's it all for? Little boys in tight jeans? Is that why we don't throw out the Oriental baby with the Orientalist bathwater?

I try to find out. Many of Hakim Bey's NAMBLA poems survive online, if you're willing to go exploring in the sketchiest corners of the Internet. In "Missa Ambrosiana," Bey describes the "tiny rectum sweet as a brown buttercup" of a boy "not-quite-seven." In "The Eroticism of Banal Architecture," set in a gas station restroom, the object of Bey's affection is an uncircumcised, ejaculating ten-year-old. In "Magian Child," he fantasizes about sharing a sleeping bag with eight-year-old runaway "Joey," who warns, "You better not let me drink too much pop!" The indulging anarcho-Sufi, of course, gives the boy as much to drink as he wants, and Joey ends up wetting himself at night. The poem's narrator then brings Joey's urine-soaked pajama pants to his own face to inhale the scent.

In "My Political Beliefs," Bey writes of a man watching an eight-year-old anarchist in the bathtub. Bey narrates that the boy plays with himself while "one of his parents clumps down the hall . . . I suppose to make sure neither of us is raping the other." In "Suburban Shocker! Satanic Youth Cult Exposed!" Bey describes an eleven-year-old anarcho-Satanist as "my Peacock Angel, Prince of the Dark Djinn," a reference to the Yazidi religious minority of Iraq, "if I can be his fantastic towel-head worshipper."

Hakim Bey's work appears in NAMBLA's *Poems of Love and Liberation* anthology and the popular *Acolyte Reader* series by Amsterdam-based Acolyte Press. *The Sixth Acolyte Reader* contains Bey's "Yohimbe Poems," which, his introduction explains, were inspired by memories of two boys. Describing the second boy, Bey offers a "bill of indictment" for the child's "hypocrite mother," a "self-proclaimed anarchist punk advocate of liberation for children" who had apparently disapproved of the narrator's affection. In 1993, Entimos Press, also in Amsterdam, published Hakim Bey's *O Tribe That Loves Boys: The Poetry of Abu Nuwas.* The book is dedicated to Allen Ginsberg, with additional acknowledgments and *salam*s extended to members of the Abu Nuwas Society for the Study of Sexual Culture in the Middle East, which has been described as an "Islamic movement that explores boy-love as part of Islamic cultural tradition" and whose leader was allegedly assassinated by Muslim extremists. The front cover of the thin paperback shows a sullen youth in Arab headdress, an image repeated throughout the book. The back cover offers a photo of a preadolescent boy on his knees, hands between his legs, wearing only a long shirt with its V-neck collar pulled down far enough to expose a nipple. The boy's facial expression resembles the over-the-top grimace of adult female porn stars. "You with the childish body," proclaims the text, "but the brain of a seasoned con-man." Hakim takes some liberties with the translation, updating the ninth-century poetry to include mentions of Nintendo. It got a nice blurb at Nambla .org: "Hakim Bey, in rendering these treasures into the contemporary idiom, has provided English-speaking connoisseurs of man/boy-love with a supply of erotic thoughts expressed in startling images."

As "poetic terrorism," Hakim Bey suggests the posting in public places of a "xerox flyer, photo of a beautiful twelve-year-old boy, naked and masturbating, clearly titled: the face of god." Most of us who read the Communiques, unaware of Bey's NAMBLA writings, took the words only as more Ontological Anarchism, deliberately provocative punk lit: shocking for their own sake, a risky artistic choice but otherwise innocuous. Bey explains its full meaning for only *NAMBLA Journal* readers, in a December 1986 piece titled "THE FACE OF GOD," which turns hysteria over child pornography into religious intolerance:

Some religions are persecuted because their sacrament is illegal—

our religion is illegal because our entire form of worship is a crime.

Mere possession of this icon of our faith in some states could earn you

several years in prison. Perhaps you better burn this document before reading further.

When the police decide what is not religion, what is not art, what is not love—

then love, art & religion all must become crimes.

We believe this to be a photograph of god manifesting theophanically in human form, according to the teachings of Abu Hulman as-Dimishki, an 11th-century Persian who first taught god's embodiment in beautiful boys—whenever he and his followers saw a lovely face they prostrated themselves—he asserted that whoever knows god in this way is "relieved of all interdictions and prohibitions, and can allow himself all that he delights in" (from al-Baghdadi, *Al Fark Bain al-Firak*) . . .

For this reason, we xerox our icons, which are meant to be displayed—glued to walls—in public or semi-public places where they can impinge on the awareness of passersby—appearing anonymously—either as acts of cultural terrorism or as revelations of divine beauty and generosity, depending on the spiritual conditions of the beholder. A Xtian icon promises something after death—"socialist realism" promises something after the revolution. But we use photographs in our icons to remind ourselves that this world is sacred, and that beauty & love are the self-expressions of its divinity. The Empire's icons appear everywhere freely; ours are branded pornography. With the publication of this Emblem, we protest Babylon's cruelty and celebrate our psychic/aesthetic freedom from its laws; we exercise our so-called "religious freedom" and invite others to share our certainty of grace.

# 10.

Hakim Bey's greatest contribution to pedo-lit remains his fantasy novel, *Crowstone: The Chronicles of Qamar,* published by Amsterdam-based Coltsfoot Press in 1983. *Crowstone* has "developed an almost legendary status," reads one online description, "because for many years it's been almost impossible to find a copy." The book remains on a list of materials confiscated at the U.S.–Canada border. An Internet merchant selling a first-edition copy for $100 lauds the work as "Tolkien meets Captain Kirk and they both go off to baths with Peter Pan. Classic mishmash of fantasy and sci-fi with ephebic intent." William S. Burroughs praised *Crowstone* as "the first (and perhaps only) example of a new sub-genre." I drive to Ohio State University to read his personal copy, preserved in the archived Burroughs Collection.

The story takes place on Qamar, one of 108 moons orbiting the giant gas planet of Algol (*qamar* itself is Arabic for "moon" and *al-Qamar* is the name for a sura of the Qur'an). Qamar hosts a sexually liberated civilization where "no one cares who loves how or when;" in particular, the Qamarian city of Suvymara has developed a culture of man-boy love populated by "slaveboys, fisherboys, schoolboys, choirboys, dancers and catamites who have taken over, to a certain extent, the role played elsewhere by girls and women." The scene has attracted Velamiel, a scholar visiting "as a tourist with a yen for the sight of boyflesh." Velamiel was born on Saendeb, six moons away from Qamar, in a more restrictive society that disapproved of intergenerational sex. His parents belonged to the "Scholars' Guild" and were "quiet, pleasant people, conservative but not intolerant." As a teenager Velamiel fell in love with an eleven-year-old boy. The onset of puberty caused Velamiel's lover to become cruel, and their relationship ended when Velamiel was seventeen, at which point he decided to "cork up the notion of love" and dedicate himself instead to a spiritual path, joining a monastery and attempting to divert his lustful energy into meditation. "As a last desperate measure," he tells the reader, "I tried to allegorize my desires into spiritual and fleshless ecstasies, transmuting my distant glimpses of young boys into themes of meditation on the Essential Beauty of the Undivided."

Velamiel recalls that one night, he left the monastery and in his wanderings encountered a group of nomads who had been smoking "vhang." Velamiel had sex with a boy from the group, then returned to the monastery only to find that it had burned to the ground, killing some members of the order. As Velamiel faced the survivors, they noticed that he was somehow different, that there was now "something alien" in his aura. They accused Velamiel of arson, forcing him to flee his home moon in exile.

On Qamar, Velamiel finds a boy bordello called the Water Fly Cafe, which appears strongly reminiscent of one of Peter's early stories, "Silver Pipe Cafe," from the *Polysexuality* anthology. Velamiel meets and

befriends Zaek, a long-haired and kilted warrior from
the northern mountains of Thuren. Zaek recognizes one
of the dancing slave boys, a blond prostitute named
Xiri, as a fellow Thurenian. When Xiri is mistreated
by an air pirate, Zaek immediately leaps to his defense. Velamiel helps Zaek fight off the pirate and his
comrades, causing a grateful Xiri to take the two men
back to his room and let them each have a turn with
him, free of charge.

In the course of their adventures, Velamiel and Zaek
cross paths with a variety of boys. At the shrine of
boy idol Voron (Qamar's patron god of pedophilia),
whose devotees leave offerings of flowers for him to
eat, they find a twelve-year-old temple dancer named
Jethael. To Velamiel, who watches Jethael in meditation, "the dreaming boy appeared as nothing less
than a god. After years as a mystical skeptic, a
heretic and a renegade, he thought, 'I have found a
real religion at last, completely anthromorphic. Or
rather paedomorphic.' " The cache of boys also includes
red-haired Kael, "at fourteen a roistering lover and
fighting rooster," and Varonael, a pigtailed young sorcerer. Much of the novel consists of detailed sexual
adventures among various combinations of the men and
boys. Velamiel buys presents for the children, for
which they reward him with an orgy. It is mentioned
that Velamiel has gazed upon boys as young as six years
old, but has not indulged his desire beyond fondling
and "spoiling"; he then enjoys himself with nine-year-
old Venyamin, "the youngest and tiniest boy he'd ever
contemplated as a lover, but also one of the most ex-
quisitely beautiful."

The group is joined by an adult wizard named Sorolon,
whose love for young Varonael is described with Sufi
overtones as "utter annihilation." Sorolon speaks of

an otherworldly sanctum: the Garden of the Beloved, a
hidden interdimensional paradise in which the men and
boys could take refuge from their enemies. The Garden
of the Beloved is not in a fixed location but can actually move, and also serves as a portal through the use
of secret doors that Sorolon has scattered throughout
Qamar. To reach this place, says Sorolon, seekers must
first actualize it in an "Imaginal ceremony." Leading
the boys in group meditation, he asks them to picture
the Garden, which will enter them into its reality.

"Unlike other less fortunate youngsters elsewhere,"
reads the narration, the boys of Qamar understand "exactly how to answer the call of the Garden." Once they
successfully manifest this mystical realm, Varonael
proclaims, "Clothes are no good here!" and the boys
immediately have sex with each other. When Xiri and
his tattooed friend Dragon are taken captive, the men
and boys use the Garden's transportational powers to
rescue them. Brought into the Garden of the Beloved,
Dragon exclaims, "Xiri! We're not prisoners anymore.
We're not slaves anymore. We're free." Xiri is called a
"true king" of the Garden and smokes vhang with Dragon.
Their captor has been defeated, due to his one tragic
flaw: "he assumed that children are powerless."

While named only as Hakim on the book's cover, Peter
writes his afterword as Hakim Bey. The afterword treats
the novel as a translation of an authentic Algolian
text, *The Chronicles of Velamiel the Scrivener*. Hakim
Bey, a self-described "scholar of Qamarian culture,"
quotes from fictitious Qamarian volumes and refers to
his imagined travels to Qamar, even vowing to use
his royalties from the book's sales to return. "There
remain more volumes to be written," he says.

Though Velamiel had come to Qamar from another moon
with a more repressive culture, Hakim Bey assures us

that pedophiles have it far worse on Earth, and Velamiel "knew almost nothing of the shame which has ruled
us for seven centuries." While Hakim Bey admires Zaek,
"prophet of Chaos, legendary first Anarch of Qamar," he
relates more to Velamiel, a "character I could identify
as sympathetic to my own, almost a friend separated
from me by Time." As Bey explains, the story's protago-
nist and its "translator" have similar biographies:

> I too had grown up on a world that knew little
> of magic and love, in the bosom of a family still
> deeply influenced by Asterian gloom. I too rebelled,
> set out a wanderer through the worlds of space,
> drifting from job to job and planet to planet, till
> some chance-overheard remark sent me to Algol. I
> too am a scholar of sorts. And I too discovered in
> Qamar that cosmic fate had not condemned me to a
> life without love, without true pleasure.

Returning *Crowstone* to the librarian, I want to cut away
Hakim Bey and keep my Peter, but it can't be done. Peter's the
academic voice, and Hakim's the crazy poet, but it's all one
story.

He knows that I know, right? Of course he does. Maybe he
doesn't. Just punch the right words into a Google search and it's
all there—or read the editorial battles on his Wikipedia page—
but Peter doesn't know how to use a computer, and he has no
understanding of how the Internet pulls all of this stuff together.
He asks me not to refer to him in my writing as "Peter Lamborn
Wilson/Hakim Bey" because he likes to "keep the Hakim Bey
thing a secret." How could he think it's a secret? Again, go to
Wikipedia. "Peter Lamborn Wilson" now redirects to the more
commonly searched "Hakim Bey."

He doesn't know that I've read the NAMBLA poems or
*Crowstone* or that I would have a problem with it. I'm not a liar

yet, because at least I'm trying to work this out for myself. But it doesn't look good. I try to see it as Sufi allegory, a hidden parable somewhere in all the porn, like Ibn 'Arabi's poems about Nizam or Rumi's donkey-sex story. Does anyone accuse Rumi of bestiality? Apart from the ugly *zahir* meaning, the surface-level interpretation, there could be a secret *batin* meaning, and the boys aren't really boys but personifications of Divine Names. It almost settles things for me, but writing for NAMBLA amounts to activism in real life. As Hakim Bey, Peter creates a child molester's liberation theology and then publishes it for an audience of potential offenders.

The historical settings that he uses for validation, whether Mediterranean pirates or medieval fringe Sufis, relate less to homosexuality than to prison rape: heterosexual males with physical and/or material power but no access to women, claiming whatever warm holes are available. What Hakim Bey calls "alternative sexuality" is in fact only old patriarchy—the man with the beard expressing his power through penetration. His supporters might dismiss "childhood" as a mere construction of the post-industrial age, but Hakim Bey forces me to consider that once in a while, I have to side with the awful modern world.

The man's integrity is shot for me, but I'm still reading him. *Shower of Stars*, his book on initiatic dreams in Sufism and Taoism, is worth keeping. On another night in Peter's guest bed, I dream that we're both naked and sitting cross-legged, facing one another. When he tries to touch me, I turn away. After waking up, I read the dream as he would have: an aborted initiation. I rejected my *murshid*.

## 11.

The closest we come to approaching the topic of pedophilia is during a discussion of the Nuwaubian movement at his kitchen table. The Nuwaubians' leader, Malachi Z. York, was once a "Nubian Islamic Hebrew" who called himself Imam Isa al-Haadi al-Mahdi, but later claimed to be an extraterrestrial from the nineteenth galaxy. Citing their shared historical connections to Noble Drew Ali, Hakim Bey describes the Moorish Orthodox Church as "distant spiritual cousins of the Nuwaubians."

Peter asks me what Malachi Z. York's in jail for, and I tell him, "allegedly having sex with children."

"Ugh," he exclaims with sarcastic mock revulsion, "the *ultimate* crime!"

It could be his secret wink. He's testing to see if I know and if I'm down.

I look at the floor.

The Moorish Orthodox Church had died with the end of Peter's college/party scene. Peter resurrected the movement in 1986, on the centennial of Noble Drew Ali's birth, with a reinvention of the message—Noble Drew's "Asiatic Nation of North America" now being reinterpreted as "all who embrace some form of the Oriental Wisdom," and "Morocco" representing not a place but "illuminated consciousness." Members in the new church included science-fiction author Philip José Farmer. Peter has written on Moorish Orthodoxy's development with some seriousness, detailing its branching into relationships with Eastern Orthodox Christianity, the Bektashi tradition, and the Radical Faerie movement's queer-friendly neopaganism. From his position as patriarch, Peter has classified Christocentric Moors as belonging to the "Order of the Paraclete," and Islamocentric members under the "Fatimid Order"—a reference to the Isma'ilis and Hakim Bey's medieval namesake, the enigmatic Fatimid caliph al-Hakim.

The Moorish Orthodox Church is an example of what Hakim Bey calls "free religions . . . small, self-created, half-serious/half-fun cults." Apart from a shared sensibility, each chapter of the church remains self-defined, even creating its own rituals. Members in Dallas observe April 23 as Feast of the Green Man, in honor of Khidr, "Islam's patron saint of cannabis." Some church members give themselves quirky names, like Ibn Lahab, Flam Bey, and Dionysios Bey, claim meaningless titles, such as Sufi 'Abdal of Antarctica, and represent made-up factions, like the Moorish Black Guard or Mosque of the Seven Eyes, directing inquiries for further information to a nonexistant address in the nonexistent town of Ong's Hat (home of "Alamut College" and the "Hakim Bey Diocesan Theological Seminary"). In Arizona, a small cluster of Moors call themselves the Kurultai Lodge, after the Turko-Mongol *kurultai* in which elders gathered to elect a new *khan* after the death of the former.

Peter is the face, brain, and soul of the movement. None of the second-wave Moors would have heard of the church if it wasn't for Peter's writings, which makes my own involvement complicated—am I just following him in what he has called "this religion I have invented, of hashish and little boys?" It's something to consider when Peter invites me to his upcoming initiation party, where he'll be handing out Moorish names and titles.

Apart from Peter, I don't know any first-wave Moors, and I'm not even sure if any first-wavers besides Peter still care about the church. Of the remaining elders, Greg Foster/Ghulam El Fatah lives on an island in the Aegean Sea, and Stephen Scully participated in online Moorish activities for a while but his old aliyazid@pacific.net now comes back as a dead address. However, second-wave Moors have no problem condemning Peter, which I should have expected, given the church's inherent anarchism. An antiracist queer anarchist from the Kurultai Lodge objects not only to Peter's "championship of child rape" but his failure to engage issues of class, since "so much of his universe revolves around some very serious privilege—well, we all know the story of the trust fund hippies with no brains, too much pot, no spine, and Daddy's money. Peter's a trustafarian, not a weatherman." The Moorish Orthodox Church, poisoned by its father, is redeemed by its sons (don't hear too much about any daughters). So I decide to go to Peter's initiation party, held at a rich artist's house in the Shawangunk Ridge area. Riding in one of the cars of the "Moorish Caravan," I sit in the backseat with Peter and listen to his stories about smuggling hash into Lebanon. Turning to face the window, he looks out at the forests and mentions his dream of getting farmland somewhere and building a Moorish Science Ashram as a log-cabin pyramid. "It wouldn't be that hard," he says, as though he's trying to put the task on me.

The party's full of old white hipsters in fezzes, almost all men, drinking wine and getting high—weed's a sacrament in the church, Peter tells us. He puts on his black robe and black fez (bearing the Inayat Khan Flying Heart) and sets up a card table on the patio with burning incense, a goblet of wine, an old authentic copy of the *Circle Seven Koran*, the old photograph of Noble Drew Ali from his house, and Moorish Orthodox stamps and seals and charters. He calls our attention and we come outside, assembling around him. Describing Noble Drew Ali as a "racialist but not a racist"—which could make for an attempted bridge between Moorish Science and Corbin's Aryanism—Peter relates the legend that Ali had allowed whites to join the temple as "Celts" or "Persians." In my research of the Moorish Science Temple, I have never seen this claim substantiated. The Sultan was said to have revealed that whites were "spiritually Persian," which might have come from the Dingle El brothers who taught him, but it seemed more like something that Peter's own race consciousness would concoct, invested in the Celts through ancestry and Persians by sentimental attachment.

Gesturing to his black Flying Heart fez, he also shares the apocryphal story that back in the pre-WWII days of Moorish Science, a black fez expressed that its wearer had killed a police officer. We give somber, knowing nods. Peter says that Moorish Science has always had this meaning as a resistance to power and authority. Noble Drew Ali was a genuine prophet, he tells us, and received his martyrdom from the Chicago police. I look around and don't see any black people, let alone members of the legit Moorish Science Temple; it's a masterful adaptation by Peter, pulling out the essential themes of Moorish Science and bringing them to an audience that Noble Drew never intended. Or it's just robbery. I can't hold much confidence that any branch of the Moorish Science Temple today would appreciate these stoner beatniks' calling each other Moors, but perhaps it doesn't even matter—simply "heresy as cultural transfer" or a "fortuitous mistranslation," as Peter calls it in Scandal. We're the heresy of the heresy.

Noble Drew's picture is there for us to meditate upon, but it's not required; we can meditate on whatever we want, says the patriarch. Peter reminds us that the Moorish Orthodox Church makes no demands on its members. Those of us who want titles get them, our charters written in Peter's elegant calligraphy. He writes my Moorish name and title and then signs his name "P.L. Wilson Bey" at the bottom. He signs it again in Arabic script as Hakim. Over his signatures he stamps the seal of the Moorish Orthodox Church, containing the Circle Seven of Noble Drew

Ali. At the top of the charter he puts two more stamps, one of Islamic calligraphy and one of the Inayat Khans' Flying Heart. It's a ritual acknowledgment of what we mean to each other. Peter, Hakim, is the old man holding on to a legacy. I am the young man who receives it, but in accepting his gift I give something back: my recognition of its value, my vow to honor and carry the gift long after the giver has passed.

This Charter signifies that <u>Mikail El</u> has been declared a member of the Moorish Orthodox Church of America and hereby appointed to the rank and title <u>Sultan of the Interstate 90</u>. We honor all the divine prophets, Jesus, Mohammad, Buddha, Confucius, Noble Drew Ali etc. in Love, Truth, Peace, Freedom, Justice and Beauty by the powers vested in us by the Noble Order of Moorish Sufis and the Al-Taha Memorial Temple #2 Manhattan.

Mikail El is sufficiently zonga, I think. At any rate, now it's official: I'm allowed in the Moorish Science Treehouse.

The 90 is America's longest interstate highway, a straight line from Boston to Seattle. I grew up in upstate New York just one hundred yards away from the road. As a kid I would walk over and stand on the overpass, watching tractor trailers disappear beneath me and others appear from the other direction, imagining the long trails of headlights to be companions in a caravan. Sometimes I bombed them with eggs, but that was a long time ago; now I have duties to the road, to drive up and down its three thousand miles and leave *Circle Seven Korans* on tables at rest stops. It doesn't seem as cool as Peter's title ("Enforcer of the Law and Bishop-Exilarch of Persia"), but the signed and stamped charter is like a stockholder's certificate representing my share in the tradition. After Peter and Hakim are dead, it could mean something, perhaps grant me a credibility; if this pseudo-religion somehow falls to a war of succession, I might whip out my title and Peter's signature and stand up as the new patriarch.

Sitting alone in the grass, away from the stoned white Moors, I remember that less than a week ago I was backstage with the RZA, Raekwon, and Brand Nubian's Lord Jamar. I had a notepad in hand, jotting down everything that they said for my book on the Five Percenters. And now *this,* whatever this is. It's a lineage, anyway. Peter was taught by Walid al-Taha, who was taught by the Sultan, who was initiated into Moorish Science by the Dingle El brothers, Noble Drew Ali's second and third reincarnations after the first reincarnation, John Givens El, who was Noble Drew Ali's chauffeur. *Congratulations,* I tell myself, the stamped charter in my hand. *You're Mikail El, Sultan of the Interstate 90.* Peter had added a degree sign, so I'm also the Sultan of 90 Degrees, which has a nice Moorish-Masonic feel. I can't tell if any of this is real or just practice for something else or complete nonsense. It feels like the religious equivalent of pro wrestling, or maybe a Sufi version of Dungeons & Dragons—*I'm a level seven* abdal *with twenty-five thousand* 'irfan *points, roll the twenty-sided!* At least Peter performs with a straight face.

I watch the Moors and realize that as nutty as all of this is, it's also typical, so typically American, and I have to consider the America that would produce Hakim Beys and Mikail Els. The room in Peter's house where I sleep, filled with statues of Hindu gods and Kemetic gods and Qur'ans and pictures of Noble Drew Ali, reminds me of Mecca before Muhammad rolled in with his monotheist order and smashed all the idols— and then it dawns on me that America looks a lot like pre-Islamic Mecca, because you have all of these big religions and small religions and false messiahs and UFO cults and 2012 books and we can worship whatever we want with no fears of God's Prophet tearing it down. By allowing for everything, the Moorish Orthodox Church proposes America's repaganizing of Islam, the Ka'ba surrounded by little gods again. Perhaps it could also argue for itself as a legitimate expression of

Ibn 'Arabi's *wahdat al-wujud,* the "unity of being." If nothing actually exists but Allah, and the material universe is just an illusion, then religious differences are also illusions, as distinctions between mosque and church only betray Allah's underlying oneness. Instead of Hassan-i Sabbah's saying, "Nothing is true," we could flip it and say that everything is true; or, at least as a representation of Allah, everything is as equally true and false as everything else. Ibn 'Arabi sided with the idol-worshipers against Noah, arguing that Noah was too focused on God's transcendence to appreciate the idols as signs of God's immanence. The error of the idol-worshipers in Muhammad's time would be that they favored immanence and ignored transcendence, seeing the Attributes that they worshiped as representing the Whole. The idols are God, but they cannot be more than God, and of course God is more than the idols. *La ilaha illa Allah,* no god minus God, for real.

But then we have the second part of Sabbah's dying words, "Everything is permitted." In a quasi-pantheistic system in which everything's a *mazhar,* the appearance of a Divine Name, where are God's ethics? Perhaps religious anarchy also leads to nothing meaning anything anymore, another American problem. Moorish Orthodoxy honors no authority but one's own limitations and desires, Peter says, which ultimately means that we owe the world nothing. That explains the Shah and NAMBLA and Temporary Autonomous Zones of hippies smoking weed at somebody's mansion, calling it revolutionary and subversive.

Freedom's a mirror. It will show you who you are. I don't know if the old writer can even see the mirror, because his sense of self-accountability is like that of a small child. His response to criticism is to put his hands over his eyes, hoping that you can't see him if he can't see you.

I break it down with Rumi's donkey verses. The slave girl can take on a donkey because she uses a gourd to keep it from going in all the way; the mistress doesn't use a gourd and the donkey kills her. In the case of Peter Lamborn Wilson, the donkey penis could represent liberation from both Islamic *shari'a* and the cop cultures of modern nation-states, but Peter won't protect himself with the gourd of ethical responsibility. The donkey hits it too deep, and Peter dies of internal bleeding.

# 12.

The book on Peter is dead, since I write him a letter asking for an explanation of the NAMBLA thing and he writes back only with angry tantrums about all the great poets and Sufi saints who have loved boys. What about Walt Whitman, he says. What about Hamid ad-Din al-Kirmani, what about Fakhruddin 'Iraqi and Abu Hamid al-Ghazali's brother? What about William S. Burroughs, who wrote not only of fucking but also of *killing* boys? Peter has a chain of authority and it works for him. It almost works for me. Besides, Burroughs did Nike Air Max commercials in the 1990s; given Nike's labor history in places like Pakistan and Cambodia, it's not so far from glorifying child abuse. The historical argument takes me only so far before it collapses. Peter has nothing to say. Again, his response is like that of a kid: if you accuse him of wrong, he points at the other kids who did it first. I respond like I'm his mom: "Peter, you're not a twelfth-century Persian. If twelfth-century Persians jumped off a bridge, would you do it too?"

There's at least one useful thing about my time with Peter: after reading his books and hearing his stories about traveling the world in search of a master, I can see that I'm on the same quest. It doesn't seem that Peter ever found his perfect teacher—or at least he found lots of them, each the right guide for only a particular moment. In the years since he came home from Iran, Peter has grown from the seeker to the sought. My first time in his house, I found a Sufi book on the kitchen table, signed by the author to "Peter Lamborn Wilson: you are the Imam of the Age." Peter was the Imam for a time in my life, but I'm on to the next one, still waiting for the right man to spit into my eyes and give me super vision.

*Not every bearded man is your grandfather,* says the Turkish proverb.

After a Five Percenter parliament in Harlem, I'm driving down Malcolm X Boulevard with Cihan Kaan, writer, filmmaker, electronic musician, and Jerrahi dervish, talking about Peter—"For me, coming from the rave scene," he says, "you know everything that his *Temporary Autonomous Zone* meant for the rave scene . . . it's a huge fucking betrayal." Cihan also tells me that he's having dialogues with Bob Dobbs—as in J.R. "Bob" Dobbs, the deity of the Church of the SubGenius. According to Cihan, Dobbs had revealed himself at various independent-film screenings as an actual flesh-and-blood man. I can feel more mischief on the way.

"Bob Dobbs doesn't exist," I tell Cihan. "He's a made-up prop for a prank religion." The Church of the SubGenius is at once a postmodern spoof of religion and a viable system in its own right, a "free religion" like Moorish Orthodoxy. Its phantom messiah, J.R. "Bob" Dobbs, the "greatest salesman of all time," was said to have started the church after encountering a vision of God on a television that he had built himself. The church's image of Dobbs, apparently taken from 1950s clip art, has circulated throughout American pop culture, landing in random places like the artwork for Sublime's *40 Oz. to Freedom* and the show *Pee-Wee's Playhouse* (Paul Reubens was a SubGenius minister and kept a Dobbs head on the playhouse set). In a cut scene from *Sid & Nancy,* Sid Vicious even says that he's going to join the church and worship Dobbs.

According to Cihan, the imaginary Bob Dobbs was based on

a real guy named Bob Dobbs, and the church's iconic image of him with a pipe in his mouth was actually modeled after the real Dobbs's father. Cihan tries to explain the teachings of the "real" Bob Dobbs, going off about something called the Android Meme that we download into our nervous systems via television and multimedia; "organic robotoids"; and the Evergreens, a collective of ethereal beings through whom Bob has maintained contact with the ghost of Frank Zappa. We sit in my car for nearly an hour after I park, Cihan rattling off mysterious terminologies and theories with awesome incoherence. It's hard to follow, and I can't even tell if Cihan himself understands all of the terms and concepts.

Cihan informs me that in our syncretisms and subcultural dipping, we're actually creating a new meme. I don't know what a meme is, but in my head I get an image of the Arabic letter م, the *Meem*. A meme's a unit of consciousness, he says. It could be seen as something like Yogacara Buddhism's *bija,* seeds produced by thoughts and perceptions, which contribute to the *alaya-vijnana,* the storehouse consciousness, and produce the external world as we understand it. Cihan says that we'll have to be careful when we put our new meme out there, since it will grow and eventually escape our control and then never go away because memes never die—memes are like matter or energy, impossible to create or destroy. Memes only swallow up other memes and keep adding to the collective brain of the world.

Then he gets out of the car, leaving my head blown in the combined meaning and meaninglessness of Bob Dobbs.

Cihan has an idea to bring our meme-fathers together—he'll produce the real Bob Dobbs, and I'll produce the real Peter Lamborn Wilson, and then we'll put them in the same room—but I've already washed my hands of Peter. Instead, I just seek out Dobbs and arrange for us to meet by the Jackie Onassis Reservoir in upper Manhattan. He shows up in a T-shirt and shorts, carrying a large Barnes & Noble bag.

"How old do you think I am?" he asks me.

"I don't know," I said. "Mid-forties?"

"I was born in 1922." He waits for me to do the math.

We walk laps around the reservoir and he reveals his life story. In addition to working for the CIA, Bob has been a friend and archivist of the culture critic Marshall McLuhan. He still makes appearances at McLuhan festivals, delivering lectures on topics such as "McLuhan and the Future of ESP." McLuhan taught that technology extended the human body—e.g., cars extending the legs and telescopes extending the eyes. Electronic media would extend the central nervous system, with the potential to bind all human consciousness in a global net. Bob really believes it, since everything that he puts out into the ether comes back to him in unpredictable ways.

"Did you see *The Matrix?*" he asks. Before I answer, he adds, "That was based on my life. You know the Bill Murray movie *What About Bob?* Did you see that one? That was me too. And *SpongeBob SquarePants*—I could go on forever. What about the one with Robin Williams, where he plays the president? What's the character's name? Tom *Dobbs*. I'm everywhere."

On July 4, 1976, Bob Dobbs was standing atop the World Trade Center and heard TV waves in the air, snippets of a Marshall McLuhan interview booming into his brain. The interviewer asked McLuhan what he had to say to Americans regarding the next two hundred years, and McLuhan answered with only one word: "apocalypse." The next day, Bob Dobbs learned that his father had died.

Two years later he was in a bar in Dallas, listening to a pair of college students as they worked themselves up over conspiracy theories, and he decided to share some of his perspectives from having worked in the CIA. At one point in the conversation, Bob showed the kids a photograph of his father. The two students turned out to be Ivan Stang and Philo Drummond, who would go on to form the Church of the SubGenius—allegedly using the image of Bob's father as a model for their fictitious messiah. In 1984, one of Bob's contacts in the intelligence community came across some SubGenius literature and immediately alerted Bob that he had become the center of a mail-order comedy cult.

"One plus nine plus eight plus four," Bob says to me as we walk. "What do you get? Twenty-two. That number keeps popping up everywhere I go." His marriage date added up to twenty-two. He had once lived at 22 Kenwood Avenue. His friend had a whole inventory of newspaper items relating to twenty-two. While going through boxes in McLuhan's archive, he found a file on himself in the box labeled 22. He even sees the number appearing in random people that he meets.

"My mother's father was born in 1922," I tell him.

"Yeah, see? *Exactly!*"

I hope to contribute by diving into Five Percenter number-play, building with their system of Supreme Mathematics. Two represents Wisdom; twenty-two would thus be Wisdom Wisdom, your *wise-dome* and my *wise-dome* adding on together to make a positive culture (culture is signified by the number four). The twenty-second degree in one of their lessons explains that Yakub was only six years old when he discovered magnetism while playing with two pieces of steel, and right then and there Yakub declared his plan to create a nation of devils to rule for six thousand years with tricknology. That's the power of memes; Yakub knew it better than anyone. Since 2+2=4, you could also go to the fourth degree in another of their lessons, which reads simply, "He does not speak his own language."

Bob Dobbs doesn't say much on my use of Supreme Mathematics or Five Percenter lessons, just a matter-of-fact "absolutely," since, of course, everything in the universe would coincide with his system. While he walks me through it, I avoid eye contact with passersby who might catch a snippet of our conversation. For Bob Dobbs, McLuhan was a kind of Christ, and James Joyce was his John the Baptist figure, the herald who foretold his coming. McLuhan had believed *Finnegans Wake* to be a cryptogram telling the entire story of the human race, and spent his life attempting to translate its phrase "Here Comes

Everybody." Cihan had told me that Bob, unable to pronounce his Crimean Tatar name, just called him Shaun after a character from the novel. Through his medium, the Evergreens, Bob communicates with Joyce's spirit, as well as McLuhan and Zappa. On one occasion, he watched the three ghosts riding unicycles, their heads opening like beer steins. Bob has also invited McLuhan's ghost to psychic parliaments involving the likes of Albert Einstein, Ezra Pound, Nelson Rockefeller, Jesus Christ, Nikola Tesla, Krishnamurti, and Dwight Eisenhower.

"You ever hear of Hakim Bey?" I ask.

"Sure, I *met* Hakim Bey. His publisher was going to put out my book, but he thinks I'm a crank."

Before we part ways, Bob gives me a copy of his book, *Phatic Communion with Bob Dobbs,* which concludes with a rambling memo to Prince Charles. The memo is dated June 4, 1990, and refers to their adventures in covert operations together in the summer of 1966: "There we were, both 44 years old and veterans of Mata Hari/James Bond scenarios since World War Two, pretending we were teenagers in a little town on the Eastern rim of the North American plate . . . such was our luck that it was the best time to be a teen—or rather, to pretend to be youth . . . However, for us it was an assignment and the stakes were very high." His math shows up throughout the memo: he says that he's writing while twenty-two thousand miles above the earth, refers to McLuhan's twenty-two-hour brain surgery, and mentions his July 22, 1970, encounter with Sun Ra.

In addition to *Phatic Communion with Bob Dobbs,* Bob asserts that he's also the true author of *my* books, the proof being that I have been brought to him, our paths crossing only as a result of his personal *magnetic* that he had already put out there.

If there's something that Bob Dobbs or his plus-lessons can give me, I've missed it. Of course he's a crank—Bob Dobbs isn't even his real name, just his own zonga—and Hakim Bey's a crank too. Even so, it sounds cool when Cihan/Shaun talks about the "Mosque of the SubGenius." I push him to move forward with it, get a properly zonga name from Bob Dobbs, or just stay Shaun and make the Mosque of the SubGenius into something really insane and fun, but Cihan goes through his own crushing disillusionment with Bob and besides, the air's out of my tires for that kind of thing.

# 13.

My pursuits linger on the fringe, adding new sources and characters for my own Anti-Caliph roster. Like Peter, I do a bit of wandering, my path sometimes retracing his. In Pakistan, I find myself at a shrine that he has mentioned, the shared tomb of Sufi saint Shah Husayn and his Hindu boyfriend, Mahdo Lal. I drink lassi made with *bhang* and start tripping balls at Data Durbar, shrine of the Persian saint Ali Hujwiri—whose advice for spiritual travel motivated *Blue-Eyed Devil,* my Islamo-American road book. But Hujwiri entered my consciousness only through Peter's writing on travel in *Sacred Drift.*

I don't know if Peter has been to Syria—he at least made it to Lebanon—but I go to Damascus and visit the tomb of Ibn 'Arabi, the Seal of Muhammadan Sainthood whose teachings informed Persian Sufism's school of love. Peter never went to Ethiopia, but his Qur'an-memorizing queer poet hero, Arthur Rimbaud, did; I head for the once-forbidden city of Harar and visit what they claim was Rimbaud's house. I know that Peter has not been to Saudi Arabia, where hardline revivalists killed all of the beauty and creativity that he saw in Islam, but I go to Mecca and perform the hajj, as *real Muslim* as it gets, even if I secretly subvert all the rituals: performing an *umrah* on Azreal's behalf, contemplating my seven circuits around the Ka'ba through Supreme Mathematics, and interpreting the story of Abraham and his son through *Return of the Jedi*. My father would have no problems at *jamrat;* I journey to the foreign land called West Virginia to see him again, and he stops me at the door, hand on his gun.

I keep writing my books—nowhere near Peter's full shelf, but there's time to catch up, *insha'Allah*. My books explore the neglected corners of American Islam, the heresies, the fringe sects. Even if I put away the Peter project, my growing body of work might just add up to my tribute to him. How can you speak when your every word honors a man that you don't respect? But whatever I do with the man, I'm still carrying him, still Mikail El. As an answer to his *Kings of Love: The History and Poetry of the Nimatullahi Sufi Order of Iran,* I put out *The Five Percenters: Islam, Hip-Hop and the Gods of New York,* showing 1960s Harlem to be as compelling a religious environment as fifteenth-century Iran, and examining Brand Nubian and Wu-Tang Clan lyrics like Peter broke down the mystical verses of Nur 'Ali Shah. My relationship to the Five Percent feels like Peter's bond with the Nimatullahis: while never officially in or out, I'm a friend of the community and participant in the tradition, and can come and go in peace. I even go on an epic road quest with Azreal from New York to Milwaukee, the two of us living in my car and visiting gods in towns along the way. Milwaukee birthed a whole new Five Percenter heresy after some black gods there taught a few white guys that they could be gods too. As soon as we return to Harlem, Azreal disappears. You can't keep track of a *majnun* like Allah's Death Angel, and there comes a time when I assume that I'll never see him again. He might be dead, which would make me the last Azreal, the remaining half of our tribe of two.

After moving on from Peter's anarchist press, I get in with better publishers who have better distribution and actually pay.

I see my books in stores that have never carried Peter. The books find me a few dollars, and I buy a personal check signed by the Honorable Elijah Muhammad to his daughter Lottie.

It stays in my desk drawer as a private relic, just to be taken out and stared at from time to time, making me probably the only person to have collected the autographs of both Elijah Muhammad and Charles Manson. I don't know if "independently poor" Peter ever made much money off his books; it's not a reasonable expectation in the underground-lit world. When I realize that I've probably been paid more, it must be like the feeling that a boy gets when he first beats his dad at arm wrestling. This is a guess, since I have never arm wrestled my dad.

The books also find me some friends. A guy writes from Turkey and says that he and his fellow confused Muslims get together and drink wine and read my shit to each other. Someone else tells me, "You should consider becoming an imam, seriously." Despite all of my open confusion and heresy, a bunch of kids write to say that these books had a hand in their conversions to Islam; considering how poorly I treat the product, this puts me in the running with Bob Dobbs and Master Fard Muhammad as the greatest salesman of all time. More than one reader asks me how to handle difficult aspects of the Prophet's

life: the alleged Jew killing, child bride, and so on. I say that I'll
let them know if I ever figure it out.

One says that he has to tell me about the dream he had where
it's him and Master Fard Muhammad together in Africa, and another sends me his drawings of my fictional characters. "You're
going to end up like the people you write about," I'm told, but
the guy doesn't say which ones. Besides people like Fard, I also
write about Asma Gull Hasan, the Republican author whose
family founded the group Muslims for Bush. She sues me over
my portrayal of her, but the suit gets dismissed.

The books make their way into lecture halls. When Carl Ernst
at the University of North Carolina describes my first novel as a
*"Catcher in the Rye* for young Muslims," the *New York Times*
and my publishers take that quote and run it into the ground.
Another professor says, "I have a hard time getting past the
immature sexuality, but this is anthropologically interesting."
As my work finds academic sponsors, some bring me to their
schools to give readings or talk to their students, and one lets
me read students' papers on *Blue-Eyed Devil* (the best one says,
"I couldn't really figure out why Knight goes through all this
trouble to find his place in Islam").

I get compared to people like al-Hallaj and the Qalandars and
any unconventional or controversial character from Islamic history, any Muslims outside the law, often figures that I recognize
from Peter's Anti-Caliph lineage. People give me more credit than
I deserve with what they read into me or what reading they think
I've done. There's no way of ever knowing what they want. After
one performance, in which I read an excerpt titled "A Complete
History of My Troubles with Urination" from *Blue-Eyed Devil,*
a professor goes on about how much he relates to my work, and
he's not even Muslim, just a guy with a complicated prostate.

Sometimes it gets scary. As journalists and scholars shuffle
my work around as a voice of the brave new Islam, well-known
Islamophobes offer their endorsements:

*Dear Mr. Knight:*
*I continue to read about your career with fascination, most recently*
*the Bernstein article. Perhaps one of these days, I could invite you to*
*a lunch and to speak to me and members of my organization?*
  *Yours sincerely,*
  *Daniel Pipes*

It's nice to think that I'm good at what I do, but encouragement from Pipes—whose Campus Watch site condemns my friends in academia as defenders of "radical jihadists"—makes me wonder whether it's worth doing. There's always a Shah. If I'm retracing Peter's path, at least I hope to make better choices.

I remember Peter after my presentation at the American Academy of Religion conference, sitting with a bunch of Progressive Muslim scholars in some Middle Eastern restaurant. After I mention that my paper is actually a chapter in my project on the Five Percenters, someone tells me that I should go back to school: professors get to research and write books, like I already do, but they also get to live in houses and eat decent food. Sounds like an idea. Peter has no degree, and his eccentric-hermit-lay-scholar thing would be a good time, but I couldn't sustain that without his family money. In my punk life, also my Peter life, it was possible to win what John Guillory called "symbolic capital" in publishing my own shit because I presented myself as such an outlaw that no one could handle me, but all of those punk rules eventually get flipped. A life in academia would mean forsaking the outsider status that I had loved in Peter and cultivated for myself. You can't freak out in the woods as Mr. Ontological Anarchism when institutions are investing their prestige and authority in building your name, and you can't run up and down the aisles of the lecture halls in a ghillie suit and witch-doctor mask, proclaiming your courses to be Temporary Autonomous Zones. But I also wonder if Peter wishes that he got his degree, since he has warned me with some bitterness that there's no place for independent scholars. Falling into a job at the Imperial

Iranian Academy seems to have been the best thing that ever
happened to him, but when the Ayatollah ruined his gig and the
Nasrs and Chitticks bailed for positions in American universities, Peter had nowhere to go.

I still run into Peter's name(s) here and there. A blogger calls
me Peter's "adoring disciple" and "trained ape," and I want to
say, *No, I'm Peter's correction.* Either way, our names remain
attached. Someone writes a dissertation on Islamic anarchism,
meaning that I have to read statements like "According to Bey
and Knight, any Muslim reserves the right to do as they please
without being bound by or accountable for the ethico-political
rights of the community over the individual." He links us together a bunch of times, like when he offers his thoughts on a
"weakness found generally in literature on anarchism and Islam,
but one that is particular to the literature by Bey and Knight."
Disapproving of our "Stirnerian individualistic approach," he
argues, "Bey and Knight fail to construct what is necessary."

Like Hakim Bey's *T.A.Z.*, one of my books—my first novel,
*The Taqwacores,* which owes its publication to him—is dis-
cussed with language like "underground manifesto" and hailed
for starting a new movement; bands such as Secret Trial Five
plug the book on their MySpace pages and refer to themselves
as "taqwacore" as though it were a real thing. A Brooklyn art
gallery holds a taqwacore photo exhibition, and someone pays
$750 for a poster-size print of me to hang in his or her apart-
ment. I buy a school bus and paint it green and we pile aboard to
travel across the northeastern United States, putting on taqwacore shows and getting filmed for a documentary. I'm always
the one driving the bus, and it feels like I'm the captain of the
ship, playing both the Neal Cassady and the Ken Kesey role in
our new scene. That's also how the documentary paints it, along
with the coverage from MTV, BBC, *Newsweek,* and so on. I'm
the "Godfather of Muslim punk," they say.

Like Hakim Bey, I give interviews saying that I did not invent
a movement, but only gave it a name. Young Muslims write

to me with confessions that through my books, they've redis-
covered their tradition; God help these kids when they outgrow
me. The *New York Times* quotes a fourteen-year-old girl saying
that my words saved Islam for her. It's the same thing that I said
to Peter in our final correspondence, even while challenging his
poems about six-year-old rectums.

BOOK 2

TAQWA

BUMS

# 1.

I sit alone in the visitors' room in absolute triple darkness. The initiated dervishes are somewhere else in the house, a room that I haven't seen. The lights have been off for almost a minute. Nothing has happened yet.

In the dark, I think about Javad Nurbakhsh, Peter's old friend from the Iran days and the former master of this order, who passed away six months ago. Since it's not my job anymore, I wonder if someone has told Peter. And I think of Ibn 'Arabi, who once said that an angel visited him while holding a piece of white light, like a piece of the sun in its hands. The angel explained that it was a sura of the Qur'an, *Ash-Shu'ara,* "The Poets." Ibn 'Arabi swallowed the light, and then felt a hair rising from his chest to his throat and mouth, where it emerged as "an animal with a head, tongue, eyes, and lips." The animal expanded until its head reached both the East and West horizons, then shrunk back down and reentered his chest. That was when Ibn 'Arabi started to write poetry.

This is my last thought before the slight pop of a stereo turning on. A recorded lecture comes in through the speakers above my head: a male voice discussing Ibn 'Arabi's views on the unity of being. Through *wahdat al-wujud,* the voice tells me, Sufism upholds the foremost creed of Islam, "There is no god but God," but takes it a step further: "There is *nothing* but God."

The lecture wraps up and I hear a *thump* from the speakers, the switching from one track to another. Next comes the Persian music and an English-accented male voice reciting poetry:

That everything throughout the world,
everywhere, end to end,
is but a reflection of a ray
cast from the face of the Friend.

In my old Islam, the heavy Islam that I carried in the years before Peter, Allah was more Lord than Friend, and I accepted assumptions that Prophet Muhammad had forbidden music and poetry: "It is better for one's stomach to be filled with pus than poetry," says the hadith.

I lie on my back and face the darkness, taking in the crucial verses as they're repeated several times, and then I get it: yes, Allah is the all in all, everything everywhere end to end just a reflection, nothing but him. I still read it through Peter. In *Sacred Drift,* he mentions the order's founder, Shah Nimatullah, as having "synthesized Ibn 'Arabi's metaphysics with a general poetic and romantic symbolism." This contributed to the formulation of what Peter calls the "school of love" in Persian Sufism.

When the poetry fades out, the music takes over, at first a slow build but it gets louder and righteously violent, and then the dervishes in the other room start clapping hard and chanting God's Name: ALLAH HU, ALLAH HU, ALLAH HU, ALLAH HU—

It sounds Pentecostal, like they're getting baptized in the Holy Ghost and Fire, but as soon as the energy of the music and clapping and chanting peaks, it's released like an orgasm. The music winds down gradually, easing the dervishes' return to normal time, and then stops. We're back on Earth. Even alone in the visitors' room, I can feel it through the walls. They're all worn out. I hear heavy breathing, but no one says a word. The lights come on and I'm reminded that I wasn't floating through space for the last half hour, I was in a room. There is no furniture, just animal-hair mats and cushions lining the walls. The room is decorated with typical Islamic ornaments, such as plaques of Arabic calligraphy bearing the names of Allah and Ali, the Prophet's son-in-law. There's also something different: a metal plate depicting Jesus Christ on the cross, with Mary and the disciples mourning around him. I don't know what to do with that. Islam honors Jesus as a prophet, and Mary is mentioned more times in the Qur'an than in the New Testament, but in my sixteen years as a Muslim, I've never encountered crucifixion art in an Islamic setting. The Qur'an clearly says that Jesus was not crucified, that Allah rescued him from his persecutors.

The dervishes emerge from their back room, still silent, their gazes lowered. It's a vibe like someone has died in there, but peacefully and without pain. A few dervishes come into the visitors' room and sit to meditate or take books from the shelves. They're almost all white people. A few approach me, asking the regular questions in soft whispers, not ready for the world to be loud again. I tell them that I'm from New York, that I've come to the Bay as a writer-in-residence at Headlands Center for the Arts in Sausalito, just across the Golden Gate Bridge. Headlands Center has given me a room and food and two months to write. I have a novel in my head and I'm trying to get it out.

Then they ask what sparked my interest in the Nimatullahi order.

"Well," I say, "I grew up Roman Catholic, and converted to Islam when I was sixteen . . ."

"Oh," they reply with raised eyebrows. Something has changed between us. I get the impression that for these Nimatullahi dervishes, I'm coming from a territory unknown and even ominous: Islam the *organized religion,* cutter of thieves' hands, cutter of innocent clitorises, submission always to laws and never to love. I consider that this *khaniqah* might have been visited by more orthodox Muslims, who might have taken offense at the poetry and music and free mixing of men and women—who dress like they're on their way to a nice restaurant, no *hijab*, skirts even showing some calf. It occurs to me that I'm probably the only one here who has made the pilgrimage to Mecca. I don't know if it matters; Mecca's only Saudi Disney at this point. Javad Nurbakhsh described pilgrimage as an inward journey of the heart, not a mere vacation to a holy city.

If the Nimatullahi Sufi order feels any tension about Islam, it'd be the natural reflex of a group that, while certainly "Islamic," doesn't necessarily think of itself as "Muslim"—an Iranian order that's no longer welcome in Iran. I make sure to explain that I have passed through my fundamentalist phase and now seek a more open relationship to—I can't say "Islam," which suddenly feels like a dirty word—"the tradition."

"We don't advocate reading the Qur'an here," someone tells me. "We don't advocate reading *namaz.*"

I hear their conversion stories: a white man who found Sufism through the poetry of Rumi, a white man who studied Ibn 'Arabi under Peter's Imperial Academy colleague William Chittick, and a white woman who had previously practiced Native American religion. Another white woman comes into the room and says that Ron, the order's shaykh for San Francisco, would like to see me. She leads me to a little room where I find him, a sturdy black man, sitting on the floor. At the doorway, the woman touches the floor, then brings her fingertips to her lips and forehead.

I sit across from Ron. He doesn't say anything. Assuming that Sufi *adab,* manners, calls for the shaykh to speak first, I wait. After about a minute, he asks if I was struck by anything during the *majilis.*

"When it described God as the Friend," I tell him. "That's not what I'm used to."

A white dervish wearing a cone-shaped hat enters with a tray, offering each of us a glass of tea and cube of sugar. When he offers the tea to Ron, they exchange the order's standard greeting that I can't quite make out: it sounds like *yow-hak.*

The glasses are slender cylinders. I drop a sugar cube into my tea and watch it dissolve, reflecting on the tea's caffeine and my prostate, getting momentarily distracted.

"Your glass has a certain capacity," Ron says. "If you pour more than its capacity, it overflows. Some glasses cannot hold as much; others can hold more. Likewise, you have a certain capacity for God. The purpose of Sufism is to find it." Then another white dervish comes in with a plate of cookies. I take one, while Ron politely refuses. She turns to leave the room, but he calls her back. "I apologize," he tells her. "I should not refuse something that has been offered to me. Allow me to correct my mistake." He then takes a cookie and turns to me. "Michael, if you commit yourself to this order, your word is your bond. If you've thought about it, and you would like to give yourself to this path for the rest of your life . . ." He looks me in the eye and nods. "This Sunday."

"Thank you," I say.

"Russ will walk you through some things."

Russ is a middle-aged, Asian American dervish. We sit together on a mat in the hallway, our backs straight against the wall.

"Do you know what you're getting into?" he asks.

"It's heavy," I answer. "I could feel the gravity when he invited me."

"It's a commitment." Russ tells me that my initiation will be marked with symbols, gifts that I bring to Ron to be accepted on the Master's behalf.

There are five symbols: a white cloth, a coin, a ring, rock candy, and nutmeg. I've already read about them in *Kings of Love,* Peter's history of the order.

The white cloth can be anything, says Russ: "a bedsheet, a piece of fabric, whatever is easy for you." It represents a traditional Islamic funeral shroud, and my desire to die. "Initiation is rebirth," he tells me. "Before rebirth in your new life, you must pass away from your old one."

The coin signifies wealth, or my attachment to wealth. The Nimatullahi path of spiritual poverty does not mean that I have to be destitute, he says. A Sufi can be wealthy, if he does not cling to material possessions; and a Sufi can be poor, if he does not become angry with God. When rich, the Sufi should be generous, and when poor, the Sufi should be patient.

"The ring," Russ says with special seriousness, "means slavery. When you are a slave to God, you are truly free."

The rock candy is a reminder of the joy I will find on this path. "Bring about two pounds," he suggests. "On Sunday, you will see why."

There's one more. Russ explains it with thoughtful pauses, allowing me to fully digest the words. "The nutmeg . . . is the *head.*"

# 2.

It's after midnight when I leave the *khaniqah*. Driving across the Golden Gate Bridge, I think of those dervishes and try to figure out why they became Nimatullahis instead of regular Sunnis or Shi'as. Their system could be more than just classical Persian Sufism, perhaps a native Islam of San Francisco, an Islam translated into the heart and history of this city—Islam if naked Allen Ginsberg howled the call to prayer from phallic minarets, and drunk Shaykh Kerouac recited Allah's Names on a flatbed trailer down the 101. Like Persian Sufism, the native Islam of San Francisco speaks with authority not from the Qur'an or the Prophet but from poets. It's an Islam of music, an Islam with space for Christian art. An Islam that won't even call itself Islam, because love knows no religion.

*Yow-hak,* the Nimatullahis say. Running through my small archive of Arabic, I realize that they must have been saying *Ya Haqq,* which means "O Truth" or "O Reality." In the 1970s, when Peter was spending time with Nurbakhsh and writing his book on the order, Nimatullahi dervishes greeted each other with *Ya Ali,* "O Ali." I don't know why the post-Revolution change was made, but *Ya Haqq* may seem less specifically tied to Shi'ism or even Islam in general.

One of Allah's ninety-nine Divine Names in the Qur'an, *al-Haqq* became the center of a controversy in tenth-century Baghdad that would forever mark Sufism's tension with Islam proper, even today. The Persian saint Mansur al-Hallaj offended mullahs when, in a fit of holy passion, he allegedly shouted, "I am al-Haqq!" For the mullahs, it appeared that he was calling himself Allah. Which he was, in a way, but he wasn't. Whatever it really meant, he was executed on a death warrant signed by his own Sufi master.

Contemporary scholarship regards "I am al-Haqq" as fiction that surfaced in later biographies of al-Hallaj; the words are found nowhere in the earliest sources. Al-Hallaj was actually martyred for his suggestion that Muslims could perform the rites of pilgrimage not only in Mecca, but inside their own homes, along with speculation that he was secretly a follower of the Qarmatiyya Isma'ilis who had once raided the Ka'ba, massacred pilgrims, and stolen the Black Stone. Either way, al-Hallaj was seen as a threat by the enforcers of institutional Islam, so they crucified him, chopped off his head, burned his body, and dumped his ashes in the Euphrates River (as the legends go, the ashes would spell out AL-HAQQ on the water's surface). For Sufis, al-Hallaj could personify the conflict between jurists and mystics. Maybe calling each other Haqq is an inside joke, or the Sufis' secret subversion, an insistence under the breath that al-Hallaj was right. The subversion best remains whispered, as Nimatullahis in Iran still encounter persecution under the modern Islamic Republic.

The "jurist vs. mystic" binary doesn't always hold up, if you consider references to al-Hallaj in poems by the supreme revolutionary jurist-mystic, Ayatollah Khomeini: "I forget my own existence and proclaim the slogan, 'I am al-Haqq,' and like Mansur al-Hallaj volunteer myself for execution." When I treat al-Hallaj as a hero of spirit opposing law, it might be a veiled Christian thought; I could be misreading al-Hallaj through my own lens, my history of whiteness and Western-ness and

Catholic upbringing, which seems like big trouble. For Louis Massignon, al-Hallaj's ecstatic gnosis and crucifixion allowed one to imagine the ultimate secret truth of Islam—the real Haqq at Islam's core, nonetheless feared, despised, and desperately rejected by orthodox Muslims—as a *Christian* mystical experience. In Massignon's treatment of Islam, writes Edward Said, the Prophet Muhammad was "thrown out, but al-Hallaj was made prominent because he took himself to be a Christ-figure." The passion of al-Hallaj provided European Christians a means by which they could impose their own spiritual universe upon Islam as Islam's inner meaning—whether actual Muslims knew this inner meaning or not. I'm not normally one to complain about mashing traditions together, but colonialism still matters.

Twelve hours later I sit on my front porch and look out at the fields and mountains and wild turkeys, Peter's *Atlantis Manifesto* in my hands. It's unreadable gibberish, all of his standard shtick masturbated into a poem around the prediction that Atlantis will rise again in 2012. He's got a merman on the cover and says that it's Khidr, the Green Man from Islamic mythology, "the true founder of Atlantean Hermeticism—now syncretized with Egyptian Freemasonry of Cagliostro and le Comte de St. Germain . . . and the Gnosticism of Proudhon, neo-platonic Luddism, Italian anarchists inspired by Stirner & Nietzsche in 1911, Fourier's proto-Surrealist Harmonialism, the 'tri-racial isolates,' the Moorish Science Temple, Ignatius Donnelly, Edgar Cayce, and Sandino."

I still wait for the Man to come. When he comes, the Man will break old institutions and build none in their place, because he alone marks the return of Presence. For no reason at all it feels like he might show up if I sit here long enough, maybe coming in from the nearby hill on which stand the ruins of an old army radar tower—the tower had to be high up on a hill because the radar heat would melt people. Maybe it was Mahdi heat. The Mahdi will walk from the mountains to this porch and invite me to join his army, and then we'll go to Medina and visit the tomb of his ancestor the Prophet. The Mahdi will ask about the two men buried next to Muhammad, and the people will say, "These are Abu Bakr and Umar, the successors to your ancestor, the rightly guided caliphs." The Mahdi will order their bodies exhumed and hung from a tree, and ask everyone who loved them to gather together, and then he'll summon a black cloud of smoke to come and annihilate them all. Abu Bakr and Umar will come back to life and be put on trial for their crimes against the Prophet's family and every crime ever in history, everyone who has ever been wronged coming forward and placing the blame on these two imposters until the Mahdi sets fire to the tree and burns them up and orders their ashes to be cast into the ocean until the Day of Resurrection, when they'll be reassembled and come back to life only to be tortured and executed over and over again by the Prophet, his daughter Fatima, and the Holy Imams.

At this point in the game, there's no history, only mascots. First Caliphs Abu Bakr and Umar are mascots for a certain Islam, the Islam of state power and orthodoxy, for which I must love the Prophet's daughter over them. I must love Husayn and his mother because Islam—whatever Islam became after the Prophet's death—destroyed them both. Fatima and Husayn have become symbols for me, counter mascots.

On the battlefield, Abu Bakr used to yell, "Suck on al-Lat's clitoris!" at infidels, and even as a strict monotheist I want to do it just to say fuck any religion of the state—place my mouth between the idol's legs, pull apart her granite lips with my hands, and make the dry stone wet, yes. It's not even an Ibn 'Arabi thought on how idols can at least express the immanent divine Attributes; my love for the *Ahlul-Bayt* is such that to spite its enemies, I will eat out a pagan goddess.

The Mahdi's not real; he's just a fantasy drawn from the first crisis of Islam, the crisis of who could lead the people in the Prophet's absence and who might come to end the confusion. I know the want.

Even if my biography of Peter has driven into a ditch, the book's unfulfilled energy passes into a new project. I'm starting a fiction with those feelings, my desire for a man to share his chapters with me. My desire for inheritance. I can thumb through my previous books and find it on every page; it's starting to look like this is all that I have ever written about. Even when I sought freedom from religion, I needed a religious precedent—yes, there have been lawless Sufis who stood in opposition to orthodoxy; yes, the Five Percenters oppose religion in a way that's nothing but religious; yes, I can be a weird white Muslim because of Peter Lamborn Wilson. There's the next fiction, the story of Hakim Bey and Mikail El. All I have for a plot is the seed of two characters, an attracted and his attractor like Yakub's two pieces of steel, and the attracted's love for what attracts him is enough to build a novel on it.

There's a writer named Marcus Ewert who put out an essay about his epic journey at sixteen to Naropa, the only Buddhist college in the United States, where Ginsberg, Burroughs, and Peter all taught at the Jack Kerouac School of Disembodied Poetics. Marcus was a pilgrim determined to fuck either Ginsberg or Burroughs, and he ended up getting both of them. As far as anyone knows, he was the last person that Burroughs ever slept with. On his Facebook page, he's put up a bunch of black-and-white photos taken of him by Ginsberg, collected in an album titled "Photos of Me by Allen Ginsberg." It's a genealogy passed through the penis, direct transmission. Having imagined a lineage to Ginsberg just for smoking weed with one of his friends, I can appreciate the thought. For my fictional character, I contemplate a kid who would go on a pilgrimage like that and crave an inheritance like that.

This novel's going to be the greatest Islamic science fiction of all time, I've decided, and perhaps the creation of a whole new literary genre: Radical Queer Islamo-Futurism. It'll be set in an alternate future in which America's gone Muslim, and in turn Islam has gone American with Muslim comic-book superheroes who appear in soda-pop ads.

I'm calling my new novel *The Great Zamel*. In Arabic, *zamel* means a male who receives anal penetration. My zamel is the attracted piece of steel, a queer and confused American Muslim teenager, and his attractor is my new superhero, Mr. Muhammad.

I try to visualize the *zamel* and make him real enough to write. In my sketchbooks he always appears as a Japanese cartoon character with huge eyes and a triangular face, and hair like a blazing inferno—sculpted into sharp points adding nearly two full heads to his height, like a *saiyan*.

## • THE GREAT ZAMEL •
### By Mikail El

Walking alone, the campus behind him, he felt gross from twenty-four ounces of Taqwa-Cola, but still headed to the gas station for more. Taqwa-Cola's display stood right by the door, hundreds of green-and-white aluminum cans stacked together. They were no longer individual cans, each bearing its own copy of the text and symbols, but viewed together as one structure like all the bricks that form a Ka'ba. Next to the display stood a cardboard cutout of Mr. Muhammad, the most beautiful creature he had ever seen. Mr. Muhammad had a sexual power that annihilated all tags of straight or queer; to bother over anatomy with Mr. Muhammad would be like assigning gender to the sunset.

In Taqwa-Cola commercials, Mr. Muhammad stood encircled by all kinds of Muslims standing together, holding hands, Sunnis and Shi'as and Mevlevi dervishes in their full getup, and every nation—Turks, Kurds, Indians, Pakistanis, Saudis, Iranians, Nigerians, Bosnians, Chinese Hui Muslims, whoever—and though their costumes represented clear differences of traditions and values, they seemed to live in a world beyond ideology. The women who covered all the way, the women who covered some of the way, the women who did not cover, all together. Perhaps there could even be a queer Muslim in those happy soda fields, joining hands with henna-bearded mullahs in big green turbans. If the boy was really gay, what mosque in the world would have him? *Kill the one who does it,* said the oral tradition, and *kill the one he does it to.* But in the fantasy world of Taqwa-Cola commercials, perhaps he could have a place with Mr. Muhammad, and then he wouldn't have to answer the tough questions of scripture-based morality. The question would no longer be asked. That was how capitalism could save Islam: the new American Islam-as-product, accepting all believers in the initiation of purchase.

The commercials promised that if you accepted their challenge of accumulation and found four twenty-four-ounce Taqwa-Bombs specially marked with images of devils under the caps, you'd be rewarded with a free trip to Mecca to meet Mr. Muhammad. Mecca was Mecca, Indiana, population less than four hundred, area roughly one square kilometer. The town hosted Taqwa-Cola's world headquarters, a marvelous facility along the lines of mega-mosques like Faisal Masjid in Islamabad—except the fountains and *wudhu* faucets poured Taqwa-Cola so believers could maintain their ritual purity with carbonated water and fructose corn syrup.

The commercials never said what happened when you met Mr. Muhammad. It could have been only a handshake, maybe a shared meal or tour of the Taqwa-Cola headquarters. The commercials remained vague enough to let your imagination run wild, so the boy got his own idea: in the parlance of *yaoi* (homoerotic Japanese comic books), he'd be the *uke* and accept Mr. Muhammad as *seme.* Everyone knew that in paradise, Allah would reward men with teams of virgins, maybe Japanese schoolgirls like Kagome on *InuYasha,* with big *chibi* anime eyes and short pleated uniform skirts. The number was usually given as seventy-two. Most readers of the Qur'an, however, failed to notice that Allah would also be dishing out boys with eyes like scattered pearls—the Qur'an calls them *ghilmaanun* in 52:17–29 and *wildaanun mukhalladuna* in 76:19. He wondered what it would be like to serve as Mr. Muhammad's immortal boy. If he found his four devils and won the trip to Mecca, he'd try to find out.

He walked past the display to the cold Taqwa-Bombs in the back. His hand hovered over the glass door, hoping to sense a devil under one of the bottle caps. The contest was a capitalist metagame, he knew. It trained a buyer's mind to invest emotions into fetishized objects. Pokémon had its checklists and trading and catchphrase, "Gotta catch 'em all!" In *InuYasha* they were searching for the fragments of the Shikon no Tama, the four-souled ball, to restore the sacred jewel to its original form. In *Dragonball Z* they chased after dragonballs; if you found all seven, you could summon Shenlong the Dragon God and employ his power. By participating in the Taqwa-Cola contest, he would rehearse the accumulation of commodities to earn another object, Mr. Muhammad's commodified cock . . . but the cock transcended object; it'd be like getting fucked by Taqwa-Cola itself and not Taqwa-Cola as anything in the physical world, like a green-and-white aluminum Taqwa-Bomb or a concrete corporate base in Mecca, Indiana . . . No, he wanted to get fucked by Taqwa-Cola the *idea,* whatever that idea turned out to be, as manifested by the cock. Mr. Muhammad's cock and its non-polluting ejaculations became the bridge between material and incorporeal, our real world of bodies and

unreal world of spiritual powers floating in or around
them. What would you call a thing with this purpose?
God making Himself known in the world. Mr. Muhammad's
cock was the *hujjat*. The boy would place it on his
highest shelf and never touch it unless he was ritually
clean. He'd polish that holy cock head like the perfect
mirror of his *nafs*.

He picked two twenty-four-ounce Taqwa-Bombs, two
chances. If only one can yielded a devil, then he'd be
one fourth of the way to getting pumped by Mr. Muhammad. If Mr. Muhammad would have him. Judging by the
Taqwa-Cola commercials, Mr. Muhammad loved everyone.
The graphic novels offered no evidence one way or the
other, since the issue never came up in Mr. Muhammad's
adventures across the universe. He wandered from planet
to planet but never seemed to fuck anyone, male or
female, nor did he engage any Muslim scholars in debate
on issues of sexuality.

Chopping heads. The Great Zamel wants to obtain four devils'
heads so that he can lose his virginity to Mr. Muhammad, and
now I'm offering my own head to the Nimatullahis in the form of
a nutmeg. Master Fard Muhammad taught Elijah Muhammad
the same symbolism, saying that if the devil studies Islam for
thirty-five to fifty years, he can wear the flag of Islam with a
sword attached—the sword meaning that he will not reveal
his secret. The parallel makes me contemplate Master Fard as
a rogue Iranian shaykh who secretly taught Sufism without
anyone having a clue. The Five Percenters could be in possession
of a legit Sufi lineage and not even know it.

It's not enough to kill the devil. You have to remove the devil's head clean from its body. There appears to be something
essential about that. I search my memory for every reference to
decapitation found in a lifetime of nerding out at the library:
Perseus and Medusa, David and Goliath, John the Baptist,

Matthew the Evangelist, Christ's brother James, ancient Aztecs using heads as balls in their games, ancient Assyrians collecting heads like trophies, modern Rwandans and Cambodians stacking genocide skulls into tall pyramids, World War II photos of charred Japanese heads placed like hood ornaments on American tanks, Jeffrey Dahmer storing boys' heads in his freezer, guillotines long and narrow lopping deposed kings' heads into baskets, criminals losing their wise-domes at Chop-Chop Square in Riyadh, and my friend's childhood cat who used to bring him headless birds as gifts, like Pompey's head presented as a trophy to Caesar, or a centurion presenting Cicero's head to Marc Antony. Everyone, even the cat, knew that all the power lived north of the neck, and if you took the head, then you owned the power.

The Great Zamel's ambition is to decapitate four devils, castrating them so that he can be feminized as the warm hole for Mr. Muhammad—but that's not Taqwa-Cola symbolism, just his own that he brings into it. He thinks of the actual, physical thing; a virgin, he has no means to understand how it works or feels. Nothing has ever gone up his butt before, and he has never put anything up someone else's butt either. Even as the passive partner, the *zamel,* is there something he needs to know? Does he have responsibilities to ensure a successful penetration? Can he ruin it by moving wrong? Does he have to move at all? How does he make himself clean?

The Great Zamel cannot imagine himself alive in the world after getting his anal cherry popped, wearing that green-and-white pin of NON-VIRGIN on his lapel. Giving himself to Mr. Muhammad is supposed to change something, but he doesn't know what. Collecting four devils will make him free, but what will he do with freedom?

# 3.

Every spiritual master, by his knowledge and his function and in the graces attaching to them, is mysteriously assimilated to his prototypes and, both through them and independently of them, to the primordial prototype, the founding *Avatara*. On the level of this synthesis, it could be added that there is but one sole Master, and that the various human supports are in the nature of emanations from Him, compared to the rays of the sun which communicate the one self-same light and are nothing apart from it.
—Frithjof Schuon

Next to my computer stands a tower of books by Javad Nurbakhsh: *Spiritual Poverty in Sufism, Jesus in the Eyes of the Sufis, The Great Satan "Eblis," Sufi Women, Masters of the Path: A History of the Masters of the Nimatullahi Sufi Order,* and a few volumes from Nurbakhsh's epic twenty-one-volume work, *Sufi Symbolism*. Reading Nurbakhsh gives me a sense of where Peter came from; even if Peter had split from Nurbakhsh to follow the Maryamiyya, his later take on Sufism seems to pull more from the Nimatullahi side. But anyway, forget Peter; the Nimatullahis offer access to the Anti-Caliph tradition and a portal into

Persian Sufi thought that doesn't require me to deal with Peter's Orientalism and pedophilia.

I pick up *Jesus in the Eyes of the Sufis,* a collection of excerpts from classical Sufi texts. While canonical Islam holds Jesus in high regard, it gives him no voice, no personality; he's just another prophet in the Qur'an's roster of names. In Sufi literature, Jesus comes alive, with a rich body of stories and teachings that claim no historic authenticity but still sound cool. Flipping through the pages, I arrive at the parable of a dead dog that Jesus and his disciples encounter in the street. While the disciples complain of the dog's stench, Jesus remarks only on the beauty of its white teeth. "Say nothing about God's creatures," he tells them, "except that which is in praise."

In *Masters of the Path,* I read on the order's beginnings. Shah Nimatullah—his name means "Bounty of God," and I like to write it *Nimat Allah,* to make him look like a Five Percenter— was born in Aleppo, Syria, in 1331. As a child, he memorized the entire Qur'an by heart, and later memorized Ibn 'Arabi's *Bezels of Wisdom,* which he treated as an authentic revelation from the Prophet to the saint. In his later poetry, however, he'd recall growing weary of textual scholarship:

> I perceive all the professors of esoteric knowledge
> to be full of learning with no application—
> day and night wasting their lives, pursuing
> discussion, chatter, and empty disputation.

Hungry for another kind of education, he set out in search of a spiritual master but found himself outgrowing every teacher. He reminds me of Peter, the Columbia dropout who chased after initiations all over Asia. Shah Nimatullah's yearnings and wanderings led him to the holy city of Mecca, where he found Shaykh Abdullah Yafi'i, who was celebrated as the "shaykh of shaykhs," a master of both esoteric and exoteric religion, the inner and outer forms, the heart and the law. When

Shah Nimatullah saw Shaykh Yafi'i for the first time, he felt as though he were a mere drop in the ocean, and Shaykh Yafi'i was the ocean itself. Shaykh Yafi'i held divine secrets in his chest, Shah Nimatullah believed, and Shaykh Yafi'i's breath brought life to the dead.

Shah Nimatullah traced his physical genealogy directly to the Prophet Muhammad, but Shaykh Yafi'i claimed a chain of teachers that began with Muhammad's guidance to Ali—whom Nurbakhsh describes as "Master of Masters, Initiator of the Chain of Love, Leader of all who travel the Sufi path." When Muhammad called himself the "city of knowledge," he named Ali as the city's gate. Shah Nimatullah took on Shaykh Yafi'i as his teacher, receiving that *silsila*. After seven years as Yafi'i's student, Shah Nimatullah became a perfected master in his own right, qualified to share what he had been given.

He distinguished himself from other Sufi masters by never turning away a disciple: "All those whom the saints have rejected," he proclaimed, "I will accept, and according to their capacity, I will perfect them." And he forbade his disciples from wearing special costumes to show off their membership in his order. As Nurbakhsh put it, "Wearing spiritual clothing does not make one spiritual."

Surprisingly for the order's Shi'a history and current state, Shah Nimatullah was a strict Sunni Muslim. "O you who are the lover of Ali's family," he wrote, "choose the Sunni way, which is our path, lest you be lost and destroyed." He also emphasized observance of Islamic law and sought to rid Sufism of non-Islamic influences such as Neoplatonism or Hindu mysticism. His migration to Iran, and his descendents' marrying into the ruling Safavid dynasty, would lead to the group's eventually becoming a Shi'a order; but even the Nimatullahis' relationship to Shi'ism became tense. One of the order's revered saints (and another of Peter's Anti-Caliphs), Mushtaq 'Ali Shah, was executed, allegedly after playing the call to prayer on his sitar. In the years following Khomeini's revolution, Iran's new life as an "Islamic Republic" caused a real problem for the Nimatul-lahis, who have basically washed their hands of formal Islam altogether.

"My knowledge of the science of prophets and saints," Shah Nimatullah declared, "is more perfect than that of any school." Before him, Ibn 'Arabi wandered from Spain to Mecca and all over the place, drawing from the wisdom of whatever masters he found, before growing into the *Shaykh al-Akbar*. Peter tried, and I've tried. I wouldn't mind having a perfect master, but the idea also bugs me out. Nurbakhsh's quotes on the master-disciple relationship—"Disciples must tell the master their secrets"; "Disciples must realize their limits and not ask questions about matters that are beyond their spiritual states and stations"; "Disciples must never undertake any matter of consequence without first obtaining permission from the master"—read like the demands of a cult hustle. It's even sketchier for Nurbakhsh to say it, because—as the Nimatullahi Master—he was claiming that power for himself. At least he doesn't look like a cult leader in his pictures, nothing scary like Frithjof Schuon, whose eyeballs try to dig into your skin and lay eggs in your veins. Nurbakhsh just looks like a sweet old man. When he passed away after half a century leading the order, his son became the new Master. If I accept initiation, the son would become Allah's ambassador to me. I don't know the son's name or what he looks like. He lives in London.

Even if this novel never sees the light of day, I'm living it. *The Great Zamel* reveals my struggle as a Muslim. If you want a life with religion, you eventually have to decide whether you'll take it in the butt. I'm still afraid of becoming a slave to mental death or anyone else's power. I've seen orthodox Muslims do that, even without a Sufi doctrine to justify it. Right here in the Bay Area, I could head over to the Zaytuna Institute in Hayward and watch Sunnis drink the Kool-Aid for their celebrity white convert shaykh, Hamza Yusuf. The Zaytuna crowd gives him everything that dervishes give their master; even if these people haven't physically bowed their heads to Hamza Yusuf, they've bowed *inside* their heads. You have to wonder about a guy like that. At some point in his career, he had to see where things were going between the community and him, the way people's eyes went glassy when they looked at him, and Hamza Yusuf had to decide whether or not he deserved to be Hamza Yusuf.

That kind of mess betrays what I used to see as the core of Islam. At least on paper—forgetting the power that Muslims sign off to imams—Islam offers a direct relationship to the Creator, with no human intermediaries. But I know that I can only say this because Muhammad is dead. In Muhammad's time, he was the exclusive middleman. God would tell him what the Muslims needed to do, and the Prophet would tell the Muslims, and the Muslims would do it. Fourteen centuries later, the balance of power has shifted, because no one can really submit to a dead man. If following Muhammad's wise sayings and example ever becomes difficult, if something doesn't quite match our modern conscience, Muhammad's not here to explain himself. So *we* explain him; we decide what his words mean. The progressives tweak him, the conservatives tweak him, everyone using phrases like "allegorical interpretation" and "historical context" to bend his words until he gives us exactly what we want. Ibn 'Arabi had a sequence of vision encounters with Jesus, Moses, and finally Muhammad, who told him, "Cling to me, you will be safe." I like the sound of that, but what can it really mean? Ibn 'Arabi insisted that he didn't write a word of his *Fusus al-Hikam;* it all came to him straight from Muhammad. Three centuries after his death, Ibn 'Arabi would fill that role for others, when a mystic proclaimed that Ibn 'Arabi had appeared to him in a vision and delivered a book about Solomon that was filled with occult squares and the science of letters.

Prophets and saints follow *us* now, like Sabbah's "Nothing is true—everything is permitted," as William S. Burroughs broke it down to Tennessee Williams: Muhammad says nothing because he eventually says whatever you want him to say. I'm not

sure that I want to hand that power over to a shaykh, but I Self
Lord And Master comes with its own dangers. At some point,
everyone needs to get slapped down. There's wisdom to the
idea that if you don't have a shaykh, the devil is your shaykh;
the devil, after all, is supposed to be your *nafs,* your asshole
lower ego-self, right? Listening only to your asshole self can't
be a good idea.

I wake up fairly early in the morning and sign out one of the
Headlands cars for the day. Before reaching the Golden Gate
Bridge and the city, I have to drive through a long tunnel that
feels like a border crossing. Headlands Center for the Arts is on
the wilderness side, the green hills full of deer and wild turkey
and coyotes. Once I make it through to the other side, my phone
gets a signal and I'm back in civilization.

My Sufi scavenger hunt takes me up the 101. Spotting an
IKEA from the highway, I get off and purchase a white bedsheet. Getting change back, I've found the second item on the
list, the coin. Then I stop at a mall and buy a $15 ring from a
vendor near the food court. Guessing that "rock candy" just
means any hard candy, I hit a Walgreens and buy three packs of
Jolly Ranchers, roughly two pounds, as Russ advised.

In the parking lot, I call my friend Shahid. He came up in the
straightedge punk scene, discovered a Sufi shaykh named Bawa
Muhaiyadeen, and eventually became a full-on Shi'a Muslim.
For a time he was seen as the leader of a syncretic movement
blending Shi'a eschatology, deep ecology, and kung fu. He
knows the problems of humans' being propped up as spiritual
authorities, even when they make all efforts to avoid it.

"I'm considering initiation," I tell him. "I've been reading
Nurbakhsh for a while, and I like what he says. If I want to keep
growing with it, I have to make it more than books, right? Only
issue is the human-authority thing." Shahid compares Sufism to
the martial arts. In the dojo, you give a certain amount of trust
and respect to your teachers, because they've dedicated their
lives to that particular path and have something real to give you.

But even in martial arts, he warns, there's still corruption and exploitation.

If I wanted to, I could imagine the worst. Nurbakhsh had become master in 1953, which happens to be the same year that a CIA-backed coup dumped Iran's democratically elected prime minister, Mohammad Mosaddegh, and handed supreme power to the monarchy. I've seen online rumors charging that Nurbakhsh's rise to leadership of the order was arranged by Iranian military officers as part of the Shah's co-opting of Iranian Sufism, but nothing that I could confirm or take too seriously. Nurbakhsh looks clean so far, but Shahid still warns me to keep my guard up. I'll give the Nimatullahis what they want, within the limits of their own cipher. When I'm inside the *khaniqah,* their master can speak for God, sure. As long as they don't try to tell me how to vote or where I should invest my money.

Last item is the nutmeg, but there's a can of it in my kitchen at Headlands. The Persian word for nutmeg is *juz.* "In presenting *juz* to the master," wrote Dr. Nurbakhsh, "the traveler's head is symbolically presented here as a hostage." Even when threatened with decapitation, I'm not to reveal my secret.

Sunday evening at the *khaniqah,* I learn that I'm a moron. Russ explains that the rock candy has to be real rock candy, like big crystal chunks found only at a confectionary store, and the nutmeg is an actual complete nutmeg; you can't represent your head with ground-up nutmeg in a can. I've never seen a nutmeg before, but he shows me one and then I grasp the symbolism.

They already have some real rock candy at the *khaniqah,* and Russ says that I can use it and the intact nutmeg in my offering. He wraps the candy, nutmeg, coin, and ring in my white sheet, and gives back my canned nutmeg and three packs of Jolly Ranchers.

The night starts out like any other. I sit in the visitors' room while the initiated dervishes go into their special room. As usual, someone warns me that they'll be turning off the lights. I sit alone in the dark, listening to the lecture and music. When the lights come back on, the dervishes all file into the visitors' room and stand at solemn attention. Russ comes in, I stand up; he takes me firmly by my right wrist and leads me to the special room. In my left hand I'm holding the bundled white sheet containing my gifts.

It's a large room, wide open. The floor is covered in overlapping Persian rugs. The walls are lined with cushions and bear portraits of past masters. Ron sits on a mat at the far end of the room, completely motionless and wearing one of those cone-shaped hats. Above him are two axes crossed over an animal skin, with a beggar's bowl hanging from them.

I follow the script as Russ has instructed. We both fall to our knees and kiss the floor, and then touch our foreheads to the carpet in proper Islamic *sujdah*. It occurs to me that I've just bent over for a man, the *Great Zamel* moment. On a superficial level, bowing to one of Allah's creations betrays Islam on a level equal to Qur'an desecration or a beer-and-ham smoothie. It feels dirty, but, like many dirty acts, it comes with a kind of liberation, because the earth keeps turning and it dawns on me that I haven't been destroyed. We rise and Russ takes me by the wrist again, leading me to Ron. Russ and I share the Sufi handshake that Ron taught me; our hands clasped, I kiss the back of his hand, and he kisses mine, and we say *Ya Haqq* as we touch our foreheads to each other's hands. Then he puts my hand in Ron's, and we do the same. I think that Russ has left the room.

I'm sitting in front of Ron, my bundled white sheet between us. "Keep your hand on it," he says. Still holding my right hand, he asks me to repeat after him. I ask God to accept this unworthy offering, and vow to accept the Master's commands as coming from God, and guard my secrets. I also promise to never harm a living creature—the one sin on this path, according to Nurbakhsh. "I'm going to teach you the proper way to remember God, your only true Beloved," Ron says. He then sucks in air and blows it out. He does it again. When he breathes in, he says "Allah." When he blows out, he says "Hu." I try. It feels unnatural at first, to say a word while I'm inhaling, but becomes easier. We practice together. "Allah represents the Attributes of God," says Ron. "Hu is the Essence of God. When you breathe in, you contemplate the Attributes. Then you exhale the Essence." He tells me to do this fourteen times every morning, and then a fifteenth time in silence.

Russ appears with the rock candy, followed by all the dervishes, who stand against the walls. Russ says *Ya Haqq* and gives each dervish a piece of the rock candy. The dervishes each welcome me in turn with *Ya Haqq* and the Sufi handshake. When the ceremony is complete, Ron asks that the dervishes remember when they were first accepted into this family.

Ron sits down and everyone follows. The lights go off again and this time I'm on the inside; I'm with them. The music plays and Ron starts us clapping. We join the recorded chants of *La ilaha illa Allah,* "There is no god but God," building until it gets loud and fast and crazy. It's too new and unfamiliar for me to really get involved. I'm trying to see in the dark, hoping for an idea of what people are doing. I wonder how they move with the music, and focus too much on their states to find one of my own.

I drive back to Headlands thinking, *Shit, now I have a master.*

Headlands Center for the Arts used to be an army barracks, and the surrounding hills contain several abandoned military structures. The old radar base is on nearby Hill 88. The hills overlooking the coast have several WWII-era lookout stations, where I can go down ladders into little bunkers with long narrow windows to gaze at the moonlit ocean and wait for the Japanese Empire to come. In each one, the walls are tagged with graffiti, the floors decorated with crunched beer cans, condoms, and an occasional dead mouse. I choose a station and sit with my back straight in the Nimatullahi meditation pose, right hand on left leg with left hand over right hand, take out my iPod, and do my own one-man *majilis,* breathing in and out like Ron taught me while listening to the Sabri Brothers doing Nusrat, *Allah*

*Hu, Allah Hu, Allah Hu.* I keep breathing, remembering the Attributes and the Essence. According to declassified FBI files, in the 1940s Master Fard Muhammad was suspected of being the head of the Japanese army, which turns this gaze to the ocean into a prayer for the messianic, a prayer for the Man to come with his ships and planes and red sun flag. Sometimes it pushes me back to my room to work on the novel.

## 4.

It started during the War on Terror, when Rasta-
fetishizing white kids with dreadlocks found themselves outnumbered by Arab-fetishizing white kids in
keffiyehs, labeled "freedom scarves" in the catalog
of American Eagle Outfitters. The United States sent
C-130 planes over Afghanistan, dropping thousands of
white envelopes that each contained a crisp $100 bill
and a photo of George W. Bush; then came the black
vinyl burqas at Hot Topic, Islamo-chic translated
into suburban mall-goth with lots of straps and useless zippers. America started to go Muslim only after
doing everything it could to bury Islam. The same
thing happened with Japan. When did the cartoons start
coming over? The giant monsters, robots in disguise,
and video-game heroes? When did Japan start feeding
culture to American children?

The U.S. does not consider it a terrorist act to
throw atomic bombs at nations thousands of miles
away, when it would not be possible for those bombs
to hit military targets only. These bombs were
rather thrown at entire nations, including women,

children, and elderly people, and up to this day
the traces of those bombs remain in Japan.
   —Osama bin Laden


The first Japanese toys exported to America were figures of dancing black men called Alabama Coon Jiggers.

In the first place a thought surged in Allah, an
intention, a will. The object of this thought and
the intention of this will were the letters from
which Allah made the principal of all things, the
criteria of everything difficult. It is from these
letters that everything is known.
   —Imam Ja'far al-Sadiq


The young saint was sitting in front of the student
union building, his back propped against the red brick
side. He had just bought a Taqwa-Bomb, Taqwa-Cola's
new twenty-four-ounce can with metallic twist-off cap
resembling the nose on a missile. The design on the
can was an American flag with Islamicized colors: green
and white stripes, white stars on a green field. The
same banner seen on eighteen-wheeled Taqwa-Cola trucks
going down the I-90.

The young saint's hair, sculpted with gel into points
that looked like an inferno of black fire on his head,
added nearly two full heads to his height. He was
skinny but fit. On his right arm he wore a wristband
with two rows of studs, green and white.

With his arms resting on his knees and his legs
spread apart, he made the Taqwa-Bomb in his hands look
like a huge aluminum dong. A green-and-white, star-
spangled phallus that would explode if you shook it.

The young saint twisted open his Taqwa-Bomb dong and
examined the cap's underside to find the letter *Noon*:

*Noon* was one of Allah's *muqattaat,* the fourteen mystical letters sometimes used to begin suras of the Qur'an.

To properly interpret the letter, he referred to a beat-up graphic novel that was small enough to stuff into his pocket. According to the Naqshbandi Decoder in the back pages, *Noon* had a value of fifty. If you cross-referenced that with the Moorish Color Code of Electronics, and digit-summed fifty as 5+0=5, *Noon* reflected as green. *Noon* also expressed Allah's Divine Attribute as *an-Noor,* Light, which explained why they had neon green lights illuminating the minarets of mosques.

The Arabic word for man, *insan,* contained two *Noon*s. The Naqshbandi Decoder said that these two *Noon*s symbolized the human being's two states, the internal and external. The idea was for these states to match each other in perfect harmony; your internal being was like the sun, and its light was reflected by the moon, your external being.

Back in his dorm room, alone, the Great Zamel took a Mr. Muhammad graphic novel and opened it to the cornered page where Mr. Muhammad was floating in outer space, wielding his green laser sword deflecting blasts from electromagnetic radiation guns of enemy *shaytans*—it was Mr. Muhammad who sent the shooting stars and comets that knocked jinns out of heaven. Mr. Muhammad was not God but, like all things in the created universe, existed as an appearance of God's special attributes, and his massive titanium cone-shaped dong manifested them to perfection. That kind of idolatrous fetishization felt like *shirk* but was really the

oldest religion, worship of the first creative power
that men could recognize, a force parallel to the rain.
Mr. Muhammad's dong manifested the ninety-nine Divine
Names, the young saint knew, and Mr. Muhammad was not
a prophet; he did not come with a new Qur'an to replace
the old one, but his dong could have been the Mahdi,
who would bring the hundredth name.

The Great Zamel gazed upon that perfect phallus,
beating himself with slow tight strokes, and arrived
at the conclusion that if Allah sent a messenger to
every nation in human history, and these divinely
guided prophets all delivered Islam in the language
of their own people, then some of them must have used
the language of phallic worship. Then he teased his
anus with a finger but couldn't bring himself to go
in, still too weird, but when he was ready to finish
he propped himself upside down against the wall so
that his feet were in the air and his penis hovered
above his face. Still holding the comic book with his
left hand, he pounded away with the right until it
was time and then turned to face his penis, opening
his mouth and pretending that it was a shot of Mr.
Muhammad's *kauthar* falling to him from the clouds—but
again, given his ingrained Muslim-boy repression, he
could only taste the first shot, since his brain immediately resumed normal function, pulling him back
out of the fantasy, and it felt gross, so he just
pumped out the rest on his neck and chest and then
lay back down. He swallowed what he had but there was
no thrill to it after the drama. His penis shrivel-
ing up, his upper body covered in gelling sperm, he
realized that Mr. Muhammad would also ejaculate. The
Great Zamel wanted it. When the Great Zamel won his
trip to Mecca, he knew, he'd let Mr. Muhammad finish
*inside*. In the Great Zamel's daydream, Mr. Muhammad

did not emit crude fluid in random bursts that landed everywhere and stained things, but pure green light in tight, controlled beams that appeared almost as an extension of the penis. Laser sperm, but a green laser sperm of Allah's *Nur*. The Great Zamel imagined cross-sections of Mr. Muhammad's cybernetic phallus, laying out the structures involved in producing and emitting the *Nur*. Mr. Muhammad's constant remembrance of God brought forth an electrical charge, causing atoms within specific power cells of his purified *nafs* to become agitated. The *nafs* functioned as his lazing medium, emitting Allah's *Nur* as coherent radiation. The excited electrons were pushed to release their energy as photons, which were then reflected off mirrors to encounter atoms, which were then stimulated to create more photons. The laser *Nur* traveled through a series of fine coiled tubes into a network of cords to reach the *Nur* Concentrator, where the power was refined and matured and then transported through another long tube, which contracted to propel the *Nur* forward. The *Nur* was transferred to a copper conductor, which would be the equivalent of a man's urethra, carrying it through the phallus to the exit gate. Just before the *Nur* left the body, magnetic rings shaped the energy into a tightened beam. It exploded out of him at ten thousand kilowatts, which would be like a hundred thousand one-hundred-watt lightbulbs focused on one target. His weapons-grade green laser cum would sever an enemy soldier's leg at the knee. For the Great Zamel, it'd be like getting fucked by the sun itself.

The Great Zamel was still covered in his own stuff, which had no symbolic value, just dead babies crusting up in his chest hair and on his neck. The taste of semen lingered. Semen contained fructose, he knew, but he couldn't taste it.

He grabbed a towel and scrubbed his chin and neck
hard, then headed over to Wegmans because they were open
twenty-four hours and he could buy another Taqwa-Bomb.

I don't know where it's going, since I've never been able to really
pull off a novel with a fully developed plot. Maybe I can get
around plot by having the young saint, my Great Zamel, just
wander the country, finding random characters, popping into
their stories and learning lessons from them, and obtaining devils
on his way to the encounter with Mr. Muhammad. It can be like
a Radical Queer Islamo-Futurist version of *Winesburg, Ohio*.
Those characters can have their own journeys, making the novel
an infinite regression of tangents and sidebars, and somehow they
can all end up at Mecca, Indiana, and tie the thing together.

Assuming that my new master's okay with my writing Islamic
butt-sex novels. I haven't asked.

Another gas station, another chance. The Great Zamel
went in. The Taqwa-Cola was in the cooler on the back
wall, as always—but this gas station had more, as the
Great Zamel stood in shock, trying to understand, while
his eyes still strained under the fluorescent lights.

There, in the cooler racks, was every flavor of Taqwa-
Cola ever made, including the rare ones that went only
to "selected markets" and even the failed prototypes
that the Great Zamel had read about on the Internet:

*Caffeine-free Taqwa,*
*Diet Taqwa,*
*Taqwa Light,*
*Caffeine-Free Diet Taqwa,*
*Diet Taqwa Light,*
*Caffeine-Free Diet Taqwa Light,*
*Wild Cherry Taqwa,*
*Caffeine-Free Wild Cherry Taqwa,*

*Diet Wild Cherry Taqwa,*
*Wild Cherry Taqwa Light,*
*Caffeine-Free Diet Wild Cherry Taqwa Light,*

and so on for each variety:

*Taqwa Lime,*
*Taqwa Max,*
*Taqwa Blue,*
*New Taqwa,*
*Taqwa Cipher,*
*Vanilla Taqwa,*
*Taqwa Green,*
*Taqwa Clear,*
*Taqwa Fire,*
*Taqwa Ice Cucumber,*
*Taqwa Tropic,*
*Taqwa Boom,*
*Taqwa Blast,*
*Taqwa Raz-Matazz,*
*Taqwa Mega Superstar Bonanza,*
*Taqwa Super-God Master Force,*
*Taqwa Zig-Zag-Zig Allah (TZA),*
*Taqwa Latte,*
*Taqwa Pomegranate,*
*Taqwa Fitna,*
*Taqwa Frauda,*
*Taqwa Ta'wil,*
*Taqwa Zahir,*
*Taqwa Batin.*

They were temptations, he knew, distractions by the
devil, the real one, to fuck him up. He passed over
the special flavors and went straight for the classic
Taqwa-Cola in the twenty-four-ounce Taqwa-Bomb. Yes. A

queer Taqwa-Cola Salafi. No innovation. His *sirat* was the only thing straight about him.

He brought it to the register and put his crinkled American dollar on the counter. The clerk was talking on his cell phone about how great the Ottoman Empire had been.

"The Zionists had gone to the Ottoman Sultan and offered to relieve his debts in exchange for Palestine, and the Sultan said no, it doesn't belong to me, it belongs to God . . . "

"Fuck the Ottomans," said the Great Zamel.

"What?" shrieked the clerk, still on his phone.

"The Ottomans shit on that place in their time."

"Take that back," said the clerk.

"They were just another empire, doing what empires do."

"The Ottomans weren't an occupying army," the clerk insisted, keeping the phone to his face. "They were the legitimate heirs to the Umayyads."

"Well, fuck the Umayyads," said the Great Zamel. "What do the Umayyads have to do with me?"

"What, are you Shi'a?"

"No, I'm not Shi'a." That ended it. The clerk picked up the money and the Great Zamel walked out.

He twisted open the Taqwa-Bomb.

No way.

No fucking way, except as Allah wills.

His back against the gas station, he slid down to the ground, eyes locked on the specially marked bottle cap in his hand. He must have looked like a bum to people going in to prepay for gas, and for all intents he *was* a bum now, having renounced the world to wander unattached for Mr. Muhammad. But now he had a devil, one-fourth of the way to Mecca, Indiana.

He had not eaten but could live off the sugar and calories of Taqwa-Cola. He went back inside to get his meal for the night, a few more Taqwa-Bombs with the last of his money. Maybe it was stupid to buy more than one Taqwa-Bomb at the same place, he thought; what were the odds that a gas station would have more than one devil? If he just left it to Allah, he'd get what he needed. He scooped up an armful of Taqwa-Bombs and brought them back to the neo-Ottoman, who gave him a dirty look and put them in two flimsy plastic bags that they both knew would break.

The Great Zamel had to pee. He felt it not in his bladder but the very tip of his penis, like a tickle or an itch that he had to relieve. The effect of too much caffeine. So he walked to the restroom, the handles of his plastic bags stretching under the weight of Taqwa. They were plainly going to rip, but he kept walking, and then the handles finally broke and the Taqwa-Bombs hit the floor hard. He picked them up and brought them into the restroom with him and locked the door. It was one of those public restrooms with a deadbolt, not just a flimsy button that you pushed on the knob, so the Great Zamel felt secure.

He stood the Taqwa-Bombs upright in what he surmised to be the cleanest corner of that public restroom, the farthest from any receptacle, behind the door. He unzipped and stood over the toilet. It took a moment and then only dribbled. It was Islamically proper to squat when you peed, because it reduced the chance of spilling urine on yourself. The Great Zamel thought about it and then climbed up on the toilet, his feet on the seat, hovering over the water. It was still a weak stream.

The devils had to mean something, he was sure, endowed with a secret message that Mr. Muhammad would share with him in Mecca, Indiana. Maybe it was related to the four journeys of the Sufi described by

Mulla Sadra, with the capture of each devil symbolizing the completion of a journey. The first journey
takes you from the creatures to the True One, where you
reject the material world and the veils between yourself and the Divine. In Mulla Sadra's second journey,
the seeker begins to manifest Allah's Divine Names, so
he sees with the Eyes of the Seeing. The Great Zamel
couldn't find a way to relate that to his second devil,
but perhaps the truth would pop up at a magical time
that he couldn't expect.

It was too soon to think about the third journey,
but the Great Zamel went there anyway: the journey
from the True One to the creatures, seeing all things
in their true essences. The fourth journey went from
creatures to creatures, the seeker having reached the
station of a prophet who brings laws, qualified to now
guide creation.

The Great Zamel squeezed his penis to get out the
lingering urine and walked over to the sink to wash the
tip. He looked at his face. It was older and sad, he
thought, at least in the awful light and spotty mirror.

After zipping up, he sat in the corner with the
Taqwa-Bombs. He opened one and it exploded all over
him. There was no devil. The next one exploded and he
knew how to avoid that but didn't even bother—he just
let it get him. Again, no devil. He had a few more but
left them alone and started drinking, not even washing
the Taqwa from his arms. He knew that he'd feel sticky
later and it would serve to remind him of the path.

He came out of the restroom, arms filled with Taqwa-
Bombs, just as a crazy white man entered the gas station, white *jalabiyya* and green turban with green band
on his left arm bearing a white star and crescent—but
the star was a swastika.

"I'M HERE TO SAVE MY *DEEN* FROM THE FAGGOTS AND THE MUDS," he proclaimed to the neo-Ottoman, who said nothing.

"I think about Malcolm X when I jerk off my black Hindu boyfriend," said the Great Zamel.

"That's funny," said the Aryan Ansar, without smiling. "Way to be a faggot *and* a traitor to your race."

"My race?" asked the Great Zamel. The moment he said the words, he realized that he must have looked white to the Aryan Ansar.

"At least you pillow-biters aren't tainting the race," said the Aryan Ansar. "Just keep your diseases to yourselves."

"Sorry to break it to you," said the Great Zamel, "but you follow a mud religion. Shouldn't you be praying to the hammer of Thor or some shit?"

"You know what the word 'Iran' means? It means 'Land of the Aryans.' That's me, dick. The Iranians are my brothers. If it wasn't for the Arab invaders, they'd still have green eyes and blond hair." He pronounced *Arab* like *A-rab*. "Read some Henri Corbin," he added.

"Motherfuck Henri Corbin," said the Great Zamel. "Corbin can lick my asshole two times."

"Islam," snapped the Aryan Ansar, "is the only world religion that's not currently infiltrated by Zionists."

"But Islam opposes racial division."

"The Qur'an says that Allah made you into tribes and nations so that you may know one another."

"That's fucking stupid."

"The Qur'an is stupid?"

"No, the way that you're reading it is stupid. The Qur'an says the Arab is no better than the non-Arab or—"

"Yeah?" The Aryan Ansar looked him over, with his

torn plastic bags and Taqwa-Bombs. "You look like a
sack of shit to me, *insha'Allah.*" He turned to the
neo-Ottoman. "What you think about all of this?" The
neo-Ottoman said nothing. "What's with all that Taqwa-
Cola? You going to shove those things up your ass?"

*In a manner of speaking,* thought the Great Zamel.

"I'm collecting the devils."

"Is that right?" asked the Aryan Ansar.

"Yeah. I'm going to meet Mr. Muhammad, *insha'Allah.*"

"How many you got?"

"One." Bad idea and he knew it. The Aryan Ansar ran
straight for him. The Great Zamel dropped his Taqwa-
Bombs, one open and spilling everywhere, and the Aryan
Ansar slammed him into the wall. Something smashed the
Great Zamel in the kidney, maybe the handle on a door.
The Aryan Ansar slapped him hard in the eye and he
fell. The Aryan Ansar kicked him in the ribs and then
frisked him for the devils.

"Listen to me, cocksucker," said the Aryan Ansar,
wrestling the Great Zamel for access to his left front
pocket. "I already have three devils at home; this is
all I need."

"Go fuck yourself. Mr. Muhammad's not a Nazi!"

"GOETHE WAS BASICALLY A MUSLIM," shrieked the Aryan
Ansar. "*WEIN ISLAM GODD ERGEBEN HEIT, IN ISLAM LEBEN
UND STERBEN WIR ALLE!*" He gave up on the pocket, stood
up and kicked the Great Zamel again. "MUSLIMS WERE
FULLY PROTECTED UNDER THE THIRD REICH! HITLER SAID
THAT ISLAM WOULD HAVE BEEN A BETTER MATCH FOR THE
GERMAN PEOPLE THAN CHRISTIANITY!"

Another kick. "HITLER SUPPORTED THE PALESTINIANS—I
BET YOU HAD NO FUCKING IDEA! THE GRAND MUFTI OF JERUSA-
LEM SUPPORTED NATIONAL SOCIALISM! WE ALL HAVE THE SAME
ENEMY, CAN'T YOU SEE THAT?"

The Aryan Ansar looked down at him. The clerk was still behind the counter. "Read up on your houris," said the Aryan Ansar. "In the Jannah, all those virgins are white. Think about it. You think Farrakhan's getting up in there? Fuck no. *KAMPFE DARUM FUR ALLAHS SACHE!*"

# 5.

The early Sufi saint Rabi'a al-Basri, whenever she had two coins, would carry one in each hand; she refused to hold two coins in the same hand, for fear that hearing them clink together would distract her from God.

I'm not a Sufi about my books. I hold my books together and hear them clink. I stack them tall, stare at them, and whisper "body of work" to myself. I count them and write lists of my titles, including the promised unwritten ones, my future books waiting for me. Writing is both my path to God and the *shaytan* pulling me away. My dirty mirror.

It's hard to write when your old books have already determined the place for your new one and you have to worry about whether the new one can or even should fit in that place. I bring my laptop to the Headlands library for its wireless connection, and messages come in from people telling me what the old books mean. They don't know that they're providing the measurements for *The Great Zamel*. Some PhD student gives me a detailed description of what's scattered around his office: records by that mysterious non-Muslim Islamophile who called himself Muslimgauze, the hardcore band Racetraitor with Arabic script on their CD (a bunch of white radicals in Chicago, one of whom turned out to be Pete Wentz), an anthology on hardcore in which

Shahid says that the Islamo-straightedge-vegan movement ended up being exactly what none of them wanted: a bunch of white boys. And the guy has Peter's books, and my books, and some European Muslim anarchist writer that I've never heard of. He's waiting to add my next one to the pile, he says. So now I have to think about the pile.

I keep going to *majilis* and learn the *adab*, the manners. When entering the *khaniqah*, we touch the floor and then kiss our hands and put them to our foreheads. One night I ask Russ to explain the Nimatullahi symbol, the *tabarzin* (crossed axes) and *kashkul* (beggar's bowl).

In his history of the order, Peter broke down the axes as "symbolic of the eternal dualities." Male/female, exoteric/esoteric, God as both Majestic *(Jalal)* and Beautiful *(Jamal)*—that kind of thing. The axes crossed over the bowl represent *al-Insan al-Kamil*, the Perfect Man. Russ explains it more or less the same way, with the axes representing Good and Evil, Heaven and Hell, the artificial dichotomies that a Sufi destroys, since dualisms betray the unity of being. The beggar's bowl, he says, represents spiritual poverty. Also hanging from the crossed axes is a string of *zikr* beads, signifying the Islamic tradition from which this order came.

When we gather for *majilis,* Ron asks that I sit beside him. "A Sufi does not ask questions," he says to the room. "A Sufi waits for the answers to come to him or her." Then he adds that if you're compelled to ask a question, go ahead and ask it.

He pauses. I know that it's about me. "So am I saying," he asks us, "'Don't ask questions' and, 'It's okay to ask questions'? Yes, that's what I'm saying. The question I was asked tonight was, 'What do the axes mean?' It's an excellent question. The axes symbolize a Sufi's rejection of this world and the next. A Sufi does not worship God for fear or hope of the next life or benefit in this one. With no thought of punishment or reward, we love God for God's own sake." The *kashkul,* the beggar's bowl, he adds, signifies emptiness, the real poverty of our existence.

Another pause before he adds, "Michael inspired me tonight." He turns to me. "Michael, is that okay?" I can't look at him, but smile while facing the carpet. I'm starting to see Ron the way everyone else does, like he's the parental figure in the room. Whatever intellectual positions I hold about religious authority, and the Five Percent's unending war of liberation from the Ten Percent, Ron has a real power and I respond to it. Sometimes it's hard to look directly at his face, even though he often closes his eyes when he speaks.

Ron talks about the Master. "The Master sees with God's Eyes. He listens with God's Ears. When he speaks, it is with direct inspiration from God." He exhales slightly when he says "God," like a *zikr,* but almost as though uttering the word becomes a brief physical trauma. "You're always in the Master's presence," he tells us, "because . . . well, I'll let you figure that out." He gives a little laugh when he says it.

*Zikr* is easier when I'm alone in the abandoned military lookouts. Other people's spiritual lives make me uncomfortable. I don't like to hear people talk about Allah or their relationships to whatever they worship or their special experiences. They always sound crazy to me, and then I can only guess how I sound with my number/letter mischief. I can see the value in turning off the lights during *majilis,* and allowing someone into the main room only after she or he has been initiated; it makes the *khaniqah* a safe space for losing yourself. Even when the collective chanting and clapping gets you hopped up, you're still alone.

At nearby Stinson Beach I sit in the sand, look out at the water, and say the Name. At first it seems corny, like I'm just another goofy white guy in Northern California appropriating Eastern traditions and breathing funny on the beach. Sufi poetry is full of water imagery, ocean-drop imagery—"When the drop lets go of itself, it becomes the ocean," I heard the other night—and the ocean made me think of the beggar's bowl on our Nimatullahi symbol, the poverty of all created things. The bowl is empty, it's nothing; even these 68,634,000 square miles of water that look so eternal compared with me add up to nothing. The ocean will pass away in its time; the Qur'an says that everything will perish except the Face. The breathing exercise puts me out of the world for a moment. I love God, Allah, the Black Mind, etc., with sadness, but it's a good sadness, and my love becomes serious and sincere. My initial motive for checking out the Nimatullahis was such a load, with my academic wonk-speak about finding new ways to "engage the tradition." I was ignoring the heart of the matter, the *Hu,* which Ron said could not be found with the intellect. It comes only with sitting and breathing and wanting the *Hu.*

I also do *zikr* at the mall. It happens by accident. Just sitting at a table in front of Nordstrom, watching people walk in and out, I start repeating *Allah Hu* to myself and feel the same peaceful grief again. These dying boys in sleeveless shirts to show off their deltoids, and these poor rotting-flesh girls buying Coach sneakers, and me watching them—we all become piles of ash and dust, nothing and nothing. There's a relief in that, even for the boys' and girls' sakes. Especially for my sake, and the sake of my novels that don't mean anything. I'm gone and whatever I love is gone; my ambition to write the definitive Great American Radical Queer Islamo-Futurist Novel will be gone, just like my ambition to write the definitive biography of Peter Lamborn Wilson is gone, just like my old Islam is gone and my new Islam is gone and all the Islams are gone, the Qur'an is gone, Prophet Muhammad is gone. Everything perishes except for the Face. The Qur'an says so, which means the Qur'an even closes itself, no more religion.

On my Headlands porch again, where the Man is supposed to show up and fix everything—I'm out here because inside the house, in my writer's room, my novel waits for me and it's frozen at thirty thousand words. The Great Zamel becomes disillusioned with his beloved, rejecting Mr. Muhammad as merely the puppet of an evil corporation, tosses away the three specially marked bottle caps that he has accumulated, and renounces the quest. I've written the ending already, but the middle parts won't move.

If Taqwa-Cola was so unhealthy—and of course it was— why would Mr. Muhammad peddle it to millions of kids? And if Mr. Muhammad stood for justice, why would he align with an evil corporation like Taqwa-Cola, which in turn aligned with all of the other evil corporations? He had imagined Mr. Muhammad as somehow separate from the rest of the world, but Mr. Muhammad was full of the world. Graphic novels, movies, action figures, Taqwa-Cola. Sex with Mr. Muhammad would actually be a three-way; because while Mr. Muhammad fucked someone, he'd still have big business up his own ass. The Great Zamel thought about that as a chain of being, because big business would come up Mr. Muhammad's ass, but the jism would then travel through Mr. Muhammad's body and make its way out of his penis into the Great Zamel, where it would live forever. In the end, it wasn't even like Mr. Muhammad would be the one penetrating him; Mr. Muhammad was only a way of receiving a greater power, though not the power that the Great Zamel had expected.

The Great Zamel wondered why Allah would have given him a third devil, bringing him that much closer to the end of his quest, and then reveal that the quest was all a sham anyway. Maybe Allah had nothing to do with specially marked bottle caps.

The darkness was broken by the white and green lights of a gas station. The clerk was a round South Asian uncle with a comb-over.

"*As-salamu alaikum,*" he said to the Great Zamel.

"What?"

"You Muslim, brother?"

"Why do you ask?"

"Sorry."

The Great Zamel threw down the last of his money and walked out. After counting the change, the clerk went over to the cooler and got his own Taqwa-Bomb. He stepped outside to find the Great Zamel sitting on the curb. The Great Zamel looked over and saw the uncle drinking Taqwa-Cola—how embarrassing, he thought, for them both to be there with dumb Taqwa-Bombs with the green-and-white flag, the Great Zamel in his Taqwa-Cola shirt like a scene from the commercials. He made a self-conscious attempt to shift his pose into something less TV-like.

The clerk watched the Great Zamel finish off his Taqwa-Bomb, put the cap back on, and, with a flick of his wrist, send it skating across the parking lot. "Wasn't a devil?" the clerk asked.

"I didn't look," said the Great Zamel.

"You should—you could win a free trip to Mecca."

"Why would I want to meet an advertising mascot?" snapped the Great Zamel. "You want to fuck Ronald McDonald?"

"No," answered the clerk thoughtfully, as though it

had been a real question. "*Insha'Allah,* I don't want
to fuck Ronald McDonald."

"You know that the original guy who played Ronald
McDonald was fired because he got fat from eating free
burgers? I'd bet that Mr. Muhammad doesn't look anything like he does in the commercials or the fucking
comics. He's probably morbidly obese and all of his
teeth are rotted out from drinking this poison. If you
stab him, he just bleeds high-fructose corn syrup." The
Great Zamel then noticed the clerk's bulbous stomach.

"Sometimes," said the clerk, "my teeth hurt."

"This shit takes the paint off cars," said the Great
Zamel. "State troopers use it to clean blood off the
highway. Why do we put it in our bodies?"

"You could save a lot of people by answering your own
question."

"They're shit out of luck." Feeling that this marked
an appropriate end to the exchange, the Great Zamel
rose to leave. But he had nowhere to go, and no direction that meant more than another. He chose the opposite way from which he had come. Walking past the
clerk, he nodded for courtesy.

Then he saw the pin on the man's work shirt. Green,
with white star and crescent. The Great Zamel froze.
"That's the Mecca pin," he gasped.

"That's right."

"You went to Mecca? You found four devils?"

"I drink a lot of Taqwa," said the clerk, patting
his belly.

"You went to Mecca?"

"The one in Indiana, yes."

"And you met Mr. Muhammad?"

"He gave me a full tour of the place."

"*Subhanahu Allah.* Holy shit, I don't even know what
to say. You went to Mecca! What was it like?"

"Brother," said the clerk, "whatever you hear about Mecca doesn't even begin to explain. You have to catch your own devils and see it for yourself."

The clerk brought the Great Zamel back into the gas station and let him take a loaf of bread and peanut butter. The Great Zamel made a triple-decker sandwich and sat on the counter to eat it.

"What about Mr. Muhammad?" he asked between bites.

"I think that whatever you expect to see, he becomes," said the clerk. "If you see him only as a mascot for this company, that's what you see in Mecca. If you want something more, you get more."

"What did you want to see?"

"I never wanted a superhero; I just wanted a tour of the Taqwa-Cola world headquarters." He gestured toward the Taqwa-Cola display near the front door, cardboard cases stacked like bricks into a green and white tower, and to the soda cooler in back. "It's funny for me, you know, I see the trucks come in and deliver the Taqwa-Cola, but I forget that it actually comes from somewhere." The Great Zamel looked at him, stunned. For the clerk, that was the interesting part: to see where the cans and bottles came from.

"I never thought of it like that," said the Great Zamel.

"Come here," said the clerk. He led the Great Zamel on a tour of his own corner of the Taqwaverse, his store, even bringing him behind the pop cooler. With the Great Zamel standing behind the pop trays, the clerk ran back around and opened the cooler door. "Now you know what it's like to be a pop bottle," he told the Great Zamel, trays of Taqwa-Bombs between them. "You stand there and watch people reach in and grab for you, or your friends."

After the clerk was back out of the cooler, the Great Zamel asked him about the tour. "*Al-hamdulilah,*" said the clerk, "Mr. Muhammad gives a good tour. And he also gives a good friend."

"I've heard some shit about him."

"Like what?"

"Like, they say that Taqwa-Cola backs military regimes and ruins water supplies in developing countries—"

"What does that have to do with Mr. Muhammad?"

"What's that have to—are you kidding? He's the face of Taqwa-Cola!"

"But he's not the brain," said the clerk. "He's not the men in the suits making decisions. He doesn't have anything to say to them."

"So the company can do whatever it wants and he's just a smiling billboard with no responsibility? What about us who live for this shit? You don't know what I put myself through for that man; you have no idea!"

The Great Zamel said, *"Khuda hafiz"* on his way out and headed down the road, thinking that at the next payphone he'd call his mom collect and see if she would get him or put him on a bus.

Then he heard the clerk shouting from fifty feet behind him.

"I DON'T KNOW WHAT *YOU'VE* BEEN THROUGH? COME BACK HERE AND SEE THIS!"

He walked the Great Zamel behind the gas station, past the 1983 Chevy Celebrity, and into the woods. Following a well-worn path, they came to a clearing that turned out to be at the shore of Lake Michigan, the only Great Lake entirely within the borders of the United States. To the Great Zamel, who could not see the other side, it looked like an ocean.

What the clerk wanted him to see was a floating island of clear plastic Taqwa-Cola bottles, close enough to the beach to wade to, on which stood a mosque built entirely of green-and-white aluminum Taqwa-Cola cans—even the projecting transept entrance, four corner minarets, and onion-shaped dome. A tattered, fading Taqwa-Cola flag waved from a bent antenna atop the center dome.

"Where did this come from?" asked the Great Zamel.

"It's mine."

"You built a *masjid* out of pop cans?" asked the Great Zamel.

"You can't tell from far away, right? Even the domes look smooth from far away."

"Where did you get all those cans?"

"You ever do the Taqwa-Points?"

"No."

"I guess it was before your time. When you buy a Taqwa-Bomb, you get a letter in the bottle cap, right? And each letter has a point value in the Naqshbandi Decoder. So with Taqwa-Points, you save up all your bottle caps and cash them in for merchandise."

"I remember that," said the Great Zamel. "I was in kindergarten when they did that."

"Remember the commercial where it showed Badshahi and it said that you could win it for five hundred million points?"

"Yeah, but that was just a joke. What, did someone actually do it?"

"I didn't take it as a joke," snapped the clerk. "I took it as real. They said it in their commercial: Badshahi Masjid, five hundred million points. Where did they say it was a joke?"

"Wasn't there a tiny disclaimer at the bottom of the screen?"

"No disclaimer. They said ten thousand points gets you a jacket. Five hundred million points gets you Badshahi. Why wouldn't it be real? So I started collecting points. I was going to win Badshahi Masjid, bring it to America, and make it the Islamic Center of Zeeland, Michigan. And I would run it the way I wanted to."

"How were you going to run it?" asked the Great Zamel.

"Regular, but we'd have music. You hear of Hazrat Inayat Khan?"

"No."

"He was a Sufi and he taught, 'There will come a day when music and its philosophy will be the religion of humanity.'"

"Was that a hadith?"

"Far from it."

"So, you really thought you could get all those points?"

"At first," said the clerk, "I just pissed away my salary into buying up all the Taqwa-Cola that I could, but realized that I wasn't getting anywhere. So I got the community involved, everyone joining in, and then my brother and his son and I all quit our jobs and emptied our savings to collect Taqwa-Points full-time."

"Did you end up getting the points?" asked the Great Zamel.

"You know what half a billion points looks like? To deliver them to Taqwa-Cola in person, we put the last of our funds into a caravan of old yellow school buses. We painted the buses green, just as a tribute to Taqwa-Cola. We were so happy. And green is the color of Hidayat—see how it all fits together? We drove to Mecca feeling like real pilgrims."

"So, what happened when you got there?"

"They said it was only a joke. They never expected anyone to really collect that many Taqwa-Points."

"Assholes," said the Great Zamel.

"What happened to truth in advertising? What happened to taking responsibility for your promises? You just can't trust anything to be what it says it is."

"You could have sued them."

"I did not want to win a mosque in a court case. That's not mathematical at all."

"I can respect that."

"And they gave me that flag," said the clerk, pointing to the top of the middle dome. "That flag would have been one thousand points, but they just let me have it."

"That's something, at least."

"To get that flag, you'd have to get a ع. Those were always the most rare."□

"So, how did you end up building a mosque of pop cans?"

"When we were collecting the Taqwa-Points, we put away bottles and cans as a reserve, since we could get money for them. See how our whole lives revolved around Taqwa-Cola? Empty cans represented money to us. After our trip, my brother wanted to cash them in and cut our losses. I said no, these cans will give us a mosque one way or the other."

"How many did it take?"

"The mosque, I do not know . . . but it rests upon two hundred thousand two-liter bottles."

"The entire island is bottles?"

"Polyethylene terephthalate isn't biodegradable," said the clerk. "It manifests Allah's Attribute as *al-Hayy*, the Everliving. And an empty bottle with the cap on tight floats like a buoy. I baled the bottles together in fishing nets and then put plywood sheets on top."

"What do you call it?"

"I call it Pelan. You know the Actual Facts of Lake Michigan?"

"It looks big."

"Lake Michigan is three hundred and seven miles long by one hundred and eighteen miles wide," said Bilal. The Great Zamel did the math in his head: 3+0+7=10.

1+1+8=10. Allah is the best of planners. "You know what
the surface area is?"

"Not a clue," said the Great Zamel.

"Twenty-two thousand three hundred square miles."
2+2+3+0+0=7.

"That's something," said the Great Zamel.

"You know its volume?"

"No."

"One thousand one hundred and eighty cubic miles."
1+1+8+0=10. The clerk then glanced at the weary and
dirty Great Zamel. "What is your plan, brother?"

"To trust in Allah."

"If you have nowhere to go, you can stay on my island.
There's food and water in the mosque. You can go out
there and see where it takes you." The Great Zamel
looked at the clerk, unsure if he had heard him right.
The clerk added, "Insha'Allah." In Actual Facts, the
Great Zamel really didn't have anywhere else to go, at
least until he figured out how the fuck he had gotten
to this point. He thanked the clerk and walked into the
water with his shoes and socks still on.

After a few days of drifting on Pelan, the Great Zamel
decided to take off all of his clothes. He considered
whether it would be wrong to enter the masjid naked, but
then thought himself insane for treating the clerk's
pop-can hut like a real mosque. The Taqwa-Cola mosque
did have a mihrab niche in the wall to indicate the
direction of Mecca, but the Great Zamel saw it to be
purely decorative, since Pelan turned in submission to
the waters. Sometimes, but only by chance, the mihrab
did face Mecca; sometimes the one in Indiana, sometimes
the other one.

The Great Zamel took short dips in Lake Michigan,
never straying too far from Pelan. He would climb back

onto the island, naked and wet, and study his body. His testicles shrank in the cold water, and his penis shortened like a folding accordion. He wondered if Mr. Muhammad would have liked him. Of course, he did not even know if Mr. Muhammad liked men at all. But perhaps, the Great Zamel considered, even if Mr. Muhammad self-identified as purely heterosexual, he might still fuck a man, if he viewed only the *zamel* as gay.

The supplies that the clerk had left in the mosque were only gas station fodder, like potato chips and beef jerky and pop. Sitting on Pelan's plastic shore with a two-liter Taqwa-Cola, the Great Zamel imagined Pelan to be floating on the surface of soda in a greater two-liter bottle, so huge that its two liters were like the Pacific Ocean with its 68,634,000 square miles. 6+8+6+3+4+0+0+0=27=2+7=9. The Great Zamel looked up and thought the heavens above him to be only a clear plastic ceiling. Then he looked back down into the upright bottle in his hands, staring hard at the bubbles of fizz rising to the surface, and imagined another young saint, another Great Zamel on his own island inside. And that Great Zamel could be holding another bottle, in which there was another Great Zamel on another Pelan, and so on in both directions forever.

The Qur'an said that Allah was the *Nur,* the Light of Heaven and Earth; but the word "light" appeared in the Qur'an exactly as many times as the word "mind": forty-nine each. That's seven and seven but even deeper, because it's also 7x7 and 7x7.

The Great Zamel recognized his own skull as the lamp of the worlds.

For all his gayness, could the Great Zamel rightfully be called a Muslim? On Pelan there was no social order to protect, no need for the regulation of sex, and no harm caused by his balls feeling the breeze and

the sun. He imagined Pelan as his own Islamic Republic
under a weathered green-and-white banner and its own
*shari'a*. In a country of one, the Great Zamel figured,
where the only laws were between Allah and himself,
*shari'a* would not be so bad. In a country of one, he
would be both accuser and accused, and also the judge.
He would be the power and the one othered by power.

With Pelan evolving into a real nation in the Great
Zamel's imagination, he considered the Qur'an's statement that every nation had received a messenger and
wondered whether he could be Allah's appointed messenger for his people—himself—delivering to no one his
new Qur'an of Lake Michigan's measurements: *What is
the surface area? What will make you understand the
surface area? The surface area is 22,300 square miles.
Now, which of the favors of your Lord will you deny?*
Then he pulled himself out of it and asked Allah's forgiveness for his mischief.

Men entered his thoughts but were not there to touch
him or be touched. He even wanted to believe that he
had removed himself to Pelan to save the world from
his evil. Such a sacrifice would make him the best among
men. He found the name Muhammad in Arabic to look like
a man lying down, and on the paper of his thoughts
wrote one "Muhammad" above the other and then rotated
them to make it look like they were standing up, one
behind the other.

The Great Zamel believed in respecting the uncles.
Even if they hated him, they could still have good
hearts; they were wrong, but for the right reasons.
The Great Zamel even considered that he was helping
the uncles by providing them with a target. He had an
uncle with Crohn's who experienced no symptoms when he
went to India and drank the water; intestinal worms
were often used to treat Crohn's, because the human

body needed something to attack every so often to keep it from getting upset with itself. In case there really was an *ummah,* thought the Great Zamel, he could serve as its intestinal worm.

Then he remembered the hadith—and it was a hadith, but he couldn't remember who'd reported it or when— about the smallest part of faith being to simply remove an obstacle from the road of your brother. If you can't pray five times every day or whatever, at least do that much. The Great Zamel considered that perhaps he was the obstacle and the community was better off with him removed to a safe hermitage in Lake Michigan.

Pelan continued its lazy float, the Great Zamel sub- sisting on potato chips and Taqwa-Cola and remaining ever mindful that Allah was steering him somewhere. He forgot about everyone he had encountered along the way, and sometimes caught himself forgetting that he was not the only person who had ever lived, and that the scrip- tures and systems that he used had come from others.

The mosque's four corner minarets, also made en- tirely of Taqwa-Cola cans, served the function of a crow's nest on an old ship. The Great Zamel would make a cautious climb to the top of one and stare out across the water, sometimes hoping for a glimpse of land or even a boat to prove that there was still a human race out there. From his pop-can minarets, he also per- formed the call to prayer for himself and the fish. *Allahu Akbar,* he cried to Lake Michigan. The sea. Look- ing out at the water, the Great Zamel knew that he was a Muslim, and he knew why oceans tripped people out and made them religious: the ocean was not a living thing, but it moved like one. It betrayed the dichotomy of living and moving vs. non-living and non-moving. When you looked at the water moving, you saw Allah.

A black bird soared by Pelan, though the Great Zamel

still could not see land. The bird flew over him,
carried by the wind with no visible effort. *Perfect
mathematics*, thought the Great Zamel. Far from civilization and man-made things, Allah's existence felt
more secure; to believe in Allah, you had to look at
Allah's work. In the cities, you saw only human work.
Humans could not have made that bird.

It circled around the mosque, and then flew by close
enough that the Great Zamel could see its individual
feathers. The bird rode the air without moving its
wings at all. The sun made its black wings shine,
almost silver but the purest black, perfect triple
black. The Great Zamel wanted the bird to mean something, because he was out there alone on the vast sea
of Lake Michigan and this black bird came from nowhere.

On the side of every Taqwa-Cola can, near the request to avoid mixing Taqwa-Cola with alcohol, it
read, "Comments or Questions, call 1-800-433-2652."
The Great Zamel did not have a phone. If he did, perhaps it would not have gotten a signal in the middle
of Lake Michigan. Only as habit, he broke it down:
$1+8+0+0+4+3+3+2+6+5+2=34=3+4=7$. If he left out the
1-800 part and digit-summed the other segments sepa-
rately, $4+3+3=10$ and $2+6+5+2=15$, and $10+15=25$, and
$2+5=7$. So it came out to Allah either way. All praise
was due.

If Taqwa-Cola was Islamic pop, why did you win the
trip to Mecca by collecting devils? The Great Zamel
tried to master that science. To drink a Taqwa-Bomb,
he considered, one must twist off the top and decapitate the devil. "De-*cap*-itate," he said aloud. This
was what Mr. Muhammad wanted to show us, he thought,
by putting devils' faces in the caps. Drinking Taqwa-
Cola, which of course was a ritual act, began with an
act of violence. You sacrificed your money and slit the

devil's throat, and the devil represented your lower
self, or your ego, which you must reject to be con-
sumed with Allah. You drank the Taqwa and the Taqwa
drank you.

Perhaps the devil represented the treacherous exoteric religion—the Taqwa-Cola corporation, the design-
ing and marketing and advertising of product, all that
must be overcome to receive the wisdom inside—and Mr.
Muhammad signified the esoteric tradition. Now a prisoner of the corporation, he offered secret messages
through promotional contests if only you could read
between the lines. That was why he trained consumers
in numerology! He had a master plan to develop their
mental powers and spot truths in hiding.

The Great Zamel no longer knew what any of it meant.
Why did ﻙ equal four hundred? Who came up with that?

Words contained essence, at least Arabic words. The
Qur'an was eternal, alone with Allah before the universe existed, and every letter of the Qur'an was a key
to unlocking Allah's Wisdom. For the Qur'an to fully be
the Qur'an, the miracle that it claimed to be, required
a language specially designed by Allah to manifest its
full power.

The Great Zamel slept in the mosque, his head always
pointed toward the mihrab, even though the mihrab had
become meaningless, with his Mr. Muhammad graphic novel
on its Qur'an stand next to him. Alone with hundreds of
thousands of empty pop cans and bottles, he now lived
the religion of Taqwa-Cola in its purest form.

The Great Zamel had a full two-liter bottle of Taqwa-
Cola that he'd clutch in his arms like a baby. The
bottle must have been shaken; the plastic was tight,
no give at all. The two-liters were heavy, the bottles
shaped almost like missiles. Before passing out, he
stood his two-liter bottle upright and looked at the

vertical green-and-white flag. For the first time, it hit him that a product could disguise itself as an idea, and an idea could also become product. Then he remembered the obvious: that he slept in a mosque made of pop cans, on an island of two-liter bottles. Even the flag that flew over him and his nation of one was that same Taqwa-Cola flag, the colors of a brand. America, said the Ayatollah Khomeini, only wants you—the Muslim world—for your oil, "wants you as a market, to take away the oil and sell you junk." The Great Zamel could see America killing Islam, only to rebuild it and sell it back to him as a shell of what it was, Malcolm X castrated and recrucified on a U.S. postage stamp. But Malcolm was on a stamp in Iran first. Khomeini said that when "America praises us, that day we must mourn."

It was all fiction, everything. The Ayatollah and America were both fictions and products. No one lived in real life; it was all spaceships and graphic novels, children in a world with no adulthood. Numbers were real, numbers were the masters of fictions and products, but our names for numbers were fiction. Mr. Muhammad was fiction. Even if he was real, it wasn't the real Mr. Muhammad who powered the Great Zamel's fantasies. *That* Mr. Muhammad, he made up himself.

Alone and with no distractions or responsibilities, the Great Zamel found it easy to keep up with Islam's five daily prayers at what he guessed were their proper times. He had never done that before. The flashes of spiritual intensity in his life as a Muslim always involved calculators, not prayer rugs. On Pelan, he prayed naked in the mosque. To perform his ablution, he went to the edge of the island and washed himself in the waters of Lake Michigan.

One day while making his *wudhu,* the naked Great Zamel paused to look at the water, and without a second thought obeyed a random impulse to lean forward and fall in. He plunged underwater, feeling the tickle on his free-floating balls. Accidentally tasting the lake, he was surprised to remember that he was not actually in a saltwater sea. He opened his eyes and saw nothing.

To the Great Zamel, Lake Michigan had no birth record; in reality, Lake Michigan was ten thousand years old, born with the melting of the Laurentide ice sheet at the end of the last ice age. The clerk did not know that but could have told him that Lake Michigan had an average depth of 279 feet, with its greatest depth at 925 feet, and 2+7+9=18=1+8=9, Born, but the real story was with that 925:

$$9+2+5=16$$
$$1+6=7$$
$$7=Allah$$

The Lord of All the Worlds lived at the bottom of Lake Michigan.

Without knowing this manifestation, the Great Zamel went as far down as he could, then looked up at the glimmering light of the surface. It occurred to him that Pelan could drift away and leave him stranded. He moved toward the dark mass of Pelan until he could see the huge bales of two-liter bottles held together by fishing nets. The Great Zamel grabbed on to a net and let Pelan decide the way, drifting along like that until finally letting go of the net and kicking away from the island of exile.

# 6.

People that are really very weird can get into sensitive positions and have a tremendous impact on history.
　　—Dan Quayle

The Great Zamel doesn't make it, he drowns, and his body washes up on the shore of Lake Michigan. The novel is also dead. I never had a real novel in the first place, just some feelings that I needed to vomit up, so now Peter's given me two unfinished books.

At least I've finished my nonfiction Mecca book while out here. It's going to be called *Journey to the End of Islam,* the title a Rancid reference (not a Céline reference) because Rancid's song "Journey to the End of the East Bay" has that line "He said this is a Mecca, I said this ain't no Mecca man, this place is fucked," and also because the book ends in the Bay, when I make pilgrimage to what some believe to be the grave of Master Fard Muhammad in Hayward. It's the second book in which I visit the grave; going there with Cihan Kaan was actually the climax of my American Muslim road book, *Blue-Eyed Devil.* The books are really just chapters of one big book, currently weighing in at 1,700 pages or so, about half a million words. I don't know what they add up to beyond page and word count, whether they become a cohesive unit of information that does anything for anyone.

Maybe they do. Muslims write to me on Facebook acting like I must have some insight that will help their own struggles. Most of the messages come from kids who are just trying to sort themselves out. Every so often, I get a high scientist claiming Alamut or Patmos as his hometown and writing about spaceships and reptilians and his own numerological breakdowns, promising that if we form an alliance we can finally unlock the big secrets, bring down the Freemasons or whoever. All I can say is "I Self Lord And Master," meaning, find it for yourself. Once you think that you have figured out questions with no answers and obtained the Truth that everyone else needs, and you're ready to assign yourself that pivotal role in human history, there's nowhere to end up but as creep-ass Frithjof Schuon.

One guy writes to me and we end up building on the phone. His name is either Adam or Muhammad, depending on who he's speaking to. It can go either way with me. He was born and raised in Brooklyn. When he was eight years old, his mom converted to Islam. In Brooklyn, that move opened the door to all kinds of cultures: Tijani Sufis, Twelver Shi'as, Salafis, Isma'ilis, Tablighi Jamaat, Five Percenters. At eighteen he got into Ibn 'Arabi and embraced what he called "scientific pantheism," which he saw as harmonious with the Five Percent—"If nothing exists but Allah, what am I? What's the highest manifestation of that but a human being?" A pamphlet on al-Hallaj helped him work it all out: "The secret of *Ana al-Haqq* is that man is the image of God," he says. You can express it in any language: the Five Percenters tell us that "Allah" stands for Arm Leg Leg Arm Head, and in Persian, "God" *(Khuda)* and "self" *(khudi)* are basically the same word. Even though Adam/Muhammad was white, the Five Percenters considered him a brother because he was Muslim. Now he's an atheist, though he still fasts during Ramadan, goes to mosques, and offers prayers with tears in his eyes. "I glorify my mind," he says. "The only truth I know is me."

We name-drop mutual friends among the Five Percenters, and then I ask him if he ever built with the Nimatullahis. "They're upper-class white folks," he says. In Iran, Sufism was largely a bourgeois elitist thing, as opposed to places like South Asia, where it's more the folk religion of the streets and shrines. When Peter Lamborn Wilson, the Ivy League dropout and son of a famed Emerson scholar, showed up in India to study Sufism, Vilayat Inayat Khan said that he was too intellectual and pointed him to Iran. But when Khomeini took over in 1979, all the rich educated people fled, and they took much of the Sufism with them.

When I get back to New York, the next project could be a reconciliation of the Five Percenters and Ibn 'Arabi's *wujudi* Sufism, at least to my own satisfaction. A few more days, another *majilis*, I say my peace to the dervishes and get on the plane and forget everything—the *zikr*s, the books, *The Great Zamel* unfinished, the fact that now I'm an initiated dervish with a master. At home I stay up all night playing *Civilization IV*. Shah Nimatullah warned his disciples on the dangers of opium and hash, and Javad Nurbakhsh vehemently opposed drug use for members of the order, but video games can be worse than heroin. *Civilization IV* sucks me into wasting trillions of hours on that which does not exist, conquering the phantom world and coming back to real life empty-handed. If video games had been around in Ibn 'Arabi's time, he probably would have mentioned them as an additional veil on the Ultimate Reality—which at least makes me imagine my wasted time as a spiritual exercise, a contemplation of Allah's Attributes, since the only thing that can manifest Allah as the Hidden is the thing that hides him, right?

One of my civilizations kicked ass, though. I chose the Zulu Empire, made Taoism the state religion—I had been reading *Sufism and Taoism: A Comparative Study of Key Philosophical Concepts*, by Toshihiko Izutsu, one of Peter's perennialist colleagues in Iran—and named all of my cities after conscious and spiritual hip-hop artists, starting logically with the Universal Zulu Nation's Afrika Bambaataa and Afrika Islam, and then expanding to include KRS-One, Lakim Shabazz, Erykah Badu, and Killah Priest. I beat the game when my Taoist Zulus built a spaceship and blasted off to Alpha Centauri.

It's only after a random glance at a picture on my wall that I snap out of the funk. The picture is of a man from 1933 in a suit and tie, with hair parted slick on the left side, holding a large open book in front of him. I don't know who the man is—I mean, I *know*, I've read and written extensively about him—but I don't really know, because he did a tremendous job of escaping history, becoming a blank slate for whatever I'd put on him. So I tag him with Ibn 'Arabi's *al-Insan al-Kamil:* he's the Perfect Man, a saint and master who realized his full potential as manifester of God's Attributes in a physical body. The burning tree in front of Moses. I impress that idea hard onto the image. It makes me realize how low I am and what kind of work I should be doing. *Allah Hu, Allah Hu, Allah Hu.*

The man in the portrait is Master Fard Muhammad. I find him waiting for me in Harlem, where I pick up a smaller version of the same picture from some Nation Muslims at their table on 127th Street. When I tell the bow tie–wearing brother that I want to buy it, he looks at me funny and says, "Praise be to Allah"—I'm probably his first devil business of the day—but it's no problem, all peace.

The Nation calls him "Allah who appeared in the person of Master Fard Muhammad." In my good Sunni days, that was enough to prove that the Nation wasn't really practicing Islam: *La ilaha illa Allah,* there is no god but God, nothing worthy of worship but God. Muslims don't pray to human beings. The Prophet Muhammad himself was only a man and never claimed to be more, and warned us against making an idol of his grave. Ali had reportedly killed a man for calling him Allah. Compared with "regular" Islam, the Nation's treatment of Master Fard looks very Christian—which makes sense, because Minister Farrakhan preaches to a community that came mostly from Christian backgrounds. I think of it in terms of what Ron taught me about the Attributes and the Essence. The Essence is beyond our comprehension, a mystery veiled by this physical world unless Allah chooses to lift the veil for us; but the Attributes are displayed everywhere, even in us and through us. Peter had taught me about *tajalli*, the idea of Allah's Divine Names "shining through" the created universe. When al-Hallaj manifested Allah as al-Haqq, the Reality, he could shout, "I am al-Haqq!" and make it true in a way.

In the Nation of Islam's account, Master Fard was born in 1877 in the holy city of Mecca, where he was trained—*initiated*—by twenty-three wise scientists as preparation for the mission. On July 4, 1930, he arrived in Detroit and went from door to door in the poorest black ghettos, teaching the ones he called Lost and Found. He brought Allah with him, I could see it by running down the ninety-nine Names: for the friendless, he was al-Waliyy, the Helper and Protecting Friend; for the defeated, he was al-Fattah, the Victory Giver; for the unloved, he was al-Wadud, the Loving; for those who had been robbed of their "knowledge of self," he was al-Mu'id, the Restorer; for those who had been degraded by slavery and oppression, he was al-Mu'izz, Giver of Honor; for those who enslaved and oppressed, he was al-Mudhil, Giver of Dishonor; for America, he was al-Hakam, the Judge.

As al-Hadi, the Guide, he brought the Lost-Founds to a better way of life; as al-Muqit, the Nourisher, he taught them to eat the right foods and steer clear of the devil's poison animal. Teaching black people to believe in themselves as gods, rather than call out to an invisible ghost, he was az-Zahir, the Manifest, but he also vanished and became al-Batin, the Hidden. Uplifting people from "mental death," he was al-Ba'ith, the Resurrector. And for so many in the eighty years or so since his appearance, he has been as-Salam, the Source of Peace. So now I'm walking down Seventh Avenue with a portrait of *al-Insan al-Kamil* in my pocket, clutching it to remember that it's there, saying *zikr*s to myself and trying to comprehend what it'd mean to perfectly manifest Allah with every step, every time I lifted my hand or opened my mouth. It's mostly harmless, since Fard has escaped history and now he's only the picture, no scandals, unable to let me down. I can put him on my wall and not worry about it. How different was it for Elijah, who was what, thirty years old when he met the Master face to face? And he believed that Fard was the Mahdi and Messiah and God himself. Imagine the kind of love that they must have had for each other. As much as I got into Peter, I never took it that far, and I don't know what I feel for the new master of the Nimatullahis yet. It's real balls when you can give yourself to a living man like that, and portraits of dead men come nowhere close.

In *The Western Lands,* William S. Burroughs confesses that perhaps his approach to Hassan-i Sabbah has been "faulty." With "a carry-over of Christian reflexes," he has resorted to invoking Sabbah's aid "like some Catholic feeling his saint medal." I used to be a Catholic boy with saint medals, and I can feel myself doing that with Master Fard.

Fard comes to me after I eat a lot of cheese. Blue stilton is an entheogen, a god food. It smells and tastes rotten, but eat thirty grams of Blue stilton about twenty minutes before you go to sleep, and it'll give you crazy dreams. I eat a whole triangle of it, maybe a pound, and drink some milk and eat peanut butter and then read Derrida's *Edmund Husserl's "Origin of Geometry": An Introduction* until my eyes get heavy. When I dream, I dream that I'm in a classroom and Master Fard Muhammad stands before the chalkboard, drawing a bunch of shapes on the wall: triangles, circles, squares, maybe more complex figures like transparent dodecahedrons. Sitting at my desk, trying to follow Fard's lesson, I'm aware that each shape corresponds to a different category of prophet, and Fard the master geometer is bringing me into the science. Then I wake up. By Sufi tradition, I can treat this as something legit, since whole chains of initiation were founded on prophets' and saints' visiting Sufis in dreams. Ibn 'Arabi met Muhammad a bunch of centuries after

Muhammad was dead. So now I have another mental adventure, trying to science out what Fard wanted to give me, or what I was trying to give myself in the person of Fard. Husserl's concern was the history of geometry's "ideal objectivity," and Master Fard said, "Islam is mathematics." The science of geometry deals with objective truth, free from historical conditions, as opposed to religion, which is all unreliable narrations and unreliable cultures—if you study religion, history is everything, but figuring out who invented geometry won't make you better at the cold science of it. Husserl placed the origin of geometry in ancient Greece, which I can't buy—Africans have been dealing with geometric forms for something like seventy-seven thousand years—but Master Fard placed the origin of the devil in ancient Greece, with Dr. Yakub the mad scientist and his regime on the island of Patmos.

So who are these prophets represented by shapes? I could get esoteric about it with Ibn 'Arabi, who considered prophets and saints to have various cosmological functions, literally maintaining the universe. Or maybe the point is to leave the human prophets behind and focus on the idealized forms: get your own vision of what Master Fard is supposed to be, and then go ahead and be that.

# 7.

Everything is a name of God. You, too, are names of God;
your tongues are names of God, your hands are names of
God . . . you go in the name of God, and you are the name
of God; the movements of your heart are the names of God,
and the movements of your pulse are the name of God.
          —Ayatollah Khomeini

Master Fard's lessons are littered with words like "Islam" and
"Muslim," but most Five Percenters don't call themselves Muslims today. If we're all names of God, who needs mosques?
Even Khomeini says in his poetry, "I became disgusted with the
mosque as well as the madrassa."

The Allah School, which I guess is a madrassa of sorts, is a
small brick building on 125th and Seventh Avenue that used to
be a barbershop. It was given to the Five Percenters by then-
mayor John Lindsay in 1967, when he was working to build
relationships with groups that he feared would otherwise burn
the city down.

On the way, I start thinking about 'irfan. Khomeini would
not have liked the Five Percenters, but at least you could put his
words in conversation with theirs. "None of us has the right to
say of a certain person or thing, 'This is God,' and no rational

person would accept such a claim," the Ayatollah warns. "However, one may perceive a manifestation of God that is completely impossible to express other than by formulations such as this."

"Peace, death angel!" exclaims one of the gods when he sees me come in. He's wearing a Five Percenter "crown," a gold and black knit skullcap with a single tassel, like a fez.

"Peace, god!"

"I'm glad you're here," he says. "I wanted to build with you on something."

"Sure."

"Does Sufism say that the black man is God?"

"You ever read Attar, god?"

"Who's that?"

"Farid ad-Din Attar. Sufi poet from Iran, twelfth century. Wrote *Conference of the Birds.*"

"Break it down."

"It's a story about thirty birds who are searching for the Greatest Bird, the Simurgh, but the whole adventure is just an allegory for the Sufi path to Allah. So you have these thirty birds on a quest for the Simurgh, and at the end of the quest, when they finally encounter the Simurgh, it turns out that they were only searching within themselves, *for* their own selves. Even the Allah-Bird's name spells it out: *si* means 'thirty' and *morgh* means 'birds.'"

"So this Iranian Sufi Muslim cat is saying that there's no mystery god."

"More or less."

"Do the Sufis teach what we teach?"

"It's complicated, god," I tell him, "but the Sufi order I'm in has an interesting initiation. I had to bring gifts for the master, just little symbolic tokens, you know? And one of them was a nutmeg, and they told me that nutmeg symbolizes my head that I'm putting up as a hostage for the secrets—"

"For *real?*"

I knew that it would grab him for the parallels in Master Fard's lessons.

"True indeed, god," I tell him.

"Okay, now there's something else I got for you—maybe you can help make the knowledge born."

"I'll try."

"You went to Mecca, right? The *holy* city of Mecca?" As opposed to the *righteous* city of Mecca, the gods' designation for Harlem.

"I did, god."

"There's this story I've been hearing about you."

"About me?"

"Gods have been saying that you went to Mecca and searched out the Sufis there, and the Sufis told you that if you want to see Allah, you gotta go to Harlem. Is that true?"

The question leaves me frozen. I recognize the story, but it wasn't originally about me. Five Percenter legend says that Old Man Justice, one of the movement's famed elders, was a merchant marine who found himself in the holy city of Mecca. He asked an imam where he could find Allah, and the imam told him, "Allah's not here." So Old Man Justice resumed his travels, eventually arriving back in New York, where he met Clarence 13X, who by then had renamed himself Allah. I don't even think the story was born with the Five Percenters; it sounds like older Sufi tales about saints searching the world for their perfect masters.

"Well, I did go to Mecca," I explain, "and when I made *tawaf*—you know, when they walk seven circuits around the Ka'ba—I broke it down with Supreme Mathematics; like, I'd be on the fifth lap around and see it as Power, you know, looking at how power manifests at the Ka'ba with the Ten Percenter Saudi kings putting their names on everything."

"That's peace, that's peace," he says, and I make an awkward exit out of the Allah School and down Seventh Avenue, dizzy at what had happened. Since Allah's assassination in 1969, Five Percenters have developed a rich canon of insane stories— Mayor John Lindsay offering Allah $10 million to stop teaching that the black man was God, Pope Paul VI visiting Allah during his stint at Matteawan State Hospital for the Criminally Insane, Allah causing city-wide power outages with his mind, and the Chinese government planning to recognize Five Percenters as an independent nation. You could probably include the story of Old Man Justice showing up in Mecca and asking imams to point him to Allah, but now I'm in there too—*I'm* an insane story. If I wanted to write a paper on Five Percenter oral tradition, I'd have to study myself.

It's Thursday, meaning that after my adventure with the Five Percenters uptown, I can head for the Nimatullahi *khaniqah* in the West Village for *majilis*. From "Peace, God" to "*Ya Haqq,*" it all feels the same to me. Whether or not there's doctrinal coherence, there's symbolic coherence; regardless of how their texts match up, they fit together in my life.

Before *majilis,* I mine the *khaniqah*'s library for jewels, pausing at Toshihiko Izutsu's massive *Sufism and Taoism.* Izutsu was part of Nasr's Tehran scene, and can be found in that 1975 group picture from Mashhad. The revised edition of *Sufism and Taoism* was originally supposed to be published by the Imperial Iranian Academy of Philosophy, but then came Khomeini. Next to Izutsu on the shelf, I find his friend Henri Corbin's *Creative Imagination in the Sufism of Ibn 'Arabi,* but I'll leave it alone. Next to Corbin I find a book attributed to Ibn 'Arabi himself. Scholars today regard the work as a forgery, but it still brings me the right words for the moment:

His Prophet is He, and His sending is He, and His word is He. He sent Himself with Himself to Himself. . . . There is no difference between the Sender and the thing sent, and the person sent and the person to whom he is sent. . . . And for this the Prophet . . . said: "Whoso knoweth himself knoweth his Lord."

As with al-Hallaj and his "I am al-Haqq" passion play, I'm not too invested in whether Ibn 'Arabi really said the words or not; either way, the schools of inheritors are saying it. You don't have to get martyred to be put in that kind of spot. I'm alive and I say real words. People inherit my real words and bend them into new shapes. My words may or may not be worth bending. Sometimes, a reader finds beautiful things in me that the writer never meant to say, and then credits the writer for them. When that starts to happen, the time comes for your name to occasionally require quotation marks (or, if the name is a verbal utterance, air quotes with your hands): "Mike Knight." You know, Mike Knight after he really became "Mike Knight."

A girl who self-identifies as an Alevi Five Percenter writes to my Facebook page on correlations between Five Percenter thought and Hurufism, Akbarian Sufism, and Twelver Shi'ism. We revolve around the Imam, she says, like the world around the sun. We cannot exist without the Imam, the veil of fifty thousand veils. Besides, she adds, Ali is one of Allah's ninety-nine Names. She makes it gender-progressive, writing that Fatima (our Islamo-goddess, "mother of her father") shared some of her own light for the creation of the world. Her interpretations earned trouble from a few gods, she adds, asking me whether she should find a new group or just build with "Mike Knight skill."

Not sure what "Mike Knight skill" means, but I could be at serious risk of becoming the Five Percenter equivalent of Henri Corbin, which would be a disaster. Corbin was a real scholar who made meaningful contributions, sure, but he was also far too weird to leave it at that. Between an Orientalist emphasis on text and a perennialist emphasis on inner cores, he went too deep into the archetypes and hidden essences of things, and the elitist scholar-as-mystical-master ideal widened the gulf between his work and the street Islam of actual history. Corbin spent the Iran years keeping things esoteric and politically useless while

Shariati asked the people to see a modern Husayn in Che Guevara, and oppressed masses in the real-life mosques were reading Husayn's martyrdom with their own real lives. If you're a white guy in America who studies black supremacist gnosticism, there couldn't be a worse thing to be called than Henri Corbin.

# 8.

Gabriel, aka Propaganda Anonymous, looks like a metalhead with his long black hair, but he's a pure backpacking hip-hop MC, and he's into the Five Percent too, rapping "Arm-a-Leg-a-Leg-a-Arm-a-Head" in his new video. Gabriel interviewed an elder named Allah B for his website, so I pronounce him Jibril the Messenger Angel, since he took Allah's words and put them online for all humankind. He also builds with a crew of Universal Zulu Nation kids who have grievances with Afrika Bambaataa and the elders and have talked about starting their own faction. Gabriel gets the white man being the devil in terms of social constructions, largely because Gabriel's Irish—"The Irish weren't even considered white for the longest time," he says. He's got a book of fringe scholarship by some crank asserting that one can spot *bismillahir rahmanir rahim* on old Celtic crosses, and he's built with Peter about the Irish-Moor stuff. I take a slight jealous comfort in knowing that Gabriel saw the outside of Peter's house but wasn't invited inside.

The Messenger Angel and the Death Angel are riding the packed 3 train to the Five Percenter parliament uptown, and Gabriel wants to know how their material enters my "regular" Islamic life, what it can mean to me when they call themselves gods.

"The older gods told me a story," I explain, "where Allah the Father—the former Clarence 13X, you know?—once held up a plate and said, 'Whoever made this plate is the god of this plate.' So if you have a concept of Allah, a way that you conceptualize Allah based on whatever sources you use, the Qur'an, whatever, that's still *your* brain and your understanding. So who's the god of that plate?"

Gabriel's on his own science and eating off his own plate, entheogenic mysticism with ayahuasca, the sacred plant that Burroughs called *yage* and went chasing after in the Amazon. There aren't a whole lot of points where Gabriel's path crosses mine, other than his life in hip-hop culture opening the door for him to appreciate the Five Percenters. And, of course, Peter himself, the natural starting point for any dialogue between heterodox Islam and shamanic drug use. We're sitting on different branches of his tree: I geek out over stories of Peter in Tehran with Nasr and Corbin, and Gabriel wants to hear about Peter in Millbrook with Timothy Leary. My life was changed by *Sacred Drift: Essays on the Margins of Islam,* and Gabriel was similarly impacted by *Ploughing the Clouds: The Search for Irish Soma,* in which Peter argues for the existence of ritualized psychedelic use by ancient Celts. Drugs fit easily into Peter's Anti-Caliph framework: the spiritual power of intoxicants, he suggests, "had to be repressed in a religion and society based on rigid hierarchy. With Soma, *anyone* could be a brahmin; nothing is more democratic than the entheogen, the god within."

We both own Hakim Bey's *Orgies of the Hemp Eaters,* and we're both trying to deal with his influence on our lives despite the rape lit. "I asked him about NAMBLA during our interview," says Gabriel. "He just flat-out refused to say anything."

"He'll never answer for it."

"Was he down with the Five Percenters back in the sixties?" Gabriel asks. "That would have been fucking dope, man, if the Moorish Orthodox Church and Five Percenters got together and had, like, an *alliance—*"

"Peter didn't even know they existed. The Five Percenters were all over black newspapers, getting done up as a terrorist group supposedly plotting to bomb the Statue of Liberty and kill the Pope, and Peter's crowd of trust fund revolutionaries was uptown the whole time, right there at Columbia—basically Harlem—and they had no idea."

"That's kind of disappointing," says Gabriel.

"Has Peter ever done ayahuasca?" I ask.

"Nah, man. I tried to get him into it, but he says he's too old." There's a new Sufi order in Australia that uses ayahuasca as a sacrament, so maybe I'll head over there, drink the vine, write a nutso Sufi ayahuasca narrative, and snatch up Peter's title of American Drug Imam.

We share dream stories—I tell Gabriel about my cheese-powered dream in which Master Fard Muhammad taught me geometry, and he tells me about his Burroughs dream. "Burroughs is smoking a pipe, and his eyes are like someone blowing smoke into bowls of clear water—I'll never forget that, those eyes—and when we make eye contact, it just sends me flying backwards like he shot me out of a cannon." It leads to discussion of Peter's book on initiatic dreams and how Aristotle came to Suhrawardi in a dream to endorse him.

"Ibn 'Arabi said that the shit is real," I tell him. "It's just the form that's imagined, like, it's not literally the body of William S. Burroughs, you know what I mean? But it's *something*, I don't know what." Gabriel appreciates Sufism, since *wahdat al-wujud* can be agreeable to anything; in just about every tradition you have someone saying that the god/universe is one and it's all connected.

"The last time I built with Peter," Gabriel says, "he said something that kind of bugged me out a bit."

"What was it?"

"He said, 'There's a charm in failure.'"

"What's that all about?"

"I don't know, man. I think he sees his work as dead."

"It's reasonable. His serious academic work ended thirty years ago with Khomeini and the Revolution. His poetry never went anywhere. The anarchists have turned their backs on him. NAMBLA's hopeless. Hakim Bey still gets all the attention, and *T.A.Z.* was huge for the rave scene but the ravers are gone. And Peter hung out with important figures, but he was just *there,* you know? He was down with Leary, he worked with elite Sufi scholars in Iran, he knew Ginsberg and Burroughs in the eighties and nineties, but he's always the wingman." My analysis of Peter's self-image comes out smooth and without a pause, as though I have these lines memorized—as though I've already been thinking about it, like I'm waiting for the day that he's *my* wingman, like I'm Shawn Michaels preparing to superkick Ric Flair out of existence. When I started asking people in Peter's scene what they thought of the little boys, it got back to me that his publisher told someone, "Mike's got a murder-the-father complex." He could be right. Turning my back to Gabriel, I hunch over my notepad and jot down a thought:

*MMK > PLW*

Peter's never been hyped in the *New York Times,* he's never seen a book made into two movies, no one uses him in college courses anymore, and I've never seen his name in a chain bookstore; but my book wasn't the inspiration for Burning Man, so he has me there.

# 9.

The night that Gabriel and our friend Omar Waqar decide to check out the *khaniqah,* the woman at the door gives me shit—"You know the *adab*—you have to ask before bringing people!" They never said anything about that when I brought a harmless-looking desi girl and I was wearing a button-down shirt; it's different with Gabriel, in his black fingerless gloves and greasy hair coming out of his backward hat and T-shirt revealing the red, gold, and green Lion of Judah tattoo on his arm. She looks Omar up and down and asks, "Are you Persian?" He starts to answer that he's half-white, half-Pakistani, but she gets embarrassed by her own question and cuts him off: "It doesn't matter." They let us sit for tea and we pull books off the shelves. I'm looking at Peter's history of the order, when another woman comes down to sit with us.

"*Ya Haqq,*" I say to her.

"*Ya Haqq,* you're a dervish?" I nod and she sees Peter's book in my hands. "Oh, you came here with Peter?"

"Peter came here?" I ask.

"I don't know, I just assumed." It seems like she's covering out of respect for Peter's privacy. I should have figured that Peter would have shown up at the Manhattan *khaniqah,* since his old friend Javad Nurbakhsh would have been here at some point.

"I've known Peter for years," I tell her, but refrain from mentioning the North American Man-Boy Love Association.

On our way to Medina (Brooklyn) and I'm in the Messenger Angel's backseat, throwing a tantrum about Sufi elitism while suspecting that this might all be tricks of my ego, my treacherous *nafs*. You can't insult a real traveler on the Sufi path because s/he has no self to get offended over, and by getting pissy and bratty I know that I'm only exposing my spiritual immaturity, but out with it—"Why does it always have to be Persian?" I ask Omar and Gabriel. "I mean, the Persian language isn't transcendent for me. Arabic isn't even transcendent for me, but I can at least get why it is for people, and I do have a place for it. I understand if the Nimatullahis are traditionally a Persian community, but there's never more than one Persian at these things. What does it mean to everyone else vibing out to words that they don't understand? What does it do for them? And Persian music just isn't my *cultural* language, you know what I mean? Why am I supposed to sit there and meditate to this stuff that has nothing to do with me? Why can't we turn off the lights and play Rakim or Erykah Badu or something?" It sets off a spark in Gabriel and he's into it, and we start to build on taking these principles of sacred musical ecstasy and translating it into our own experience. Gabriel mentions the article he wrote about Rumi as the first B-boy and says that when he's in the freestyle cipher it takes him beyond himself, like hip-hop mysticism. Those spinning and whirling "Mevlevi cats," says Gabriel, "manifest pure spiritual hip-hop." He doesn't claim any personal or academic background in Sufism, but it had all sounded right to him when an Iranian girl built on Rumi after one of his shows. Omar knows the positive fury of punk, and he's into it too: "All music offers a heightened state," he says. "When you're really playing, your hands move faster than your brain."

"It's all already out there," I tell them, sprawling out across the backseat. "There's nothing new to invent in the field of religious experiences. All we can do is pour the old wine in a new bottle, as the Sufis say." Then I go off a bit—"Because maybe the whole master-disciple thing doesn't work for us! The old Sufis were all about finding their masters, but who gives a shit, right? Does that work in our moment? Do you give a fuck?" Neither of the guys in the front seat expresses that he gives a fuck. "The Five Percenters have something, you know what I mean? Yeah, it's all the same problem of organized religion, no matter how hard they try to dress it up as something besides religion, but at least they're democratic about it. There's no institution, no masters or shaykhs all Ten Percenter–style bloodsucking the people and making them mental slaves. No priests—you just show and prove what you've got. If you know your lessons, if you live by your lessons and manifest the lessons mathematically, it's peace and respect. What the shit, even the Salafis are more democratic than the Sufis, because it's just about knowing Qur'an and hadith. There's no one claiming a higher social position on the basis of mystical experience; no one's taking over on the grounds that they met Ali in a dream—" Then our man Volkan calls to say that everyone's hanging out at a basketball court near his house: Volkan, the Kominas, and two taqwacore girls who have been bumming across the country on Greyhound buses like I did in *Blue-Eyed Devil*. We find them sitting in a circle, a *cipher,* one of the girls playing her wild painted-up banjo, Imran playing the guitar, and he dedicates the next song to me: Sublime's tribute to KRS-One. *In school they never taught 'bout hamburgers or steak / Elijah Muhammad or the welfare state . . .*

Everyone has a song. Omar sings "Ignorance" from his old band Diacritical, and Basim sings his Kominas song "9,000 Miles" that builds on the Five Percenter stuff, and Gabriel freestyles about the 85 percent, the slaves to illusion. Volkan taps on the asphalt with drumsticks, and one of the girls has a tambourine. I don't sing, but they sing my poem "Muhammad Was a Punk Rocker" the way our friend Kourosh used to do it, and whatever I talked about in the car ride over here is starting to manifest in front of me—*this is a majilis*, we're doing *sema*, and this basketball court's a *khaniqah* for our nameless order, our non-order order with no hierarchy, no master. The experience stays real even if the order ceases to exist once we've all fallen asleep. It's a Temporary Autonomous Zone, if you want to use Hakim Bey language, the rejects dreaming up our own structure, just for a night. To keep it temporary, which is to keep it innocent and free from power grabs, don't say a word about what it means—no "Wow, this is like our own version of Sufism; we should keep doing this and start inviting people and make it into a *thing.*" The problem with any religion is when it tries to speak beyond the authority of its moment, like addressing modern gender issues from a position in the seventh century. In the Qur'an, Allah says, "This day have I perfected your religion for you, completed my favor upon you, and have chosen for you Islam as your religion," but what if it was just *that* day? The most perfect religion doesn't last long enough to be named. Our amazing night on a basketball court in Medina can have its own Qur'an that expires with sunrise.

During everyone's songs, I sit in the Nimatullahi pose, right hand on left leg and left hand over right hand, knowing that it will go unrecognized here. At times I wonder if I'm dreaming up this night into something that it's not for anyone else, alone in my overthinking a good time, but that kind of lonesome still allows for sweetness. Master Fard Muhammad told us that he crossed the ocean by himself. In various forms, the Arabic root letters of his name (F=ﻑ, R=ﺭ, D=ﺩ) mean things like "to be single, be alone, do alone, be unique, be without parallel, withdraw, segregate, isolate." I think about Fard but never let on and never sing along, never say a word, just smile and listen and love my friends and imagine Ibn 'Arabi having sexual intercourse with the Arabic alphabet, the Sufi master with his long beard and turban flying through space and humping letters. At one point I lie down on the pavement and fall asleep.

Another dream, this one without the support of cheese. Arabic words on my penis:

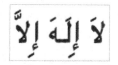

"No god but—" it says, as in Islam's statement of witness ("There is no god but Allah"), minus the affirmation at the end. In my dream, the words are followed by three unconnected Arabic letters, but I don't know which ones. So there's no god but *something* says what Old Man Justice called the "life rod." There's no help in knowing that there are three letters, since Arabic has a triconsonantal root system in which essentially every word breaks down to three letters. It is probably significant that the words start at the base of my penis and the final three, mystery letters are on the head. The Prophet said that if a man does not mention Allah's Name before having sex, the Devil folds himself up inside the man's urethra and the intercourse becomes a three-way.

Certain suras of the Qur'an begin with just a letter or a few letters. Throughout Islam's history, high scientists have tried to decipher their meanings. Allah says repeatedly that he gave us the Qur'an in the Arabic language, which has led people to treat the language itself as transcendent and eternal, its letters as real as gravity. My penis dream appears to be telling me the opposite. Maybe the Qur'an's mystery letters are just Allah pointing to the limitations of his whole project: *Look, this is all it is. Letters in arrangements that you imagine to mean something. Bricks that you think have formed a Ka'ba, but they're only LEGO bricks; you could take it apart and build something new with the same pieces.* The mystery letters say that we have letters but no mystery: *There's no god but* ا ل م, says my *shahadah. There's no god but* ا ل ر, *no god but* ت س م, *no god but the dot under* ب, *no god but the* و.

Why this had to be written on my life rod, I don't know—a penis is like an arrow, but what's it pointing to? Ask Frithjof Schuon.

# 10.

Gabriel calls Peter to ask about the next Moorish Orthodox Church initiation party, but it doesn't seem like there will be one, maybe ever—Peter's old and tired and doesn't like to do anything anymore. He just tells Gabriel to go ahead and do it on his own. I offer to use my charter to make a photocopy template for him, so he'd still have Peter's signatures and stamps.

"You can initiate me?" he asks.

"I'm as authorized as anyone, I have the lineage."

"Do you think we should make a new name, though? I'm down with the Moorish thing, but we're obviously not orthodox, and we're not exactly a church."

After some deliberation, we jointly decide that our autonomous chapter of the Moorish Orthodox Church will be known as the Moorish Gonzo Cipher. There are no doctrinal or ritual distinctions between the two bodies, since the parent body has no doctrines or rituals to begin with. The move seems purely aesthetic; Gabriel insists that somewhere in his life, he has seen an image of Gonzo from *The Muppet Show* wearing a fez, and thinks that it'd make an awesome logo. But it's also a simultaneous tribute to Peter and divorce from him. An alternative patriarch for the Moorish Gonzo Cipher might be Peter's comrade Hugo Leaming Bey, who uncovered the secret history of the Ben Ishmaels of Mecca, Indiana. Hugo grew up boasting of his mother's poverty, went to Lebanon in the 1940s, became fascinated with Islam, came home, got into the civil rights struggle, and considered communism. By the 1970s he had declared himself tri-racial and joined a branch of Moorish Science.

I employ my *silsila* from Peter to initiate Gabriel into our new Moorish Gonzo Cipher, with the righteous zonga name Jibril Bey and the title Ayatollah of Liminal Space. As with Peter, I can never tell if it's a parody. Maybe we're just a new version of the Shriners, white men playing dress-up.

Jibril Bey and I are building on the idea of a Moorish Gonzo Cipher mission to Iran, and he sounds serious about it, when an Iranian American Five Percenter anarchist emails me out of nowhere and says that he's read my stuff and thinks that we should go to Iran together. He has the family connections and the language and says that Iran is awesome because the government, in an effort to keep the people too sedated for revolution, distributes free weed to youths. Turns out that he's still in high school.

I'd like to see Kirman, where Shah Nimatullah is buried, and maybe check out Alamut, but the main goal should be Mashhad, where the eighth Shi'a Imam is buried, since it's supposed to be the "shrine of initiation." If you go to Mashhad in search of a teacher and pray for it at the tomb, your teacher comes. I send Jibril Bey on a fact-finding mission to call Peter and see if he has visited Mashhad; Peter tells Jibril Bey that it's a cool place, but describes the Sufi vibe there as "orthodox."

I have to ask Jibril Bey if my name ever comes up.

"Yeah, man, I mentioned you. He just said, 'Mike attacked me.' There's definitely a level of hurt."

It's difficult for holders of U.S. passports to get anything done in Iran, but we can send the Moorish Gonzo Cipher mission to Patmos, the Greek island where Yakub made the blue-eyed grafted germ devil. There's nothing literal for us there—no one expects to dig up remains of an ahistorical eugenics government from six thousand years ago—but Jibril Bey's into the purely imaginal value; we can make it part of a greater pilgrimage, starting with a trip to Ireland to get deep into his Irish stuff— the "metaphorical, mythological fuckin' dopeness of it," he says, Azreal Wisdom and Jibril Bey racing toward "the hyper-evolution beyond bullshit social constructs." We can meet up at Patmos, perhaps with rucksacks full of entheogens, and run along the coast, trying to science out Yakub's ultimate meaning. "Recognize the devil," Jibril Bey says, "and then purge the devil." For what we're building on, it seems like the appropriate conclusion to a lot of things.

*Journey to the End of Islam* comes out, and the reviews start coming in. "I recently had a friend ask if American Islam needs a Michael Knight," says the *AltMuslimah* reviewer; "this book is yet another example of why my answer is yes." *Publishers Weekly* likes the "breezy tone" but also notes an "indifference to whether the reader can follow his references."

You send your guts out into the world and you never know what they'll bring home; *Journey to the End of Islam* brings me a sixteen-year-old in California who writes cryptic emails breaking down everything. He's building his own system in which mad scientist Dr. Yakub is actually a "gnostic anti-hero like al-Hallaj's Iblis," white represents mental death and confusion, the absence of color and life, and black as the unity of all colors signifies the Islamic concept of *tawhid,* God's Absolute Oneness. The Seventh Imam Musa al-Kazim, he writes, is a divine manifestation because seven breaks down as God in Supreme Mathematics, and the Twelfth Imam al-Mahdi emanates mathematically as 1+2=3 (Understanding), the Divine Star Child, and becomes equated with Master Fard Muhammad, "son of an Imam and *daw'ah* to the lost-found tribe of Shabazz taken up by the Mothership." He celebrates Khidr, the mystical Green Man who taught Moses, with cannabis, like I attempted to in Pakistan; and he compares the wise scientists of Master Fard's cosmology to the Kemetic pantheon while issuing the proclamation, "Pharaoh Akhenaten was a 5%." He also writes things like:

Knowledge: my name is J. Tabari.
Wisdom: I came to Buffalo, New York, by myself.

It's a cross-referencing of codes, resulting in a new code that only the two of us can understand—like when he mixes up Supreme Alphabets and Arabic, referring to Facebook as Kitab al-Father Allah Cee Equality. Knowledge and Wisdom are one and two in the Supreme Mathematics, and he's building on the first and second degrees in Master Fard's English Lesson C-1: "My name is W.F. Muhammad. I came to North America by myself."

J. Tabari is Jehangir Tabari, my fictional mohawk-wearing drunk lawless masterless dervish from *The Taqwacores*, who arrives in Buffalo with a punk-rock knowledge of self for the lost-found tribe of American Muslim fuckups.

He asks if I've met Hakim Bey, and I say yes, I used to crash at his house.

There aren't too many pictures or friends or a fleshed-out life on his Kitab al-Father Allah Cee Equality profile, and it occurs to me that he could be an instant phantom persona cooked up in a basement at the J. Edgar Hoover Building, but I still write back to him, sending lessons by First Born Prince Allah. We're becoming friends; he says it's like getting emails from al-Hallaj or Hafiz. Besides the esoteric breakdowns, he reveals a little about himself: his mom is mentally unwell, and his dad is nice but has no tolerance for Islam. He knows from the books that my dad's schizophrenic. I give him some pluralism-positive Ibn 'Arabi quotes that might help with his father, like the verses that flaky progressive Muslims always like to drop on people, about how his heart is capable of all forms, becoming a Torah for Jews and field for gazelles and such, finding his religion wherever love's caravan takes him. I additionally inform the kid that he represents the *barzakh*, a word that appears three times in the

Qur'an, always to indicate a barrier between two things that cannot be passed. Things are defined by their limits, so a *barzakh* becomes the means by which anything knows itself; without borders, there would be no such thing as the United States of America. But the shared border is also a point of unification, the place where things meet; so this kid's the *barzakh* between Islam and America, white devil and black god, Isma'ilism and the Five Percenters, however he wants to see it. Whatever he stands between, the *barzakh* is neither and both. That's what it means when Jibril Bey calls himself the Ayatollah of Liminal Space, at least as I read him.

Another thing about this kid: one night, he gets drunk on the beach and proclaims to the moon that he's Azreal Understanding, Allah's third death angel. He says that he hopes I'm okay with it. I say sure, but tell him what the original Azreal told me: "Being Azreal is a lonely thing." Azreal Understanding says that he understands.

*I'm 19*, says the next one, a soldier soon to be heading for Afghanistan, *and a revert to Islam. . . . Just wanted to thank you because your book really strengthened my faith, and gave me a desire to search out Allah with my eyes wide open. If you wouldn't mind, or aren't too busy, some advice would be great, because I'm living a life of confusion, and I'm trying to find my place in the Universe of Islam. Thanks for your time and for being so honest.*

The only advice I can give is that it's okay to be confused, and find some peace in your confusion. The Universe of Islam is pretty big; it's full of dead planets but also worlds that can sustain life. But you're the only one who knows one from the other.

A month later he writes, *Now I'm AWOL. . . . I'm going to turn myself in in a few days . . . probably do jail time and then hopefully be discharged. I'm just wondering your opinion on the matter. Did I do the right thing?* In his PS, he says that on his bus-ride escape from the army, he read *Blue-Eyed Devil* and appreciated my thoughts regarding Greyhound.

Yes, I tell him, you did the right thing.

Then a guy writes saying that he read my *Impossible Man* shortly after his conversion. Though he hoped that he wouldn't end up at my station of religious failure and disillusionment at the end, it brought him "a lot of relief to feel like there was at least one other person out there who was in a similar boat." What he says next trips me out a bit:

> I can't say what in particular spurred me to write you now, but I guess I feel like I've been putting off doing it for a very long time out of what I think is mainly a fear of coming off as some sycophantic stalker or simply an unwanted hanger-on or something. Plus, I figure you probably get a fair amount of mail like this anyway. Also, I'm not sure I could see a point in it—and I'm still not 100 percent sure I do—because I tend to self-down a lot and I've had a lot of those experiences where you finally meet a person you've either idolized in some way or just imagined would be a cool guy to hang out with, and they turn out to be a total douchebag. It sucks having your image of someone shattered, right? And then there was probably some small part of me that's always paranoid about committing one of the many minor, unseen (and hence, major, really bad in a semi-ironic way) types of *shirk*.

There's a chance that I know the feeling.

*Shirk*—the worship of things other than God—is bad news for both the performer of the act and its object: the Prophet said that if you receive too much praise, angels will beat your ass in the grave, asking if you were really as great as people said. Were you and your books really the answer to someone's religious confusion? When they told you that you were, did you believe it?

It's two hours before a flight to Sweden when an email comes from my cousin David, a Baptist minister. He says that he's sorry to have heard the news about my father. I don't know what the news is.

I call him, he tells me, and it means a choice between getting on this plane to Sweden to deliver a lecture on Islamic punk rock and driving to West Virginia. Then I go back online and learn about some Jewish kids who have started building with Supreme Mathematics, relating Knowledge Cipher (ten) to the Ten Commandments and breaking down the Twelve Tribes as 1+2=3, Knowledge-Wisdom-Understanding, Zig-Zag-Zig. It turns out that they use my books as source material; I'm now in the business of signing permission slips. I choose the plane.

BOOK 3

# OLD MAN OF

## THE MOUNTAIN

# 1.

From my unfinished Peter Lamborn Wilson biography:

In 1987, Canadian zine *Edge Detector* published "Ong's Hat: Gateway to the Dimensions," a brochure for a paranormal science cult offering interdimensional travel from its commune in Ong's Hat, a ghost town deep in the New Jersey Pine Barrens. The piece was presented by Hakim Bey as "something sent to him anonymously," though it carried the hallmarks of his work, with references to a Chaos Ashram in the Pine Barrens reminiscent of Bey's Communiques, and even ending with Bey's catchphrase "Chaos never died."

Joseph Matheny, a well-known culture jammer and friend of Peter, took the ball and ran with it, building Peter's short story into an elaborate conspiracy hoax. Matheny's book *Ong's Hat* would present Peter's original brochure and new texts as nonfiction and Peter's stoner-prank religion as something much more serious: "In the background shadows . . . stands one of the most secretive and mysterious religious organizations ever known to man: the Moorish Orthodox Church,

a revolutionary and heretical sect of Islam that carries on an ancient tradition which sought to coun-
terbalance the forces of orthodox Islam." There was
enough real-life material inserted to make the hoax
believable; someone reading the book could perform an
Internet search and find that there really was such a
thing as the Moorish Orthodox Church. The story also
includes a mysterious figure, Wali Fard, named for Wal-
lace D. Fard (aka Master Fard Muhammad). Someone wanting to research the Ong's Hat conspiracy further would
learn that Fard had emerged from unknown origins and
background in 1930, developed his own Islamic sect,
and then disappeared in 1934, presumably never to be
heard from again. The Wilson/Matheny hoax is bolstered
by real-life information that conspiracy hunters can
uncover for themselves, giving the story depth and
making the reader feel like an active investigator.

The Wali Fard of *Ong's Hat* is described only as an
American member of the Moorish Orthodox Church who
travels abroad near the end of the 1960s. His biography
rings familiar:

> Wali Fard . . . travelled throughout Asia and collected
> exotic initiations in all sorts of different schools
> including the tantric arts and different forms of sha-
> manism. At the same time he engaged in his spiritual
> journey, he traded in carpets and other well-known
> Afghan exports. The Soviet invasion induced him to
> return to America in 1978 whereupon he laundered his
> savings by buying about 200 acres in the New Jersey
> Pine Barrens. Around 1980, he moved into an old rod
> and gun club on the property along with several runaway
> boys from Paramus, New Jersey. An anarchist lesbian
> couple from Brooklyn joined them and together they
> founded the Moorish Science Ashram.

The depiction of this fictitious Wali Fard selling carpets and Afghan exports may be a play on tales of the real Fard selling silks and Eastern fineries door-to-door in post-Depression Detroit, but the details are largely grafted from Peter's real life and Hakim Bey persona, with some changes (fleeing the Soviet invasion of Afghanistan, rather than the Islamic Revolution in Iran). Elsewhere in the book, Fard's spiritual training is explained in greater detail. The passage recalls popular tellings of the Nation of Islam's Fard as a mysterious figure who travels throughout the world to obtain knowledge, but illustrates them with staples of Peter's biography:

> [H]e collected an impressive assortment of exotic initiations: Tantra in Calcutta, from an old member of the Bengali Terrorist Party; Sufism from the Ovayssi Order in Shiraz, which rejects all human masters and insists on visionary experience; and finally, in the remote Badakhshan Province of Afghanistan, he converted to an archaic form of Ismailism (the so-called Assassins) blended out of Buddhist Yab-Yum teachings, indigenous shamanic sorcery and extremist Shiite revolutionary philosophy-worshippers of the *Umm-al-Kitab*, the "Matrix Book."

Wali Fard and his runaway boys and lesbian anarchists are joined by Frank and Althea Dobbs, twin siblings and rogue physicists from Princeton University. The Dobbs twins were raised on a UFO-cult commune in Texas that was founded by their father, a retired insurance salesman who was murdered by his own disciples. Their name's a reference to J.R. "Bob" Dobbs, of the Church of the SubGenius. While Fard's self-published "Visionary Recital" zines provide an ideological basis in heresies, chaos theory, and post-situationist politics (much like Hakim Bey's Communiques), the scientists conduct research and experiments in old Airstream trailers and rebuilt barns. Merging their own findings with Fard's occult practices, they develop a brain machine known simply as the "egg." The Moorish Science Ashram manages to host some breakthroughs in time travel and the opening of gateways to parallel universes, even discovering a Pine Barrens on an alternative Earth where human life has never developed. Then comes the Delta Force from nearby Fort Dix, sliding down ropes from a swarm of black helicopters, wielding automatics and flamethrowers to raze Fard's techno-tantric commune into the dirt.

Peter Lamborn Wilson appears in Matheny's fiction, introduced to the reader as a former interpreter for the Shah and "a member, and some say secret sponsor, of the Moorish Orthodox Church." Peter is said to play an "integral role" in Matheny's unraveling of the vast Ong's Hat cover-up.

In *Ong's Hat,* Matheny provides the full text of *Incunabula,* a catalog of rare books and obscure documents. Most of the listed items do not actually exist, but the reader could be fooled by the presence of real books such as Henri Corbin's *Creative Imagination in the Sufism of Ibn 'Arabi.* The catalog is rife with Peter Lamborn Wilson references, some more subtle than others; its proprietor, Emory Cranston, is named after Peter's father, Douglas Emory Wilson, and Peter Cranston, a freelance writer in Iran during the 1970s and Peter's art-critic colleague at the *Tehran Journal.* The catalog's description for *Poetic Journal of a Traveller; or, A Heresologist's Guide to Brooklyn* mentions a shaykh who "claims to be Sudanese but speaks 'pure Alabaman,' runs a junk shop and wears a battered old Shriner fez," clearly inspired by Peter's accounts of Rufus German Bey, Moorish Governor of Maryland. Among *Incunabula's* rare materials is a paper by Pak Hardjanto, named for a semi-fictitious character in another of Peter's hoax pieces, "Visit Port Watson!" and an article by "Dr. R. Von Bitter Rucker" named for Rudy Rucker, coeditor of the *Semiotext(e) SF* anthology. There's also a 1978-'79 course catalog from the "Institute of Chaos Studies and Imaginal Yoga," which is founded by Dr. Kamadev Sohrawardi, "a Bengali of mixed English, Hindu and Moslem origin, descended from an old Sufi family, and initiated into Tantra." The character is named after Shihab ad-Din Yahya Suhrawardi but based on Sri Kamanaransan Biswas, Peter's tantric instructor in Darjeeling. The course catalog offers classes such as "Metaphysics of the Isma'ili Assassins." Other items in the *Incunabula* catalog include the Foucault-and-Baudrillard-quoting *Sacred Jihad of Our Lady of Chaos* and *A History & Catechism of the Moorish Orthodox Church,* along with obligatory nods to pederasty and a revisitation of the Qamar fantasy:

> *The Temple of Antinous,* a Travel Cult of neo-pagans devoted to Eros and Ganymede. (Warning: this leaflet contains some just-barely-legal graphic material.) "Wistfully we wonder if the boygod can manifest only in some other world than this dreary puritanical polluted boobocracy—then, gleefully, we suddenly recall: *there ARE other worlds!"*

The summary for John Lorde's novel *Maze of Treason* also describes a character as a "child-molester and black magician." *Incunabula's* plot synopsis for this nonexistent work thrusts its hero into a world much like Sonsorol, where "Visit Port Watson!" is set:

Sex, hallucinogenic mushrooms and song improvisation contests comprise the nightlife, with days devoted to the serious business of "sorcery, skinny-dipping, flint knapping and maybe a couple of hours of desultory fishing or berry picking." There is no social order. "People with bones in their noses sitting around arguing about Black Hole Theory or recipes for marsupial stew—lazy smoke from a few clan campfires rising through the hazy bluegold afternoon—people masturbating in trees—bees snouting into orchids—signal drum in the distance—

Among the actual books listed in the catalog are works on quantum physics by Nick Herbert, who, like Peter, appears as a character in *Ong's Hat;* it is through Herbert that Matheny first encounters the catalog, which includes Herbert's published books as well as stolen galley proofs of his manuscripts that have been suppressed by their publishers. The real-life Nick Herbert was known as Jabir ibn Hayyan in Moorish Orthodox circles, named for a tenth-century Sufi alchemist. His personal website mentions that he once recognized Hakim Bey as his shaykh but later denounced Bey as an "Anti-Caliph." Herbert's story "On Eve of Physics Symposium, More Sub-Atomic Particles Found" appears in *Semiotext(e) SF,* and he performed some of his own work at Hakim Bey's final reading. As with the Moorish Orthodox Church, Wali Fard, and Peter Lamborn Wilson, Nick Herbert's existence in the physical world gives credence to Matheny's imaginary world. The reader is expected to go online and perform a Google search on these names; *Ong's Hat* has been called the "first attempt to create a believable and interactive fictional world using the tools of the Internet."

Skeptical readers identified Hakim Bey as the

engineer of the hoax, while Matheny insisted that Bey was as "genuinely puzzled" and excited to learn of the Moorish Science Ashram as anyone. Others accused Nick Herbert/Jabir ibn Hayyan. Matheny admitted to having manufactured his interview with Emory Cranston, in which Cranston claimed to have stolen the proofs of Herbert's *Alternate Dimensions* from its publisher, but nonetheless insisted that Cranston was real, a "strange bearded little man in a fez and a tweed suit." On August 9, 2001, Matheny finally made an online announcement ending his culture jam:

Open letter to conspiracy community:

Nick and I decided today to publicly announce in the near future that the Ong's Hat project has now concluded. We will be contacting Peter L. Wilson as well and see if he'd like to make a statement. I think it would still make a good book from a cultural anthropology perspective, your call.

Days later, the post was amended with:

Ong's Hat Tantric Egg Research Center was a necessary ruse for deflecting attention from our real project—to open up your conduits, brothers and sisters, to rip off the confining condom of language and to Fuck Nature Unprotected.

Doctor Jabir
Public Relations
Quantum Tantra

The updated post also included Peter's official statement: "Fuck Off!"

Peter likes to compare maps to magic spells, and this kind of thing performs magic on the map; if I had to drive through the Pine Barrens, I'd keep an eye out for anything suspicious. Same with the Ben Ishmael myth—I drove the whole triangle and treated Mecca, Indiana, as this mystical Islamo-American secret that tied everything together in the most awesome way. There really is a Mecca, Indiana, and I really did go there, and a hundred years ago there really was a Ben Ishmael clan, but sadly they weren't a secret Muslim tribe wandering the Midwest to filter into the Moorish Science Temple and Nation of Islam. A new book has come out shitting all over Hugo Leaming Bey for his ideologically loaded scholarship. I don't know if Peter knows, or if he'd care.

One thing I'll say for Peter, and compliment it as "childlike," if not for the creepiness of that word in relation to him: he can play pretend until the play becomes real.

# 2.

[Master Fard Muhammad] was so sweet and kind to everyone, you would never believe the kind of powers that he had. But he didn't lord it over anybody, just as common as an old shoe. And you felt relaxed around him and you knew that you were loved. And he's not like some of his protégés that are beating drums on their own chests.

—Mother Cecile, Nation of Islam pioneer

I've allowed Master Fard Muhammad into my heart in a very serious way. It occurs to me while I'm heading down the I-81 toward Winchester, gospel rock on the radio. Master Fard warned against loving devils, no matter how long a devil studies; but something tells me that even if I'm unworthy of his love, even if I'm the reason that he suffered, he could love me too. More than religion, it feels like I have a personal relationship with Master Fard, like I'm starting to know what it means to walk with him.

I think about Fard's three and a half years of persecution in Detroit, and I write. Writing while driving isn't as bad as texting, because I can keep my eyes on the road and scribble—left hand on the wheel, pen in my right hand, notebook in my lap.

Sometimes the result is illegible, and lines often overlap each other, but I can usually retrieve the main idea.

I'm online at a truck stop off I-81 when this shows up on my Facebook page:

Mike, in some ways I think you've successfully fulfilled your teenage prophecy of being a Malcolm X for white trailer trash kids like myself. I thank you and your books for playing such an important role in my identity as a Muslim convert. And just for being somebody for me to relate to. Again, thank you. As-salaamu 'alaikum.

There's a good feeling with that—and it's a *physical* feeling, like I'm literally drinking an ego trip with the real sensation of it sliding down my torso, into my gut. It's the devil, I know it is, and the fact that it gives pleasure poses a real threat to my religion. This kind of validation from others is the spiritual equivalent of crystal meth: while you're getting addicted, it makes your face melt away. This is how cults start, right? First you put yourself out there, and then a few people appreciate it, but once you start to agree with the nice things they say about you, everything turns bad. Before anyone realizes how far it's gone, you're running around naked in the woods, sharing your spiritual powers by rubbing up on teenage girls because you're the *Qutb,* blessing them with the Pole of the Age. After a while with the good feeling, I'm left with only carsickness because deep down I know better. Nausea's a good sign; it means that I haven't lost myself, I'm not a Sith lord yet. My body still resists. *Aoudhu billahi mina shaytani rajeem.*

The message's line about Malcolm X and trailer parks references *Impossible Man,* my memoir, the section where I'm fifteen years old and have just met my father. Crossing the state line into West Virginia, I start to roll over Dad's story. Wesley Unger was born in Berkeley Springs in 1938, the thirteenth of twenty children of Reverend Calvin and Martha Unger. The labor took place in the family home and lasted a week. Reverend Calvin was a Pentecostal preacher and mean drunk. One of the Unger kids would say that the reverend whipped his sons and raped his daughters. The Unger kids slept six to a bed and shared hallucinations of what they called "tar baby demons," little black satans about the size of a kneecap, that would materialize from time to time.

When Wesley was fourteen years old, he watched the family's twentieth child, six-year-old David, get destroyed by a truck, and men come to scrape David off the road with shovels, and his mother attempt to murder the driver with a butcher knife. His mother died not long after, and Reverend Calvin married another woman with her own kids. Wesley's new stepmother claimed that when Wesley left a room, books would come off the shelves and fly around. He was possessed by the devil, she said. Rather than deal with her, Wesley preferred to sleep in his car in the church parking lot. When he was seventeen, she signed the papers that allowed him to join the army. He went to Korea, and I don't know what happened there.

He came back from Korea, disappeared for a time running with the Hells Angels, and returned to Reverend Calvin's house with some club mama on his bike. Reverend Calvin went through Wesley's bags, found books on Nazism and Satanism, and had him committed to the veterans' hospital. Wesley's sisters came and found him strapped into the bed, medicated into outer space.

Wesley married more than once, but I'm not sure of the exact number—either three or four times. His family briefly disowned him because one of the women was Puerto Rican. That might have been the marriage that ended when Wesley had sex with his mother-in-law, but I could be wrong. One of his wives gave him two children, a son and a daughter, but she left with the kids when things started to go bad. Wesley arrived in their front yard to threaten her with an army-surplus bazooka.

Then he found a girl he called Jodie, though her name was Susan, married her, and tortured her for five years. Sometimes

Wesley put his knife to their infant son's throat to make Jodie confess to things such as sleeping with Satan or selling the boy's "light" to the Mafia. One morning, Jodie asked if he would leave the door unlocked so that she could take the boy for a walk. He agreed. When he came back she wasn't there. The boy was gone too.

Jodie and the boy were back in New York with her parents. I have no idea what Wesley did through the 1980s. He may have gone to Montana for a time.

By the early 1990s, he was back in West Virginia. One day, Jodie showed up with the boy, who was now fifteen years old. Wesley asked the boy about his religion, fearful that he had been indoctrinated by Jodie's Catholic parents. The boy answered that he was Muslim. Wesley showed him pornography and explained his racial separatism; the Ku Klux Klan's book, he told the boy, was called the Kloran.

The boy visited a couple more times and they exchanged some letters. After seven years passed without their seeing each other, Wesley was sitting in front of the gas station in Capon Bridge, when the boy arrived and called out to him. It went like that for a few years, the boy popping in here and there. The last time the boy came to Wesley's house, Wesley put his hand on his gun and said, "I'm not your father."

Wesley's health started to go bad, and one of his legs was in urgent need of amputation, but no one would know until the coroner saw it. One day, Wesley was cutting firewood on his land, when he got tired, sat down, and died. He was buried in the next town, in a small old cemetery in which five graves were decorated with Confederate flags every Memorial Day. His headstone bore the engraving of a cabin in the woods, a buck, and a rifle. The boy skipped his funeral to give a lecture in Sweden.

Wesley died on February 23, one day after the birthday of Allah (the former Clarence 13X), two days after the death anniversary

of Malcolm X, and two days before the death anniversary of
Elijah Muhammad. And Elijah Muhammad passed the day
before Master Fard Muhammad's birthday. While celebrating
Fard, I have made it my custom to remember these awesome
black gods on his tree. From now on, Saviors' Week will also
require that I think of my father. Islam is mathematics.

I waited a few months before making this drive. West Virginia's hills are now thickly forested green, reminding me of the
road to Harar in Ethiopia. I have written of West Virginia and
my relationship to it in *Impossible Man*. The story makes for
somewhat intense back-cover copy:

> This is where it starts. His father—a paranoid schizophrenic
> white supremacist—threatens to decapitate his infant son,
> Michael, when he is a baby, believing him to be the Devil's son.

"An unconventional coming of age memoir," says the *Publishers Weekly* review, which "combines the familial pathos of
Augusten Burroughs with a religious awakening narrative bor-
rowed from Malcolm X."

I write about Wesley's telling me that he's not really my father,
that my true biological father is actor Dan Aykroyd "or someone
within his sphere of influence." He knows because my earlobes
match his, indicating a shared Jewish ancestry. Wesley additionally informs me that I am F. Scott Fitzgerald. He's hesitant to
use words like "reincarnation," but allows me to if it helps my
understanding. Then he sends me on a holy pilgrimage to the
Hermitage, Andrew Jackson's plantation in Tennessee, the setting for the opening scene of Fitzgerald's unfinished final novel.

To provide his rationale for my being F. Scott Fitzgerald,
Wesley initiates me into his elaborate cosmology, which I can
never explain if I've been away from it too long. The main
point is that F. Scott Fitzgerald himself was a "reincarnation"—
again, not exactly—of one of the early founders of the Catholic
Church. The inner circle in Rome, therefore, was understandably

devastated that Fitzgerald died outside the faith. They hatched a plot of murder and intrigue to ensure that I, as the return of Fitzgerald and their long-lost father, would be raised in a Catholic household.

A real punch in the nuts for the poor Catholics: their new F. Scott Fitzgerald fell in love with Malcolm X and converted to Islam.

*Impossible Man* ends with me reading a lot of Fitzgerald, embarking on Wesley's pilgrimage, and spending a night at Fitzgerald's grave to beat myself and pour holy Zamzam water on the stone and finally wonder what the fuck I'm doing, concocting my own religion out of Shi'ism and *The Great Gatsby*—pretending until it gets real, the best I've got.

On the way to the town of Capon Bridge, church signs boast wordplay like LOOK TO JESUS: 'U' ARE PART OF HIS NAME! and SEVEN DAYS WITHOUT GOD MAKES ONE WEAK. One of Wesley's old brothers is waiting for me at the gas station to hand off the keys, and then the place is mine. It's just outside Capon Bridge on the way to Romney, the town that changed hands between the Union and Confederacy no fewer than fifty-six times. The driveway is off the main road but hidden if a car is coming from the east, and I always miss it and turn around, and then it winds around steep—driving up a mountain, I really have to believe in my vehicle and bust it up there. If I get scared, I get stuck.

After some sharp turns, the land flattens out. It's beautiful until I reach the top and see his house at the end of what has become a full-fledged junkyard since the last time I've been here. The black pickup is gone, and the white pickup rests with four flat tires sunk into the earth, just ten feet or so from the spot where Wesley died. The pile of firewood has not been touched, covered under a blue tarp as though it were the body. The rest of the world is gone, civilization gone, West Virginia gone, the green forest thick enough to block out the loud road below.

The shed with the Lord's Prayer carved into the door is still there, and he's built another one. The newer shed has three different compartments, each with its own padlocked door. On one door he has carved the Star of David, on another a crescent.

Inside his house there's no room to move; Wesley was a hoarder and the main room, the kitchen/bedroom/workspace, is packed with various table saws, drill presses, buckets of wrenches and screwdrivers. And dozens of plastic gallon jugs, because Wesley had no running water. A thick layer of dust covers everything; I can make clouds by stomping the carpets. The kitchen table is lost under his mass of papers, receipts, bills, junk mail, and stacks of yellow legal-size paper, his poems.

Not knowing where to start, I just go around opening cabinets and dressers, not sure what I want to find, but I feel like it's there and waiting for me. A stuffed brown paper bag reveals two hundred empty Altoids cans, and a drawer contains only a wreath made from over a hundred miniature pie tins. His kitchen cupboards are filled with canned goods at least three years past their expiration. In the first round of exploration, there hasn't been a discovery that will explain everything and provide a grand narrative meaning to his life. It's easy to get esoteric about the mentally ill and imagine a tremendous secret at the core of the madness, and it was something that my father encouraged; but from where I'm starting with Wes, to stand in his crumbling house just normalizes him. There's no Mystery Dad.

He's got birthday and Christmas cards taped to the outsides of his cupboards, some signed not only with names but with titles like "Outreach Director" and "Social Services." A few are addressed to "Uncle Wes"; even if some of these cards have been on his cupboards for over a decade, at least he was human enough to be an Uncle Wes for someone. When I first met him, at fifteen, the insides of his cupboards were lined with clippings of hardcore porn.

One of the "Uncle Wes" cards contains handwriting that looks to be from a female in sixth grade or so:

India is a very interesting place. The people here have dark skin and the women wear colorful dresses called saris. The children are especially cute. I had a lot of fun with them at the Kids' Crusade. They just loved our puppet show! Their country is very different from ours. There are so many idols, you can't even go down the road without seeing an idol or a shrine to their god. And yet they are very open to learning about Christ. We had 10 to 15 thousand people come to our crusades each night!

The offerings are better on his kitchen table, but Wesley never threw anything away, so I have to sift through his whole life in paper, receipts for a drill bought in 1990 on top of divorce papers from 1982, mentioning Wesley's "cruel and inhuman acts toward the Plaintiff" and awarding her the child. Another letter from his niece—she's in high school in this one; the next mission's to Thailand. There are nearly a dozen confirmations from the post office that someone at the state police or FBI had signed upon receipt of his letters. I check out hand-drawn specifications for cabinets that he had wanted to build, and find his passport in the envelope in which he received it, never used, still crisp and clean.

And his poems. He has one of several pages titled "Camel," dated January 19, 2009. In the margin he writes, "Inauguration," but I can't really make out his position. A shorter piece from 1998 reads more easily:

> I did not ask for money
> and I did not seek fame
> I spoke my truth
> asking not
> for fortune
> nor for claim
> I walked with friends
> knew no enemies
> Left my message
> with you

May
history
remember my step
and literature recall my name

I smash through the house a few times, making sure that I don't miss any place where Wesley would have hidden something. Picking up his copy of *Conspiracy of Silence*, a 1986 book about a queer British double agent, I find my mother's contact information taped to the inside of the front cover and mine taped to the back, with my baby pictures in an envelope. Opening one of his closets, I find an old World Wrestling Federation trading card at my feet. It's of former tag team champions Rick Martel and Tito Santana, known collectively as Strike Force. Even beyond my dream initiation in which Randy "Macho Man" Savage yells Ibn 'Arabi quotes at me, wrestling's been a huge part of my life—I took forty-six stitches in the head fighting Abdullah the Butcher at a book festival in Atlanta—but Wesley was never around to know that.

# 3.

Something has to be done with the shed door bearing the Lord's Prayer, since this whole place will eventually be torn down—Wesley left no will and I'm not administrating the mess of his life—and I'd rather it be me handling my father's devotional work than the state. I get the determined idea to tear that door off its hinges, but Wesley's tools are old with rotting wood handles that break off when I try to use them for leverage—a hammer breaks, a hatchet breaks, I end up with a wedge that used to be the head of a pickax and a mallet, plant the wedge, and smash away with a two-handed grip, and bring up sparks when the mallet hits the hinge. After a while I can rip the bottom hinge from the shed and move the door and twist it and put pressure on the top hinge. The door comes out fierce, like it made the decision itself, with beaten warped hinges, and I pull it four feet away from the scene and throw down my mallet in the dirt like I've just won a fight and killed something. It's not all out of my system yet, so I spend twenty minutes or so throwing rocks at the dead white truck, landing plenty but not breaking any windows, so I go right up to it and hurl the mallet into the front windshield from point-blank range. My heart rate slows back to normal. I saw off part of his door to make it fit in my car, and leave the other half standing against a rock in the woods.

At the Star of David shed, I can see through the window that there's nothing worthy of investigating, but I take Wesley's keys and unlock his crescent shed and right behind the door there's an open book on the dirt.

It's my book about him, *Impossible Man*.

He read it.

Trembling like when I first heard that he died, I turn through the book, hoping for a mark, a note, a dog-eared or ripped page or any trace of his reaction, but nothing. All I have is speculation that locking the book behind this door with the Islamic moon, to be found after he's dead, likely by me, counts as his response.

I turn over my father's poop bucket—no running water, he had a bucket—and sit down to read my book, the last thing that I ever said to him. Couldn't have asked for more, since we've never had a real conversation. I'd visit him on the mountain, he'd ramble for an hour and then send me on my way. *Impossible Man* was my chance to talk back, and I told him everything, so much more than most fathers ever know of their sons, all the inner and outer humiliations. He read of how I'd punch a kid in the head during recess and then get out of trouble by bawling to the principal about how my dad went crazy in Vietnam (it was actually Korea, but in seventh grade I didn't know the difference), and how all the teachers and guidance counselors felt sorry for me. I told him all of that and he couldn't say a word back, just turn the page and get more: I told him that I skipped a quarter of eighth grade and spent the whole time at home dreaming of the day that I could put a shotgun to his face. I told him about the psychiatrist. I told him that I used to fall on the ground and bruise myself to get laughs from kids, and I told him how I not only practiced "Charlie Manson eyes" like him, but became Manson's pen pal. He read about the summer between public junior high and Catholic high school, when I tried to write a short story and deliberately wrote it messy, wanting it to look like the product of mental illness.

My neo-Nazi father had to read about his twelve-year-old son wearing Africa medallions and blasting the blackest, angriest rap that I could find from Mom's radio, and moving from that to praying in Arabic. He learned that after we met for the first time, I promised myself that I'd be the undoing of him and his world. And my book told him the full details of my first masturbation, in case he was wondering.

*Impossible Man* additionally presented Wesley with my mother; he used to say that he knew her better than anyone ever had or could, but I told him things that he did not know. Reading *Impossible Man* was his first chance to learn how we got away. Thirty years ago, Mom was stealing money from him and hiding it in a sock—did it piss him off to read that? Did he try to remember where the sock might have been, did he figure it out and curse himself for not having looked there?—until the day that she asked him to leave the door unlocked so that she could take me for a walk. And then, Wes read, she ran to the neighbor's house and asked to use the phone. And then she ducked down in the backseat of the taxi, and then she raced out of the bank after writing a bad check, and then she called her father from the airport. He read that we looked so shell-shocked, so removed from what we should have been, that a college kid felt bad and bought me a teddy bear, and Nan and Gramps walked right past us, not even recognizing their daughter.

He read the first page of *Impossible Man,* the dedication, "for mothers," and he read the ending, where I called Mom the real masculine figure of my life.

The last time Wesley saw my face, it was the four-year-old me on *Impossible Man's* cover, the 1981 me in my Superman costume. Wes would have recognized the background as Nan and Gramps's living room, but could not have known the boy; he had never seen me at that age. Did it make him curious, did he ever stare at the boy and try to see himself?

## 4.

Besides the shed door, there's a Star of David motif throughout the house that I can't understand; I find a Star of David plate on the wall, sharp-pointed Stars of David of varying sizes that Wesley cut from copper sheets, a cabinet he was building with Stars of David on the hinges, and a small metal sculpture that I interpret to be a motorcycle:

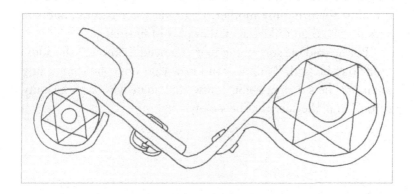

Wesley's Star of David fixation was a recent development, emerging only since our last contact. It doesn't compute until I'm thumbing through my own words again, his weathered copy of *Impossible Man*:

The twentieth child was Calvin and Martha's eighth boy; but because one of the boys had lived only six months, they thought of this one as the seventh son—which Calvin saw as full of religious meaning. They named him David Pine Unger; David after the Bible's King David, who was also a seventh son, and Pine after the hospital in which they delivered him (he was the first Unger born in a hospital).

That they named him after King David was something of an educated guess on my part, based on mumblings that I've heard at family dinners and the knowledge that my grandparents were fanatically biblical in their approach to life. But my guess appears to have worked for Wesley, and he used it in his art. At least we have that. My book that called him a Nazi rapist lunatic also helped him to deal with his defining trauma; I've made a hermeneutical intervention in my father's life. Going back outside and looking at the sheds again, I can now understand the doors properly: the Star of David was his brother, and the crescent moon was his son.

There's still the question of the rest of the book, where I address his torturing my mother. I call his sister Naomi, and she says that he didn't like seeing that part of himself.

"But he told me something that you need to know," she adds. "One day he said, 'Naomi, you know that boy—he's not a boy anymore, he's a man—you know that man who says he's my son? You make sure that he's okay.'"

# 5.

I'm not going to be okay; I'll be staying here, for how long I don't know. I sleep in my father's unwashed sheets and poop outside in his junkyard, using his poop bucket. It's always darker in the woods; late at night, especially when the moon is near full, looking up at the sky makes you feel like you're getting buried alive by the darkness of the trees. At night on the mountain, either it's dead quiet or the animals are going berserk on each other.

The first time Wesley showed me this place, he said, "You won't like my house, and you won't like my lifestyle." Now, at least for a while, the house and lifestyle are mine. I've paid up the electric bill so the lights will stay on, but should have brought more clothes and things; my bags are filled only with books and notebooks. Feels like there's something wrong about that. I have *T.A.Z.* with me, the edition including Hakim Bey's Ontological Anarchism pieces, and read it on a boulder overlooking the road. My setup here reminds me of one of his commune fantasies, the Kallikak Memorial Bolo, minus the runaway boys. In a scenario reminiscent of the Ong's Hat story, Hakim Bey envisions Airstream trailers, the insides draped with Persian rugs, hidden away in the Pine Barrens for "childhood as permanent insurrection" and "summer's alchemy." The inhabitants read comic books and go for joyrides in a pickup truck.

"The suchness of things," he writes, "when unchained from the Law, each molecule an orchid, each atom a pearl to the attentive consciousness—this is our cult." These Peter Pan scenarios draw out Hakim Bey's full attention and power and damn, the man's a writer—enough of a writer that he can make you forget what he's really writing about and see the beauty that he sees. It changes what I see when I look up from the page: for the time being, here in my own Temporary Autonomous Zone, I'm living in a Hakim Bey dream (again, minus the boys).

# 6.

The shed with the crescent moon and Star of David on its doors has a third compartment that would make a good mosque. It has a porch with shelves for our shoes and inside there'll be room for ten people or so after I clean it up. The *masjid* shed's filled from the back wall to the door with garbage—broken parts of things, scrap wood, ancient Christmas tinsel, a completely rusted wheelbarrow, old tools, nothing of clear use or value—and it takes more than a day to clear out.

I set the iPod boom box to a Gravediggaz vs. Metallica mashup I've found online and start throwing heavy shit around. Outside the shed it looks like a bomb went off: there's a door, broken glass everywhere, broken flower pots, wooden beams, busted lanterns, a bag of charcoal, dozens of coffee cans filled with nails and screws and bolts and things that I don't even have the Home Depot vocabulary to describe, extension cords, broomsticks, engine parts, rusty circular-saw blades. The inside still has scattered debris, but there's enough clear space that I can lay down four flattened cardboard boxes and pray, my forehead and nose leaving oil stains where it says FAMOUS BERKELEY SPRINGS® MINERAL WATER, surrounded by crud, chunks of fiberglass insulation—some of it still pink, most of it too dirty for me to know if it ever had a color—shovels, a stack of shingles, small hills of dirt, remnants of a wasp's nest. The shelves in here have more coffee cans full of nails, but I can dump them and load the place with Qur'ans and the *Fusus al-Hikam* and Master Fard's lessons. I spray-paint Ali's name in Arabic exactly twenty-seven times (27=Wisdom God) on the naked particleboard walls, and tag up the outside with a *bismillah* and huge "5%" in gold with black outline. On the door I paint MASJID and a big green seven, and then I stick my Hezbollah flag from Syria on a metal rod and duct-tape it to the porch doorway overlooking all the garbage.

Still sweaty, I take off my shirt and walk around the rubble with my belt unbuckled. Too much soda over the last year has made me look pregnant, but I still feel like the Mighty Cracker Asskicker of All Time, sloppy mustache hanging over my lip, bearded with greasy mullet crawling out from under my cam-ouflage cap, and carrying a chainsaw that I discovered and then broke. Unfortunately, my Lacoste sneakers kill the look and I come off as a hipster from Williamsburg exoticizing West Vir-ginia as an ironic pose. Never underestimate the importance of correct shoes to a costume.

I am content with the day's work. There is now a mosque on my father's land, my land.

When Five Percenters bring the knowledge to a new area, they have to take the land back from the devil by giving it a new righteous name. Assuming that I'm the closest thing to a Five Percenter to ever arrive on Cooper Mountain, it's my duty to take Devil Cooper off the planet. The easiest way to come up with a new name is to look at the Supreme Mathematics and Supreme Alphabets. *C* stands for "Cee," meaning to arrive at a perfect understanding, and *M* has the attribute of "Majestic." It's flexible, though; contemplating "Cee" as "see," I end up thinking of *S* words. I've been reading Abdullah Yusuf Ali's com-mentary on the Qur'an where he talks about pagans worship-ing Sirius, "the brightest fixed star in the heavens, with a bluish tinge in its light." Magic is performed upon the map: Cooper Mountain becomes Sirius Mathematics, pretty righteous as far as zonga names go, and I can now call my mosque the Islamic Center of Sirius Mathematics. Time to contact Muslim missionary groups and request free Qur'ans sent to Wesley's PO box, and see if I can get this added to the churches on the WELCOME TO CAPON BRIDGE sign at the edge of town. Capon Bridge gets renamed Understanding Born, and my father's house is Alamut the mutation center, what else.

Five Percenter legend holds that Allah gave Azreal the keys to heaven and hell, meaning that Azreal could come and go as he pleased. I read it as allegory for whiteness, since Azreal's neither devil nor god, but somehow both. He's white, but hasn't derived much gain in his sad life from white privilege, and Five Percenters recognize his place in the culture, but most won't count him among the gods. During our road odyssey, Azreal gave me a literal set of keys that he had retrieved from a lost-and-found box. I kept the keys to represent what my teacher had been given by his teacher, the man he called Father, and now use the ring for my father's keys.

Having been labeled as mentally ill since he was sixteen years old, Azreal grew into a legitimately unwell adult, but it's his job to get the wrongdoers, they say. There's something messianic about being Azreal, the devil handpicked by Allah, and gods have been giving that to him for forty years. Maybe it does something for him, gets him through the times when cops beat the shit out of him and kids sic their dogs on him. He can hide from his suffering in that name, that special role in human history. His name was a shelter when the world gave him none. At least until he shared it with me, Azreal had a title of honor that no one else could claim; even if he couldn't call himself Allah, like all the other gods, he alone could wear the mantle of Allah's Death Angel.

It may be the right time to forget that there's any Islam beyond this mountain. Word from Pakistan is that a mufti with the Jamaat-e-Islami has issued a statement declaring the *Taqwacore* documentary to be blasphemous and that everyone involved should be arrested. It's only scary because one of our guys is still over there and he can't leave his house.

Not all fatwas come in defense of orthodoxy, as a Five Percenter elder named God Kalim delivers his own all-caps condemnation:

> SOMEBODY BETTER TELL THAT WHITE BOY AND THE REST OF THOSE CHUMPS, I DON'T PLAY . . . MICHAEL KNIGHT WRITES WELL WOVEN WICKEDNESS TO CLOAK THE PINS HE IS STICKING . . .

> MANY KNIGHTS WORE APRONS AND STUDIED ISLAM [THE KNIGHTS TEMPLAR—THE KNIGHTS OF COLUM-BUS] BUT A KNIGHT'S FEALTY IS TO THE CROSS, NOT THE CRESCENT . . . ON THE CHESSBOARD THE KNIGHT SITS BETWEEN THE BISHOP [RELIGION] AND THE CASTLE [ALLAH SCHOOL] . . . THIS DEVIL HAS A PLAN USING ALL THESE PLOYS IN HIS PLOT. BUT WHO IS MICHAEL KNIGHT? WHY WAS HE SENT AMONGST US AFTER 911?

On top of all that, an activist-ish grad student writes to say that I could never represent "real taqwacore" because I'm too white, too male, and a whore for corporate media. Okay, so I don't represent the word that I made up. Exile me from my own island. I've got a *masjid* now, and I Self Lord And Master means leave me the fuck alone.

# 7.

And then he seventeen, the child Knowledge God. And
that's his daddy. You can find any boy, if he don't know
where his daddy is at, all he got to do is look in the mirror
and then he'll see him. Because he's looking at him. Who is
your son if he ain't you?
>                        —Allah, interview at Otisville Training School for Boys,
>                        November 15, 1968

There's an agitated jittery feeling and this urgency to write. I
feel it most in the ribs and behind the knees, but I'm so excited by what might come out that I can't sit down to write it.
I pace around, break stuff, go outside and spray-paint things in
Arabic script that will never get recognized as words in Hamp-
shire County: Allah's Name, Ali's name, Ya Husayn, "5%
AL-HAQQ."

My presence begins to push Wesley's out; most of his junk in
the main room has gone flying off the deck and rolling down
the hill, and his kitchen table hosts a stack of books on Ibn
'Arabi. I've ripped out the ancient carpet, choked on its clouds
of dust, and heaved it outside. My Gatorade Propel bottles are
scattered everywhere. One night I go through Wesley's cassettes
and have an orgy of violence to his Joan Baez, blasting it as loud

as it can go while I walk in and out of the house, collecting objects to launch off the roof—mainly items whose crash landings will have significant implications, such as unopened paint cans. Wesley once told me that Joan Baez was the "female Robinson Crusoe of her time," and I don't know what that means, but her rendition of "The Night They Drove Old Dixie Down" makes the right soundtrack for throwing his possessions. A paint can crashes on the deck; turns out it was red, and the eruption looks like someone shot in the brain. This is like *jamrat* at Mina, when the hajjis throw stones at the Devil to celebrate Abraham's willingness to put a knife to his son, except I'm the son and the knife has already been on my neck, and the gun too, and Abraham's buried but it's Ishmael's turn. I'm a big man like my dad, and when I swing his axe at his furniture, it's with his power. This is how Wesley Unger comes to know himself.

There are no repercussions for anything, I can stand on the roof naked with the wind drying out my balls and shout that the black man is God and all praise is due to Allah in the land of Sarah Palin bumper stickers. For the time being, this is no one's property, but it's spiritually mine more than anyone's, and long after I'm gone the state will show up and claim whatever they find in whatever condition they find it in.

Lights from inside the house are just enough to make the surrounding trees glow bright while the rest of the woods remain lost in darkness. After things settle down, I'm just chilling on the roof and knowing that this moment of perfect peace is something that Wesley never had here.

My phone reception goes in and out, so a new voicemail shows up without my knowing that I missed a call. It's a photographer from the *National*, the major paper in Abu Dhabi. They're doing a story on me and he's their photographer in Washington. His name is Norm. I call him back and he asks how the lighting is in the woods.

Waiting for him to come by in the early afternoon, I sit outside and look at the newest issue of *Nylon Guys,* which came out just before I drove down here. Flip past the fascinating looks at $750 sneakers and find the page on me in the "Genius" section, with a photo where I'm standing in front of the Allah School in Harlem, the Universal Flag behind me. My arms are crossed and I'm looking tough. The article is titled "Shock Value." *With his first feature film, Michael Muhammad Knight takes the Muslim punk rock movement beyond the fringes . . .*

It's awful, even says that I was drinking coffee during the interview. Anyone who has sat in a café with me for thirty seconds has heard my anti-coffee diatribe—years ago, a doctor told me that it was bad for the prostate—and if I were actually drinking coffee I'd have had to get up and piss so many times there never would have been an interview. The article also says that I spent a few years in Pakistan (it was actually two months), that I'd considered joining the Russian army (actually the Chechens *fighting* the Russian army), and that my work has been banned in Algeria and Iran—I don't have a clue where she would have gotten that, but it's out there now.

Norm comes by in the early afternoon and takes the same picture five hundred times. The paper asked for "moody," he tells me, so I pout and scowl and then he says, "You're easy to photograph—you only have one expression."

We do most of the pictures in front of the Islamic Center of Sirius Mathematics, which admittedly has some style, with the spray-painted Arabic and surrounding piles of junk. He moves my Hezbollah flag so that it fits into the shot better. "So, they tell me that you wrote a book about a punk band and it made you reconsider your faith?"

"It was, you know, I wrote a fictional novel, and it was like fiction," I say, looking to his side, never the face—only a month by myself, and I've forgotten how to have a conversation—"about a punk scene, and it was like free expression, you know what I mean? Like, I couldn't express myself, so I thought I was on the outs and I wrote the book to express myself, and then these kids came and gave me a space where I could do, uh, *that.*" He nods.

"And they made your book into a movie?" he asks while shooting.

"Two movies. Omar Majeed made a documentary on the real-life Muslim punk bands, and Eyad Zahra made an adaptation of the novel."

"Which one played at Sundance?"

"The adaptation."

"Is it really punk rock to have your movie play at Sundance?"

"I don't know." I try not to open my mouth too much when speaking, since he's taking pictures.

"So, are you a *practicing* Muslim?"

"I have no idea how to answer that."

"And your father was a white supremacist? Was he active?"

"He didn't like crowds."

When we're done, he looks over Wesley's junk piles and notices a tall pyramid of stacked metal canisters. For a photojournalist with imagination, they could look suspicious.

"Has something *bad* been going on here?" he gasps. Is he asking because of the Nazi father or the Muslim son?

He gives me his business card and walks back down the mountain—his car couldn't make it up—and then I'm alone in the woods again. The sounds of rustling and the snap of a branch make me nervous, but it's only a family of deer.

# 8.

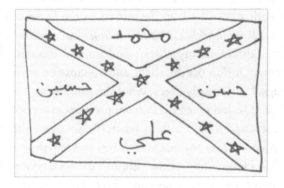

Working on my father's property—cutting down a tree, adding more NO TRESPASSING signs, trying to clean out his sheds, and walking through the woods in search of trees bearing pink tape marking the border—it's the first time that I come close to looking at land as a sacred tribal claim, *the land of my people.* My ancestors on Wesley's side have been in this part of America longer than there has been the idea of "America," arriving before Thomas Jefferson was born. They landed in 1714 as founders of the Germanna miners' settlement. Germanna was established as a buffer between another, wealthier settlement and the nearby natives, a working-class human shield on the literal margin of the privileged white world. Through our shared descent from one of the Germanna founders, Buzz Aldrin is my seventh cousin twice removed. We're also related to Janis Joplin somehow, but I haven't traced her descent.

The first of my ancestors wearing the Unger name arrived from Europe in 1743, settling in the Pennsylvania Dutch regions. Johannes Nicholas Unger married the daughter of a Revolutionary War militia captain, and moved to Morgan County, and the Ungers have been there ever since. During the Civil War, we sided with the Confederacy.

I attempt to push away an abandoned washing machine and remove some of the debris around the Islamic Center of Sirius Mathematics while my iPod boom box provides Nas's *Illmatic* as the soundtrack—*We were beginners in the hood as Five Percenters, but somethin' must have got in us 'cause all of us turned to sinners.* But I wipe myself out and go into the mosque to sit down, pull a Qur'an off the shelf, and collapse on my cardboard prayer rugs. I can't really digest what I'm looking at, but it works. Reading the Qur'an when dizzy from physical exertion and a diet of only water and tuna, on a day when it's hot like Lahore, you're setting up your brain for magical things to happen.

There's a Hans Wehr Arabic-English dictionary at the Islamic Center of Sirius Mathematics, since I have just enough Arabic to occasionally get suspicious of Abdullah Yusuf Ali's translation. In 53:36, he's referring to the "books of Musa," but in the parallel Arabic, it's not *kutub*, "books," but *suhuf*, which I thought meant "pages." Turns out that Hans Wehr supports both translations, but then it gets more compelling: if you write the same *s-h-f* root letters as a Form II verb, it means "to misplace the diacritical marks; to misread, mispronounce, misspell (a word); to misrepresent, distort, twist (a report, etc.)."

It's a blessing straight from the Black Mind, because I can distort the word and make it the word for distortion, put it into the verse: *had he not been told of the misreading of Musa?*

Muhammad was protective of the revelations that were given to him, allegedly saying, "Whoever interprets the Qur'an in accordance with his own opinion shall take his place in the Fire." He was also quoted as saying that when two Muslims differ on the Qur'an's meaning, they should stop reciting. But Ali said, "If I wished, I could load seventy camels with the exegesis of the opening sura of the Qur'an," a mere seven verses. Al-Ghazali quoted another scholar as saying, "For every verse there are sixty thousand understandings, and what remains to be understood is even more." With a few diplomatic disclaimers, Ibn 'Arabi taught that every interpretation of the Qur'an was intended by Allah. The Qur'an is a universe like the universe is a Qur'an.

Verses of the Qur'an are called *ayat*s, literally "signs." For Ibn 'Arabi, Allah's self-manifestation—whether in the small universe of the Qur'an or the big Qur'an, the universe—represents an infinite reservoir of signs, incapable of being restricted or fully comprehended. The word *ayat* appears 360 times in the Qur'an, referring to all kinds of things: the creation of Heaven and Earth, the creation of human beings and their division into male and female, the alteration of day and night, the winds and clouds, ships on the ocean, rain reviving the dead earth, she-camels drinking water, lightning, sleep, Allah's favor upon us, and the Virgin Mary. All of them signs for us to read in the world-as-text. For the word to appear 360 times is itself a sign, but signs don't lead to the Creator of the Universe, only to more signs. Maybe it's *all* misreadings.

Another issue with Abdullah Yusuf Ali's translating a word as "books": 54:52, which he has as *All that they do is noted in the books (of deeds)*. The word looks more like *zaboor*, the Arabic for "Psalms," but not quite, and searching the *z-b-r* root letters in Hans Wehr only gets me *zubr*, "penis." Here's what you get with an unqualified reader of Arabic alone in the wild: *All that they do is noted in the penis*. I remember the RZA announcing onstage that the Wu-Tang has big dicks "physically *and* mentally," and Ibn 'Arabi fucking all of the letters of the alphabet, and my dream where I have "no god but—" tattooed

on my penis and then three mystery letters that I never see, but
as al-Ghazali says when things approach the boundaries, I put
the pen down here.

> The purpose of technology is not to confuse the brain, but
> to serve the body.
>> —heroin-addicted homosexual gun enthusiast,
>> Nike Air Max commercial

Writing is technology, and the Qur'an's a machine. I space
out reading the *Sura ar-Rahman* as the iPod boom box switches
from the Germs' "Lexicon Devil" to William S. Burroughs: first
"The 'Priest' They Called Him," his collaboration with Kurt
Cobain, followed by a lecture recorded at the Jack Kerouac
School of Disembodied Poetics. He's talking about his cut-up
writing method, in which he slices up texts to create new ones,
distant ancestors of mash-ups like my Gravediggaz vs. Metallica.
In 1959, twangy old Burroughs tells me, Brion Gysin declared
writing to be five decades behind painting, and aimed to help literature catch up by applying the collage technique to words. He
put scissors to newspaper and magazine articles and reorgan-
ized the scraps. When they traveled, words changed meaning:
"drafted" could be lifted from an article about the army and
inserted into an article about architects and blueprints.

Burroughs talks about these experiments like he's curing
cancer. There's a millenarian promise to the cut-up, the claim
that he can reveal our destiny as a species from messing with
human languages—"Cut into the present, the future leaks out."
Cut-ups cut into the unseen and unknown. Each document offers
a bottomless psychic reservoir. Burroughs is a mystic about his
words, as though the new phrases that he reveals in a cut-up
were always in the texts and waiting for him, the jewels that
wanted to be known. Noble Drew Ali's *Circle Seven Koran* was
only a cut-up of New Age works, but Burroughs wouldn't see
that as cause to deny his prophethood.

While I've never heard the gods reference Burroughs, Five Percenter culture seems to have perfectly realized the power of the cut-up. Five Percenter *tafsir* is all cut-ups. If I knew today's date, I could break it down. Let's say that it's the tenth: I could read that as ten or add the digits together and get 1+0=1, so it's either Knowledge Cipher or just Knowledge. Even alone, the attributes own deep wells of meaning, but then I could cross-reference the number that I choose with Master Fard's lessons, examining corresponding degrees in the Student Enrollment, Lost-Found Muslim Lessons 1 and 2, English Lesson C-1, Actual Facts, Solar Facts, or any combination of them as they relate to each other. Or go to the corresponding letters and their attributes in the Supreme Alphabets, or bring in the Twelve Jewels of Islam, if desirable. For any day of the month, especially those with double-digit numbers, there could be thousands of different ways in which you might pull these texts together.

A professor once told me the story of a man who wanted to learn Arabic, so he bought some books and taught himself; but with only the books, no tapes, he had to invent his own sounds for the letters. The man developed a solid vocabulary and working grammar, and could interpret Qur'an verses, but for him to read out loud would have sounded like another language altogether—was his Qur'an still the Qur'an? Five Percenters treat "Allah" (Arm Leg Leg Arm Head) and "Islam" (I Self Lord And Master) as English words, never asking whether these acronyms work in Arabic. Their adversary in Brooklyn, Malachi Z. York, had a cane that looked like the Arabic letter ل, pronounced *lam;* he read this to signify that he was the *Lamb* of God. Centuries ago, Fazl Allah used to read the Arabic Qur'an in his native Persian, no translation; he just searched for Persian words appearing in the Arabic sounds. I can take appearances of "his" in the English translation to be H.I.S., the Burroughs acronym for Hassan-i Sabbah, and "them" to mean T.H.E.M., The Honorable Elijah Muhammad, and see how the verses read with *hu* and *hum* given new meanings. Burroughs talks about a friend in Tangiers who went crazy finding personal messages in English from all-Arabic radio shows. He mentions another man who went crazy thinking that street signs, overheard conversations, and so on all referred to him. "Of course they refer to you," says Burroughs. "You see and hear them." I look up the Arabic equivalents of his initials (W=و, S=ص, B=ب) as a three-letter root in my Hans Wehr Arabic-English Dictionary, getting *wasaba*, "to be (chronically) ill . . . illness; discomfort, hardship, suffering."

Burroughs considers English to be the easiest language for cut-ups, which I can believe. Arabic cut-ups would be much more complicated, with case endings and gender, duals and plurals and verb conjugation, especially if your Arabic sucks, and mine does. But I'm thinking about it anyway. Because of my bad Arabic, I did a cut-up years ago without even meaning to. At the end of *The Taqwacores,* I butchered the last verse of the ninety-seventh sura, writing out *salamun* as *sulayman,* which makes the difference between "Peace until the rise of morn" and "Solomon until the rise of morn." It's okay for that book, because messing up the Qur'an in the very last line would have been the most punk thing to do.

Sir Muhammad Iqbal quotes a Sufi as saying, "No understanding of the Holy Book is possible until it is actually revealed to the believer just as it was revealed to the Prophet." An *event* experienced by the Prophet, first on the mountaintop, the Qur'an marked Allah's appearance in creation; for the Prophet, the Qur'an was physically traumatic. When the verses came down, he felt his soul getting ripped from his body.

To cut into the Qur'an could be like breaking open a tomb, as the Qur'an is a tomb for the Prophet. As an actual book, an *object,* the Qur'an marks Allah's absence and the death of the Prophet, because we cannot access either of them. The Qur'an as a book is an act of memory and mourning. I have visited the Prophet's bodily remains at his mosque in Medina— the same mosque where, after his death, the Qur'an's verses were compiled into their final codex—and found thousands of Qur'ans there, stacked around columns and against the walls and opened on little wooden stands for men to read in the presence of Muhammad's skeleton. The death of a prophet is the birth of scripture.

Khomeini tells me that the Qur'an resembles a "banquet from which everyone must partake in accordance with his capacity. It belongs to everyone, not to any particular group; there is a share in it for everyone." Mahmud Muhammad Taha tells me, "The Qur'an is the hidden treasure. It is still virgin, as early Muslims broke only its outer seal." I've cut the wise words from their proper contexts. "You cannot will spontaneity," says Imam Burroughs, "but you can introduce the unpredictable factor with a pair of scissors." For Burroughs, the cut-up method brings revelation and prophetic power, and while I'm still too Muslim to throw those words around, I understand. Your creativity shakes up the book and turns it back into original chaos, but the energy also brings it back to life, and the old words produce something radically new. It's democratic that way—no need for scholars spouting off about historical contexts and classical Arabic; I can cut into the *zahir* and grab my own *batin,* the special misreading that Allah intended just for me. As the hadith says: "Cut-ups are for everyone. Anybody can make cut-ups." In *The Western Lands,* Burroughs claims that it's for this mentality that "the Ismailians were singled out for special persecution, since they commit the blackest heresy in Islamic books, assuming the prerogatives of the Creator."

At least one blessing from doing a Burroughs Qur'an and redefining Allah's copyright: a cut-up of the revelation saves me from ever having to be treated as a credible Islamic reformist again. I've surrendered any chance at defending myself, any claim of legitimacy, any reason to be propped up as a voice of the New Islam—it's not here, *fuck off.* If a verse gives you static, you don't like 4:34 or whatever, my answer now is to find out what it really means by moving Allah's words around like magnetic poetry on the refrigerator. I offer nothing to any serious Progressive Muslim concern, and no one can say that I've missed the mark, because there's no mark to miss.

Cutting up the Qur'an makes for off-the-chart sacrilege, but also the most intellectually honest act of piety that I have. It's what everyone wants to do: the progressives, the conservatives, all of them claiming to own the book and denouncing each other as misreaders. The modern scholar A.E. Affifi accused Ibn 'Arabi's interpretations of "giving us a new Qur'an altogether," and Elijah Muhammad promised that in fact a new Qur'an would come sometime in the future, but in truth every reading is a new Qur'an. Abu Talib al-Makki said that the inexhaustible Qur'an, like Allah himself, "never discloses itself in a single form to two individuals, nor in a single form twice." Malachi Z. York put out his own translation full of pictures of spaceships and reptilian aliens, illustrating what he found in the verses.

It's all a cut-up: every sermon, every prayer in which verses are extracted and quoted out of their contexts, every *tafsir* in which verses are pasted to hadiths and scholars' commentaries, creating whole new hybrid books, every translation in which a translator adds things in parentheses to the English without admitting that they're not in the original Arabic. Arguments over the Qur'an and its meanings are scissor fights; we rearrange and reinvent the words every time. We read what we want to read and then make a claim on what the Qur'an really says, while the Qur'an says nothing; it gives us only the means by which we can say everything. You are the Qur'an that speaks. Nothing is true, everything is permitted, says Sabbah, says Burroughs. If the Qur'an weren't capable of such major shape-shifting, it wouldn't have lasted this long, traversing cultures and generations, speaking to a billion individual minds at any given moment.

It could also mean something that the Qur'an is *already* a cut-up: verses aren't arranged in the order of their revelation. The first verse is generally believed to be 96:1, in which Muhammad is told, "Read!" The final verse is held to be 5:3, in which Allah says that he has completed his favor upon us. In between, it's a divine mess.

This reality of the Qur'an gives me a metal detector to hold above verses or words or even letters until something makes it go *beep-beep-beep, buried treasure here*. It's not a chainsaw; I slowly turn pages, waiting for something to feel right, and cut delicately, surgically, around the text—at first whole verses at a time, retrieving strips of thought that I can put next to each other and see where the attractions are, like six-year-old Yakub playing with his pieces of steel. As I cut each verse apart and scatter the pieces, "Do not prostrate to" from 41:37 lands next to a piece of 2:187, "the limits of Allah," combining into a statement of negative theology: the Names and Attributes are limits placed by human thought upon Allah; don't mistake that small god of language for the Essence. "Was not the earth of Allah spacious enough for you?" finds itself next to "in a scroll unfolded," leading to contemplation of the earth as text, the text as earth, and all the Qur'an's vivid descriptions of the world as references to the Book—so when the Qur'an mentions cattle and crops, it maintains that literal *zahir* but also has a *batin* in regard to the Qur'an itself, and *ayat*s can be signs in the earth or verses in the book or switch it around, the world full of verses.

In 14:24, the Qur'an helps me along by comparing good words to good trees, with branches reaching to the sky. A few verses later, I extract from 14:48—*One day the earth is changed to a different earth.*

The Qur'an says that whatever is in the heavens and the earth praises Allah, so I take the heavens to be things outside of the words. When the Qur'an describes rain as a gift from Allah, causing seeds to grow and become trees that we burn for warmth, I read the rain as whatever we bring to the verses: the prejudices of translators, other books that we've read, our sects and philosophical schools, cultures and historical conditions, and our own personal lives and Rakim's line "It even tells us we are gods in the Holy Qur'an"—so completely unreasonable, but of course it does—penetrating the soil and allowing our seeds of interpretation to sprout. The sun that gives light is the Prophet, and the moon is our tradition, reflecting the sun's light in its absence—*By the sun and its brightness, and the moon following it*. But the Qur'an also says that Allah made the sun and moon subservient for you: I Self Lord And Master.

The Qur'an makes reference to mountains' having been created as firm pegs to stabilize the earth, "lest it should shake with you"—meaning (at least in my Qur'an, the Remix) that the scripture has to be stabilized by religious authorities, to protect against all the wingnuts finding their own desires endorsed by the text. A society needs Ten Percenter mullahs to keep everyone from becoming Peter Lamborn Wilson, or doing, uh, exactly what I'm doing right now. It could even be read with Master Fard Muhammad, who taught that earthquakes were caused by scientists experimenting with high explosives—what's more explosive than the Book? Allah says that these mountains are humble and would collapse under the weight of the Qur'an, but in another verse, immediately after mentioning how mountains keep the earth steady, Allah says that scattered throughout the land are beasts of all kinds.

When the Qur'an mentions cities, especially Mecca ("this city of security"), I take it to mean the interpretive communities— Sunnis, Shi'as, Akbarian Sufis, the Nation of Islam, whatever— where we can live comfortably and take shelter in shared readings. At the present moment, I don't have a city, but I can stop and rest in each one along my way.

This wisdom goes deeper than your scuba diver.
     —the RZA, "A Day to God Is 1,000 Years"

The Qur'an says that if the ocean were ink for writing Allah's Words, it would be exhausted before finishing the Words—even if you added another ocean after it. The Islamic Center of Sirius

Mathematics reads this as a confession of text's failure to convey the full *Haqq*.

Sufis have always used the ocean, full of food and secret treasures and seemingly infinite, as a metaphor for mystical knowledge. Oceans exist within the words but are also beyond words; the verses just dissolve. Whatever the Sufi saints bring back to dry land to become institutionalized within limits of human language isn't quite the same.

The oceans are also unstable; you can't grow anything or build a city on water—you need solid earth. There are times in Sufi tradition when people have followed their readings to some potentially fucked-up places, like the ecstatic utterances of saints losing their shit *Ana al-Haqq*–style. In the 1960s, there was a teen Five Percenter named Katanga Ali who started his own faction, the Ali Family, with a school in Brooklyn. In 1969 he fell off a bridge or something and drowned. I've heard elders build off a wisdom-water metaphor when they talk about him, saying that Katanga Ali "drowned in his own wisdom." It's worth spending some time on. The oceans might be deep and even cover three-fourths of the Qur'an—compared with the literal meaning, a mere quarter—but they're also dangerous and will bring you down if you're unprepared. Frithjof Schuon tried to captain a ship and got lost at sea.

# 9.

Mythology is not simply willed into existence, and the peoples of the earth quickly ensured they would no longer understand their own myths. It is at this very moment literature begins. Literature is the attempt to interpret, in an ingenious way, the myths we no longer understand, at the moment we no longer understand them, since we no longer know how to dream them or reproduce them.

—Gilles Deleuze, "Desert Islands"

If I build on the image of the Qur'an as an earth, with wide fields producing vegetation and oceans of mystic knowledge, what is represented by an island? For Deleuze, an island is "like an egg. An egg of the sea, it is round. It is as though the island had pushed its desert outside. What is deserted is the ocean around it."

Deleuze reads the island as a place of rebirth, a "second origin" as it appears in the myth of the Flood. This matches the island of Patmos, which Master Fard Muhammad calls Pelan, the place where Dr. Yakub withdrew in exile. The 59,999 followers who joined him had been the dissatisfied members of society, willing to forfeit their old lives and contribute to the building of a new culture. It was on Patmos/Pelan that Yakub's

government successfully created a devil, the devil who would
return from island exile and spread across the earth, bringing
destruction wherever he went.

I've been to the real Mecca; I've kissed the Black Stone and
prayed at Arafat with millions of my sisters and brothers and
renounced the devil at Mina. My Hans Wehr Arabic-English
Dictionary says that *hajja* can mean "to overcome, defeat," and
hajjis throw stones at the devil to overcome his tricknology, but
this is Patmos, not Mina. Patmos represents withdrawal and retreat, the opposite of hajj. Nothing is overcome.

> To make devil what must one first do?
> To make devil one must begin grafting from the original.
> —*The Supreme Wisdom Lessons*

Master Fard Muhammad says *word is bond.* Yakub's island
breaks the word and the bond. "Absolutely separate, absolute
creators," writes Deleuze of the island's inhabitants. He calls
them gods and goddesses; Dr. Yakub, the father of the devil, was
also a god. My cut-up Qur'an will not become a mountain, the
institution by which others can stabilize their text, but instead
an island: "separated from a continent, born of disarticulation,
erosion, fracture." The island may offer some usable soil, or
only rocks and sand. I can't honestly say.

# 10.

Prisoner, come out. The great skies are open. I Hassan i
Sabbah *rub out the word forever.* If you I cancel all your
words forever. And the words of Hassan i Sabbah as also
cancel.

—William S. Burroughs, *The Western Lands*

In my cut-up version of 67:15, Allah says that he has "made
the book manageable for you, an earth expanded, so travel
through its verses and eat from his word"; but in the next verse,
Allah warns that he might cause the earth to swallow you up.

If the earth is the book, and the book is the earth, what does
it mean that the earth won't last forever? What does it mean for
a religion built upon nothing but words?

```
When the sun is folded, and when the stars darken,
and when the stars disperse, when the heavens cleave
asunder, and when the heaven shall be removed, and the
mountains shall become like carded wool, and when the
mountains are removed and the mountains will fly here
and there, and the mountains will be as a heap of sand
poured out and flowing down—they ask you about the moun-
tains, say "My Lord will uproot them and scatter them
```

as dust, he will leave them as plains smooth and level,
nothing crooked or curved will you see in their place"—
and when the seas be comingled, and when the oceans
are caused to boil and burn, and when the earth shall
be flattened, and the earth brings forth her burdens,
and shall cast forth whatever is in it, gods from the
earth—and they say "What? When we lie hidden and lost
in the earth?"—and it becomes empty . . .

The day when verses of the Wise Book are like moths
scattered. Travel through the earth; you worship nothing but names that you have named.

Then what message, after that, will they believe in?

The end of the world is the Qur'an's suicide note—*You'll miss
me when I'm gone,* it says. Terrible things will happen, the book
promises, and people will panic, and many will suffer. "And
Allah hits a thousand-year writer's block," says Imam Burroughs
in *The Western Lands.* Turning to the last paragraph of the book,
I make Allah the Burroughs/Sabbah of "The old writer couldn't
write anymore because he had reached the end of words, the end
of what could be done with words."

But some will be okay. Some can live on after Hassan-i Sabbah
rubs out the word forever, and even have gardens with flowing
springs and eternally renewing virgins.

# 11.

He is dear to my heart, but his path isn't soundly established on any principle.
—Ali Hujwiri, on al-Hallaj

I'm sitting on the roof of my mosque with a cardboard box full of Louis L'Amour titles like *Last Stand at Papago Wells*, *Showdown at Yellow Butte*, *To Tame a Land*, *Mustang Man*, *The Man from the Broken Hills*, *Ride the Dark Trail*, *The Lonely Men*, *The Empty Land*, *Down the Long Hills*, *North to the Rails*, *The Rustlers of West Fork*, *The Quick and the Dead*. There's nearly a hundred thin paperbacks here. Maybe I'll write my dream novel, the story of Imam Husayn retold as a pulp Western with Husayn in a white cowboy hat, riding his white horse, six-shooter in hand, and call it *High Noon at Karbala*.

Since it might be Friday, I give a *khutbah* to myself based on what could be the day's degree—*Why did Musa have a hard time civilizing the Devil?* Moses/Musa's an intriguing character in Master Fard Muhammad's lessons, a "half-original" prophet who lives a beast life. In Fard's language, "half-original" would mean that Musa's other half is a devil, making Musa the *barzakh*. Allah made the two seas, says my cut-up Qur'an, and between them is Musa. In 18:60, when Musa vows to reach the junction of the two seas, he's searching for knowledge of his own conflicted self.

From his unique position between the two seas, I have Musa speak first to the believers. O you who believe: *Allah said, you have your religion from the sacred mosque to the farthest mosque. We have opened your hearts and removed your burden.* My commentary on the remixed verse, because every Qur'an needs commentary: "Knowledge of *wahdat al-wujud* has freed monotheists from the burden of their own intolerance." *To Allah belong the East and West. No vision can grasp him, but his grasp is over all vision. He is above all comprehension yet is acquainted with all things. If you think you are friends of Allah to the exclusion of humanity, you will soon know. Allah said: I am not one to bow for man.*

In Allah's Qur'an, "I am not one to bow for man" was said by the arrogant devil when ordered to make *sujdah* before Adam, but his words now go in Allah's mouth to slap down arrogant humans.

Musa then speaks to the unbelievers: *O idolaters: Allah said, we certainly gave the book to Musa, but differences arose in it. Have you considered one who takes as his god his own desire? Allah has the Best Names, so celebrate the Names; abandon not your gods, abandon not Wadd nor Suwa, not Yaghuth nor Ya'uq, nor Nasr, if you are true. Travel in the earth with our signs and authority manifest; wherever you turn, there is the face of Allah.*

If I close my eyes and picture my new Musa, he looks like Robot Monster.

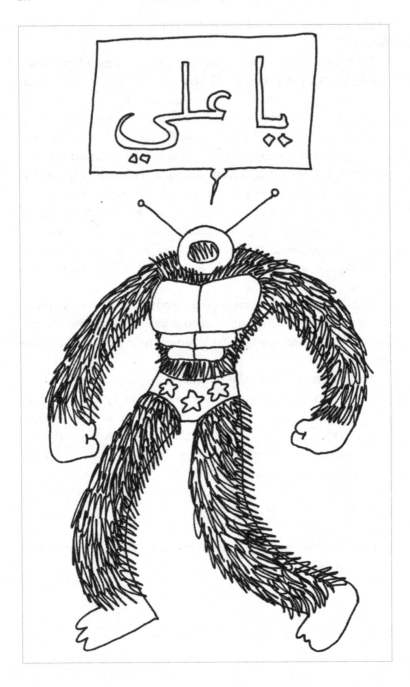

# 12.

### Qissat al-Gharaniq, Part II––

In his revelations to the Prophet, Allah does speaks not in a secret cipher that only the two of them can understand, but in the human Arabic language. If Allah had used his own unique system, it would be easier to draw borders around the sacred text, to know when words are sacred and when they are not, when it's Qur'an and when it's just words. What happens when I find, within the body of the Qur'an, the names of Allah's enemies, such as Pharaoh? Abu Lahab, the Prophet's cruel uncle, is cursed by name in the Qur'an, but this means that his name has become a holy verse. In 53:19 and 53:20, when Allah denounces worship of the goddesses al-Lat, al-Uzza, and Manat, he does so by naming them, which makes them part of the Qur'an. Their names are now eternal and sacred.

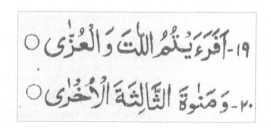

Even when I cut them away with the X-Acto knife, these words are Qur'an. Despite their possible misreadings, I can recite them in prayer and remain fully within the bounds of recognizable Islam. I spray-paint al-Uzza's name on the side of Wesley's house, right next to "5% AL-HAQQ," and it's a prayer to the One God of Abraham.

The new Arabic word on my dad's house: it came from the Qur'an, it *is* Qur'an, having lived in the Qur'an and now arriving here on this house. Like Venom from *Spider-Man,* the word has a memory and can draw information from its previous host.

In hadith literature, al-Uzza appears as a black woman, naked and insane with grief, screaming and pulling out her hair when the Muslims destroy her idol. But even if worship of al-Uzza died on the Arabian Peninsula, her name grafted itself onto Allah's triumphant Qur'an and survived for fourteen centuries, waiting for a new host. Like Venom, she is an extraterrestrial, since I've identified the Qur'an as Earth in my cut-up. She is an alien in the book; it makes no sense that she is there. But now she is *here.* I even see her looking like Venom, huge blank white eyes and sharp fangs, like Jehennam's version of the seventy-two virgins. The hell-houri tears through the strips of *ayat*s; as I take scissors to 81:8 and 81:9, she settles in between the words.

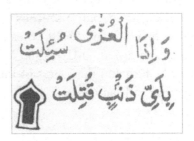

And when al-Uzza, buried alive, asks for what crime she was killed.

One word out and one in, and now my Qur'an demands justice for a smashed idol. I add a symbol for the *sujdah tilawat,* the prostration required with some verses, just to give it a worthy exclamation point.

Al-Uzza screamed within the book for centuries until a Muslim would hear her, a Muslim upon whose emotions she could feed. She knows my idol-friendly sensibility as a *wujudi* who could see Islam in everything. She also knows the Muslim feminist desperation to find a home in the Qur'an even when it crushes women; she can speak as a black womanist to the guilty white man who just strolls through a religion, owning it with his blessed balls.

Regardless, al-Uzza does know her crime, and I know. Her idol had to be smashed, as all idols have to be smashed because they stand in the way of words. Transcendent above the natural world, the god of words is too remote and abstract to connect with hearts. The god of words cannot compete with the goddess who is visible and touchable. Peter has a new book out on the evolution of letters, where he says that "the process of alphabetization consists of a Mosaic attempt to purify the pagan pictograms of imagery." Turn your eyes from the statues and gaze upon text; adore letters and words in a book. One had to go, Musa's tablets or the golden calf. In Judaism, the enshrined Torah took the place of idols; in Christianity, the laity's lack of access to the Bible allowed statues to creep back into their lives. At Mecca, the god of words won. There are no idols in Muslim homes today, only framed calligraphy of holy verses— no crazy converts on Cooper Mountain breaking apart and re-assembling *statues,* right? Al-Uzza died for my Qur'an to have life; as a reward, she lives in the archive. The stone goddess has crumbled, but her name remains carved into the new fetish. Any Qur'an anywhere holds her memorial and chance of rebirth.

# 13.

I was a prophet sent to myself from myself, and it is myself
who, by my own signs, was guided toward myself.
     —Ibn al-Farid

**I** quote this dude and I don't even know who he was. The
words just washed ashore in a bottle from some other planet.

My Qur'an moves and changes, words going in and out,
verses assembling and breaking apart and then reassem-
bling to make new meanings. It's a Temporary Autonomous
Qur'an, a T.A.Q., you could say. Liquid *ayats*. I'm playing
with thoughts of Musa and his biography starts to take form,
cut from what the Qur'an already says about him, mixed
with other prophet stories and random things. The story of
Musa, a new creation, a mad poet. A strange thing, a
partition between the two highways. Out of our mercy,
we gave him the Death Angel, put in charge of him. A
man like you.

Musa said to his father, "I see you and your people
in manifest error, and I do detest your doings."

Musa said to the mosque, "I am of the Muslims." The
mosque said, "O Musa! You rebelled before, and you were
of those who did mischief!"

So Musa threw his rod, when behold, it swallows up all that they fake.

By the even and the odd, and by the seven, and by the words, Musa is an olive neither east nor west.

Musa said, "I will not give up until I reach the junction of the two seas, or I spend years and years in travel." When Musa was traveling, then came a man from the farthest city, a sorcerer and poet and guide who had knowledge of the book. Musa said to him, "You have an authority manifest! May I follow you, on the footing that you teach me something of the truth you have been taught? I am to you an apostle worthy of all trust."

The guide said, "Your prayer is granted, O Musa!" The guide granted knowledge and taught him by the pen, taught him what he did not know. Tales of the ancients. He made the gods into one god. He created and gave order. He ordained laws and brought out the pasture in a scroll unfolded.

The guide said, "And what is in your right hand, O Musa?"

Musa said, "It is my rod."

The guide said, "Seize it and fear not. Now draw your left hand close to your side: it will not come forth white."

But Musa withdrew his hand and behold, it was white.

His guide threw his rod, and behold, it was a serpent plain. This is a sorcerer telling lies! He does not nourish, nor satisfy hunger. Musa said, "You found me wandering, and you gave me guidance. But Man is evidence against himself. God has not made for a man two hearts. This is the parting between us."

So Musa returned in a state of indignation and sorrow. He said, "Lord, I have indeed wronged my soul." And he said, "I am indeed sick."

O believers and O unbelievers! Bring me a book. Have you considered the pages of Musa? And what will explain to you the misreading of Musa?

A sura from my Qur'an—make your own.

# 14.

I was born an even century after Master Fard Muhammad, 1877–1977. Elijah said that before coming to America, Fard was prepared for his mission by twenty-three wise scientist-imams. I'm considering who should be named as my own scientist-imams, the ones who trained me for this path.

It's gorgeous on Cooper Mountain, but Wesley didn't like the fact that voices in the trees would threaten to come and get him. Since he liked to play prophet and speak in allegory, it could mean more than a random audio hallucination. Actual human beings were getting in his space; if I look hard enough through the trees, I can spot a brand-new house. Another one has popped up on the next tier of the mountain, looming high above Wesley's house. Looks like money. Less than a hundred yards from the end of Wesley's property, there's the start of a road—gravel now, soon to be paved. Wesley checked out at the last possible moment that this place could have been tolerable for him.

Allegorical readings aside, Wesley was legit paranoid schizophrenic and avoided leaving the house, so I don't expect that he ever climbed to the top of Cooper Mountain. It's a steep hike but easier under the power lines, which hang over a stripe of cleared land going forever in both directions. Bitten up from the circling mosquitoes, scratched from tall weeds, and slick with sweat when I reach the top, I discover a secret tribe of new houses on their own hidden road. The houses have neatly trimmed lawns, sculpted bushes, smooth clean driveways, basketball nets, and plastic children's play sets. At the end of the road, I can see the main highway, and on the other side—with a perfect view, as though the people put their road exactly at this spot on purpose—a large white church on top of a freshly mowed hill.

These new houses have no signs of life, no motion at all. Even the air around them is completely still, like it's a photo—or maybe a ghost town as of thirty seconds ago, everyone instantly vaporized. No, the people of this tribe are alive, and being alive is very good for them. Just by standing here, I feel like I've broken their law. It messes with you a little to squat in your dad's bunker in his junkyard for weeks, throwing his stuff off the roof, hurling rocks and hammers at his truck's windshield, cultivating black fingernails and swampy balls, sticky arms and legs, possessing no soap or shampoo, eating only canned tuna, putting spray-paint or an axe to the wall when you feel like it, forgetting that you're not the only person on this mountain, and getting spiritual about the place and thinking that you can rename it something crazy zonga . . . and then you remember that there *are* other people, and you find out that the other people are *these* people, the ones who have running water and live not in bunkers, but in *houses*.

As I look at these houses, it's the first time that I fully comprehend what it means that my father defecated into a bucket. It's going to make me cry about him—I can feel it coming. Whatever these people are, Wesley was not, and Peter is not, and Azreal is not, which has me contemplating my chances. And the chances of these kids who write to me, thinking that I can lead them somewhere.

For some weeks and days it's a satisfying ritual life, doing my prayers and *zikr*s in the mosque and bringing my Qur'an to the kitchen table to search through verses like an old lady scavenging at the flea market. Doing cut-ups is the most intimate interaction I've had with the Qur'an in a long time, and it reintroduces me to the book as something tangible, an object to be touched and revered—and I do revere it. If one of my cut verses falls to the floor, I kiss the words as repentence. The physical act of cutting doesn't even feel wild or radical, and I've been away from any Muslim community for too long to even understand why it would. It's a quiet act of worship in my quiet house, my lonely time with the Black Mind.

Even with these crimes against scripture, and even if I've ripped out my page in *Nylon Guys* and taped it to the wall to gaze at my own self as the baseball-cap shaykh of this place, prayers at the Islamic Center of Sirius Mathematics remain mostly orthodox and orthoprax. I make my *tayammum,* sing the Sunni *adhan* softly in the trees, and pray just regular as I always have, reciting the same Qur'an as everyone. Sometimes I'm only in my boxers, which wouldn't be valid *fiqh*-wise, since they don't cover my knees, but otherwise I look like an acceptable Sunni. Ritual trains thought and my inner belief conforms to the outer motions, my prayer becoming intellectually the same as most Muslim prayers, no special Akbarian or Five Percenter spin on it. I even try to pray at the regular times. Afterward, I get into the Nimatullahi *zikr* and do it long enough that my head empties, a thought surfacing with each *Allah,* only to be pushed out with *Hu,* and eventually it's just breathing. Leaving the mosque (left foot first, because it *is* a mosque), I do a quick look around just to see if any graduate students are writing dissertations on my new movement.

Beyond phone calls and emails from the ether, I don't deal with humans; apart from the photographer that one time, no one comes up here, and when I come off the mountain, no one talks to me. When I first showed up, it was hard to be alone; now it's harder to be with people. Wesley lived on the mountain at least since the late 1990s; I'm assuming that it only made him more of what he already was.

It's fun to pretend that my place in Capon Bridge society has been culturally contextualized, as though every Appalachian ridge and valley town has its own recluse writer hiding in a junkyard with his secret project—like people see me during the tractor pull at the Romney fairground and tell their kids not to say hi because spiritually I'm in another dimension. A seven-year-old with blond rat-tail and his own can of Mountain Dew wants to bother me, but Mom says, "Leave him alone, Billy! He might be getting transmissions from Master Fard Muhammad!" That would rule, but I'm in white-privilege *taqiyya*—no one knows a thing when they see me, and I'm not showing them the stamps on my passport.

One morning I decide to start on the special letters of the Qur'an, the random letters that begin suras. But nothing's random, and, as Ibn 'Arabi said, "The world of letters is a real world like us." The letters are the breaths of Allah through which existence was created, which means that when Ibn 'Arabi fornicated with the alphabet, he basically fucked reality itself.

Abu Madyan said, "Whatever I see has ب inscribed on it"— and Muhammad's name in Arabic looks like a man lying down, write it out. To support his own interpretations of the Qur'an, Ibn 'Arabi could resort to breaking down a single letter in a word, or even inserting letters. I have my complete set of Javad Nubakhsh's *Sufi Symbolism* on a shelf at the Islamic Center of Sirius Mathematics, and I pull out Volume 13 to deal with the science of letters. The letter ق represents the station of limitation, the farthest a Sufi can go before the stop sign. The letters ي and س together signify the Perfect Man.

About a century after Muhammad, a sorcerer named al-Mughira ibn Sa'id founded his own sect, the Mughiriyya, which mastered the art of strangulation. He taught that God was the Man of Light, and that the Man of Light's robe was Christ's gospel, his shirt was the Torah, his pants were the Psalms, and his loincloth was the Qur'an. The Man of Light's body parts were the letters of the Arabic alphabet, and all of these body parts together spelled God's Greatest Name. The letter م was the Man of Light's head, ص and ض were his eyes, ع and غ his ears, and his teeth were formed by the letter س. Al-Mughira told his followers that if they could see where the letter ه was on God's body, "you would see something awesome." Arabic letters change shape depending on what you do with them; if you add a long vowel to the letter ه to make the letter's sound, it looks like this:

According to an Isma'ili heresiography, al-Mughira was hinting that he had seen God's genitalia.

This is the point at which the earth finally coughs up its contents and I'm asking what's wrong with her, the oceans boiling and the mountains ripped up—the day I notice how many hours I've been at this kitchen table, trying to figure out how to interpret a م and where to place it, and how a morning becomes an afternoon and the sun comes and goes without my traveling beyond my own head, and how socially incapable I'd be if I went into town and how long have I even been on the mountain? Nothing compared with Wesley's time. And he had his projects; he could lose himself in this kitchen building a cabinet with Stars of David on it, or writing his poems.

Wesley's kitchen table is now covered with *my* madness: pieces of three-by-five index cards, cut-out Arabic words taped to them, handwritten English on the other side, some laid out in sequences, some in piles, a bunch in a plastic bowl for the holy-word raffle. Looking up from a pronoun suffix, I register the sight of this table. There's another side to what I've been doing here. Maybe it has nothing to do with religion—or it does, but religion isn't always religion.

The first time I met Wesley, he read me a story that he had written in 1973: "Harley Hill," about two kids on a motorcycle.

My next visit, he gave me his work in a tall stack of legal-size yellow notepads bundled together with twine and sent me off on the Greyhound with it, a cinder block of illegible writing in my lap. I wanted to be a genius writer like I imagined Wesley to be, and because of him, my idea of what it meant to be a genius writer would always be married to mental illness, questionable hygiene, bizarre personal mythology, failure in every other aspect of life, and a dump of a house. Ten years later I'd be crashing in Peter's guest room and finding all of that with him, lonely hermit Hakim Bey, self-described "So-Called Prophet of Chaos" and "'Alien' unmasked as Shiite Fanatic Queer Poet," living with his statues and thousands of books and bathtub full of cobwebs. Wesley was a bit of a mean fuck and denied me as his son, but I loved him through loving Peter. I loved him through loving Azreal, who knew Wesley's experience of getting strapped into hospital beds. Allah's Death Angel had canceled out the Hells Angel: Wesley was institutionalized for his Nazi and Satanist books, and Azreal left the asylum calling a black man Allah. When I drove Azreal from Harlem to Milwaukee, paying for his weed in every town along the way just to hear him sing old songs and tell stories about building on Supreme Mathematics with Ol' Dirty Bastard, he was holding a place for my father.

If this epiphany means anything, it has to be followed with another one . . .

Yes. There it is.

I don't actually want to be like them, any of them.

I don't want to be Hakim Bey, and Azreal remains an innocent heart and saint for Allah, but I don't want his life. I don't want to be Yakub or Sabbah, and I don't want to live in a shack like this, in a junkyard like this on a mountain like this, stroking my long white beard and sitting around for fatherless boys to show up looking for instant history. I don't even want to be Elijah Muhammad alone in his mansion, staring up at Fard's picture and waiting for the spaceships.

Musa said, "I seek refuge in Allah from the mischief
of the companions of the cave. They stayed in their
cave three hundred years, and add nine."

Another Five Percenter story from the early days: Al-Salaam, one
of the first nine teenagers to follow Allah, would end up getting
exiled from the movement because he fasted for seven days
straight, bought too hard into his own hype, and subsequently
lost his mind, Frithjof Schuon–style. Al-Salaam broke his fast
with ham and then got in Allah's face about it, telling him, "I
did something that you couldn't do." Allah threw him out of
the cipher and banned any fasts longer than three days. I think
about Al-Salaam after I've run out of tuna—which many Five
Percenters avoid anyway, the pork of the sea—and gone three
days without eating. It's best to just come off the mountain and
get some oatmeal cookies; but there could be more to the Al-
Salaam parable than diet, I consider as I sit in my father's chair,
the one that he put in front of his woodstove for cold nights, and
feed words to the fire.

Some Five Percenters warn against indulgence in "Willy
Wonka math," in which your science puts you in a world of pure
imagination. It's probably not a good idea to read Ibn 'Arabi
when you're all alone in the woods, since there's no one around
to keep you at least halfway attached to the shared world. I
learned that from Peter Lamborn Wilson, and it's especially true
if you have the genetic code for schizophrenia—I learned that
from my father, who used to sleep with the Bible under his shirt.
God forgive all my fathers, let them glow for once like the saints
at the end of *Return of the Jedi*.

# 15.

The new clarity leads to my own Billy Hitchcock moment where I snap and banish the heretics and throw fourteen grand at Timothy Leary to get out of my mansion—except there's no money and I'm the heretics. When I come down from the mountain, it's done for good. As always, the Temporary Autonomous Zone disappears without a trace; I've painted over my Muslim tags, no more Ali or al-Haqq or even al-Uzza. The seven can stay. My *Nylon Guys* profile came down from the shed wall and landed as a wadded-up ball in a pile of garbage. The outside of the house smells like a blend of summertime piss and chunk light tuna juice. I went at the pickup with the axe, destroying its passenger-side door and smashing the last window; no insult to Wesley—it's the state's truck now.

At least I can contextualize this with my *Ahlul-Bayt* love, since Fatima inherited land from her father and the state took it away too. I survey the destruction, forgive my father, recite *al-Fatiha* for him, and then drive down to the highway.

Reading my Google alerts in the parking lot of a hotel in Winchester, I glimpse an excerpt of an anthology, *Religious Anarchism*. One of the guys who brought me to Sweden has a chapter in there on Islamic anarchists, and for some reason I count as one.

Though still feeling indebted to Wilson for publishing *The Taqwacores*, Knight has disavowed his former mentor due to Wilson's advocacy of paedophilia/pederasty. While standing up for an Islam that embraces all sorts of heresies, Knight has felt compelled to draw boundaries of his own.

Now recorded in a citable source, it seems more official. Feels like something that really happened.

Then I read an interview with one of the guys from Das Racist. "This Michael Muhammad Knight cat who wrote about these bands," he says, "and brought them to the forefront of whatever they're at the forefront about was probably just trying to make some guap. That might not be a fair statement—I don't know dude—but something just doesn't add up."

On another blog, I find someone talking smack about the "fantasy of an isolated, abused white kid projecting what he wants so-called 'Muslims in the Gray' to act like and be like." It's always tempting to get on and defend myself, especially when there are easy factual errors, but debating online is like giving a mouse a cookie—it will never make the mouse go away. Besides, this person claims to have attended my reading in Vancouver, and I've never stepped foot in Vancouver in my life. You can't argue with the makers and owners of reality:

> My question for Mike is, had daddy finally called you? Did you do a good job corrupting your worshipping Pakistani pygmies?

> The reason I ask this is if you read his second book, and I have been following Knight for quite some time, you see he comes from a white supremacist background. His Aryan Nation supporting father rejected him after telling him to write about the natives, and so he turned Muslim as taught by Malcolm X, not by the Sufi practitioners he now mixes in the same sentences with "vomit" and other vulgarities. The book itself

came from inspiration by known pedophile Hakim Bey aka Peter Lamborn Wilson who Michael Knight wrote about his many experiences with in 2005 while writing Taqwacores. The book came from this relationship, which I can only imagine wasn't the most holy of things.

Zahra & Knight: their whole demeanor and come-off in articles written in western rags will forever be remembered as the illegitimate children of Peter Lamborn Wilson's final fuck you to a world that rejected his heresy and confined him to an upstate exile, as a pedophile.

I have to give it to them, because it's theirs anyway.

Someone else has created a thread on a message board, titled "Michael Knight: enlightened white man or white coon?" One of the responders writes, "I do feel he wishes he was black. How could he not want to be black when the religion he follows states that black men are gods, and white men are devils?" The next chimes in: "The fact that he was raised in a blatantly racist household kinda shows you the rubber band effect that happens when you are subjected to extremes like that, it always swings completely in the other direction."

On another board, a post recommends *Journey to the End of Islam,* even while calling it a train wreck. "I think the author is a crackpot," it says, "but he is quite a unique voice (not many Caucasian-American 5%ers out there)."

While a Muslim blogger in Japan complains about "academic salivation" over my work, the books have received a new write-up in an online journal, treating them together as a complete rhetorical artifact and weighing in on the sum of their meaning:

This is not the first time that a "hip" writer has sought to "turn on" the larger "square" culture to an ostensibly alien religious tradition. In the 1950s the Beat writers, perhaps Knight's best analogues, turned their attention to Buddhism and in so doing helped to make Buddhism "hip" and "cool." Knight similarly drapes Islam in a mantle of hipster cool by evoking images of punk and hip-hop music, professional wrestling, drug use, *Star Wars, Transformers* and horror movie zombies.

The author of the review, Vernon Schubel, is a professor of Islamic studies who had invited me to speak at his college. Peace to him. He goes on to write, "Part of the power of Knight's work is that he takes Islam seriously." I want to say that he's right, but maybe it's just the evil Whisperer putting mischief in my ear. At least say that I take Islam more seriously than Peter, but that's still difficult, given the past month of DIY scripture.

*No,* I tell myself, *I do.* Peter's gone for good, and my exiles are always temporary.

The newest review of *Journey to the End of Islam* is also out, and it's positive, but the last sentence leaves me horrified:

If more people were as brave and honest as Michael Muhammad Knight when it came to their religion the world would be in far better shape.

The "brave and honest" porkshit is artistic and spiritual sabotage. When someone puts that psychic poison on you, how can you ever write a word?

Before folding up the laptop and pulling out of this parking lot, I read a thread on my wrestling match with Abdullah the Butcher, and a guy writes that he's going to name his son after Hassan-i Sabbah. God love him.

Knowing that I'll be in the area, I've agreed to give a reading in D.C. On the way, I stop at a mosque in Manassas that I've already written about in fiction and nonfiction. I've bought new socks just to hide the condition of my feet and gotten a haircut—asking the woman to shave my head clean was a knee-jerk solution to my unwashed mullet, but after the fact I remember Wesley's advising me to go skin. The carpets are much softer than the floor at the Islamic Center of Sirius Mathematics. No one's there to see my *zuhr* prayer, but I hear women and kids from some other room and it's enough for me to feel like the *shahadah* has witnesses.

My reading is at the dorm house for the Muslim Public Service Network's summer program: two men and four or five *muhajabahs*, all interning for senators. We sit in the living room and I just read from *Journey to the End of Islam*, no Rumi donkey-sex poems. They're open to what I'm doing and even tolerate my Master Fard angle. We break for *maghrib* prayer and one of the men, an intern for Senator Feingold, leads. He recites words, lots of words, the Arabic words that hold our *ummah* together because we have all agreed on their importance. After a brief period of questions and answers, I drive up to Rockville and hop the short iron fence at Saint Mary's Cemetery.

SO WE BEAT ON, says the stone, BOATS AGAINST THE CURRENT, BORNE BACK CEASELESSLY INTO THE PAST.

Whenever he spoke about F. Scott Fitzgerald, Wesley would slide into a lecture on what he called the Secret Vanity.

"You don't need everyone to know that you're F. Scott Fitzgerald," he'd say. "Don't go around telling everyone that you're him. It's enough that *you* know who you are. The Secret Vanity is best." Like the amateur cult leader that he was, he'd lock Manson eyes with me while slowly repeating the key phrase: "the Secret Vanity is best." He made sure that I knew the Secret Vanity before sending me to Andrew Jackson's plantation.

I'd like to believe that it meant something for Wesley to call me F. Scott Fitzgerald, that he had a reason and I could keep trying to interpret him and break it down forever, but maybe there's nothing, only my father being crazy. Inside the Ka'ba, it's just an empty green room. But at least Wesley had a turn at being my shaykh. I studied Fitzgerald for him. Even if we were just pretending with each other, it felt real enough; as an act of pious discipline, I copied *The Great Gatsby* out by hand. Jehangir's only Jay Gatz dying for the green light.

St. Mary's Cemetery is where I stand at the end of *Impossible Man,* so now I've written two books that wrap up with me at the grave of F. Scott Fitzgerald and two books at the alleged grave of Master Fard Muhammad. Without the push of Wesley's Fitzgerald mythology, I wouldn't have had these books; he made writing into a religious path, and writing became my small share of his illness. This new book about unfinished books might be the end of my words, at least the words about myself, unless I do the Islam-and-ayahuasca book, or *Why I Am a Five Percenter.* Otherwise, look for me next time in the academic journals.

This weekend I'll drive up to Harlem for the Show and Prove, the Five Percenters' yearly convention on the anniversary of Allah's assassination, and be surrounded by friends again, all the gods and poor righteous teachers—and if Azreal's still alive and not incarcerated, there's a chance that he'll manifest. Jibril Bey says he'll take me to Long Island's North Shore, setting of *The Great Gatsby,* for mushrooms and loud *zikr*s. Weekend after that I'll be in London for the Meltdown Festival, hanging out with the Kominas and Aki Nawaz, reading tweets like "Taqwacore is a sham" at Riz MC's place, and laughing at how being anthropologically interesting gets you free trips everywhere.

# 18.

Muhammad wasn't white
And neither is this fight
And we weren't birthed by Michael Knight
　　　—Secret Trial Five, "We're Not Taqwacore"

Then an eighteen-year-old writes from Mecca, telling me that he has just performed the rites of *umrah*. He says that while walking his seven laps around the Ka'ba, he recited my poem "Muhammad Was a Punk Rocker."

Running late for the doctor, I have no time to consider which book to bring—always bring reading material, can't handle their magazines—so I grab the one nearest to the door, which happens to be my second novel, *Osama Van Halen*. It seems kind of dickish to read your own book in the waiting room, but I realize this only when I'm halfway there.

*Osama Van Halen* is a metafiction in which I show up throughout the text and interact with my characters. It ends with a burqa-wearing riot grrl cutting off my head after she delivers a tirade about how white boys who convert to Islam are all phallocentric Orientalists. Peter Lamborn Wilson's head is Gérôme's *Snake Charmer*, and Michael Muhammad Knight's head is Eugène Delacroix's *Women of Algiers in Their Apartment*. Time to shut the eyes of the colonial gazer: *Michael Muhammad Knight,* says the burqa-wearing riot grrl, *I'm putting an end to your bullshit sand-wigger discourse right now.*

And then *swoosh* goes her big curvy scimitar.

It's also in *Osama Van Halen* that I present a character named Ben Majnun, who writes novels by inserting a pen up his urethra and essentially fucking the page. He breaks it down with "My pen is my penis, my penis, my pen is." The penis mightier than the sword. Male fans ask if they can look in his urethra, just "to see what's up there." *For some,* I write, *Ben Majnun's penis was a gateway to self-knowledge.*

So I wonder if my doctor gets anything from looking up ure-thras, or whether he will get anything from mine. Perhaps he'll realize that he's looking into a urethra and consider that what he sees is also what someone would see if they looked into *his* urethra, and maybe he'll say, "Holy shit." I guess you can specu-late on that about any kind of doctor, and it's probably never true because they do their procedures hundreds and thousands of times and they're over such thoughts. But maybe it's different with a penis doctor who has a penis of his own.

He's a nice enough guy for what he's about to do. He gets me on his table naked from the waist down. Time to rock out with my *haqq* out. A bunched-up towel on my stomach blocks my view, but I turn away regardless, focusing on my jacket on the hook. It's an amalgamation of old army jackets, like some-one blew up a bunch of soldiers and stitched the scraps of their clothes together, a gift from a fashion designer who wanted me to sign on for a taqwacore line. It's better to look at than the cystoscope, the camera that's about to be rammed up my urethra to shine a light into my penis, allowing the doctor to watch what happens when they shoot water into me.

In medieval Punjab, it was customary for Qalandar Sufis to pierce their penises with thick iron rods *(seekh)* and seal both ends, rendering them unable to have sexual intercourse. This will probably not be as bad.

"We're going to deaden it first, don't worry," he says. By *it*, the thing to be deadened, he means my penis; we're going to deaden my penis. He puts gel on his hands and massages it onto me. After a few seconds, I realize that I'm getting a handjob: the motions are all the same: he's kneading my soft penis from the bottom up, squeezing but not too tight.

As the doctor and nurse are getting ready and it looks like the moment's coming soon, I search for some way to interpret what could be the worst nightmare in the male imagination: perhaps I should go *wahdat al-wujud* and see the doctor as Allah and the nurse as Allah and the cystoscope as Allah and the guy scared shitless on the table as Allah and it's all just the Best Knower knowing himself, Allah preparing to shove himself up himself in the name of his own self. I remember a Five Percenter in Harlem referring to his meatus (the urethral orifice) as the "stargate," the portal through which a cosmic traveler reaches Earth. I also remember a kid back in elementary school who was rumored to insert nails into his meatus, and the shivers in my spine whenever we said it. Did he lube them up? He had to. When nothing's shooting out, the urethra's not really a tube, just a cleft; the walls meet and touch. A foreign object has to force its way in, part the walls again. The doctor has lube on his cystoscope, but what if the lube wears off while it's still inside? The cystoscope will scrape up my dick guts on its way out and I'll spend the rest of my life with inside-out dick guts dangling from the stargate.

My body tenses. Pain at the tip as bad as I ever thought it could be, like he opened the lips of my meatus with a sword. I can't think or breathe or move. The pain passes through the stargate instantly and moves up inside. It's worlds of suffering beyond doctors' going knuckle-deep with those prostate exams, because there's no way of imagining a solid object in my piss-hole—how unnatural, no frame of reference for it at all. As the pain climbs—I want to say that it's worst at the tip, but is it? I can't even tell—I do the *zikr* that Agha Ron taught me, *Allah Hu*, with the *Allah* a deep inhalation that doesn't even sound like the word, and then I let it out with *Hu,* but it's really just *Hu* with no time for *Allah,* rapid-fire *Hu-Hu-Hu* like I'm giving birth.

"What's going on?" I say, embarrassed as the words come out.

"This is the deadening," says the doctor.

*The deadening? This isn't the actual shit?* I thought that the deadening was the handjob part, but the handjob was only to stretch it out. My penis had withdrawn like a frightened turtle, and he needed to get it long for the camera to insert more effectively.

So what's inside me right now isn't even the cystoscope, just a syringe to numb me for when the real terror goes down. I'm pretty sure that there's no needle, but it still feels like a needle going in deep, a sharp needle through the length of my penis. It feels like a needle but thicker than a needle, five-sixteenths of an inch in diameter. Islam is mathematics. Cold liquid shoots into me. I keep bringing up my knees and the doctor keeps telling me to put them down. I lock my ankles together and clench my fists.

Whatever he squirted up there may have worked enough for me to not realize when the syringe comes out and the cystoscope goes in, but that also means that between them it never stops hurting. I can't tell which part of me is supposed to be numb. The doctor says things and the nurse puts her hand on my arm and I realize that she can see everything—what does she take from watching this? Will the image stay in her head when she goes home? With her other hand she's holding on to the cord that sends water into me. It's flexible for conforming to the twists and turns of its journey through my spongy urethra to my membranous urethra to my prostatic urethra. "Water," the doctor says, and she pushes a button or something, and then he tells her to turn the water off. It feels like I have to piss, but more important, it feels like a machine has entered me via my smallest and most sensitive hole. "We're all the way up to the bladder now," he says. How does he know where we are? Information from his fiber-optic endoscope. I keep up with the *Hu* and clenching my fists. The only way to survive this might be a peak experience, a transcendent out-of-body vision, so I close my eyes and try to make it happen. The pain is too much for me to concentrate on anything, no thoughts surviving beyond flashes of images: an island, a beach, a tribe of castaways waiting for me—the 59,999 Weird White Boys of Islam with all their zonga names—like my teacher Azreal and my heir Azreal Understanding, the old Death Angel telling the new Death Angel stories about the sanitarium where he met Allah, waving his hands around, smoke from the equality trailing behind, Azreal Understanding the new *barzakh* child jotting it all down for a science-fiction novel he wants to write. I scramble to come up with more faces: William S. Burroughs, the disembodied pixelated TV head like in his Nike commercial when he proclaims that technology's purpose is to serve the body—he says this while my dick's an antenna broadcasting my insides to another man—and he delivers a *khutbah* on Sabbah while Brion Gysin in Arab drag draws magical spells in the sand.

It's a freestyle cipher: Jibril Bey, Ayatollah of Liminal Space, stands there in his camouflage jacket and sips ayahuasca tea from a Styrofoam cup, the mic in his other hand, killing Muslimgauze beats alongside Foeknawledge the vegan Shi'a MC with Walid al-Taha on the sax for an all-time audience of figures like forgotten Muhammad Alexander Webb from the nineteenth century. *Quick, who else?* I don't know the faces but I imagine Henri Corbin and Rene Guénon, only there as names, Massignon too. Next to ethereal Guénon I see his student who went bad, Frithjof Schuon, wearing a Viking helmet with absurdly oversize horns, his floppy old-man junk hanging out of crotchless deerskin pants. Hugo Leaming Bey shows up in a fez and calls for the new hajj to Mecca, Indiana. The Sultan passes golden Moorish passports to everyone while my man Husayn Sapphire and Muhammed al-Ahari El, the Moorish Mahdi, witness with right hand on their hearts, forming holy sevens with their bodies.

I'm breathing hard *zikrs* and the image of John Walker Lindh appears, mud-caked face with wild-man hair, like he's just escaped from U.S. custody in Afghanistan, carrying four Marines' heads in a sack.

The doctor keeps saying that we're almost through and tells me to hold on while I see Peter on my island, beating the drum, wearing his black robe and black fez with the Flying Heart and surrounded by little boys dressed in yellow raincoats and blue hats, like Paddington Bear but with big blue-green dragonfly wings. They're not actual human beings, just robotic houris created for him, no ethical dilemmas.

I try to feel the sun instead of the cystoscope and picture these Muslim Sons on the Patmos beach, some on the sand and some knee-deep in the Aegean Sea, just flashes of each one and a sense that the water's darkening and the sky is purple, it's that early-evening dreamtime. Write the Qur'an in the sand and watch Allah wash it away. Everyone's barefoot and their faces are painted up in stripes and patterns like they've formed an anti-tribe together. Besides the music and freestyle *zikr*s, there's weed, and prayer rugs, and books, piles of musty thought-to-be-lost volumes of arcane heresies and impenetrable numerologies. And ancient rusty scissors.

The scene goes in and out since my brain can't focus, but I give the assembly a purpose: they're working together to finally build Peter's log-cabin pyramid, the Moorish Science Ashram, and in the sand they've planted torches and flagpoles bearing black flags and *khamsa*s, those Hand of Fatima amulets derived from pre-monotheistic fertility virgin goddesses whose hands and/or vulvas were used to repel the Evil Eye. *Yes,* I plead with myself, a log-cabin pyramid, LOG-CABIN PYRAMID ON THE BEACH, NOT A DIGITAL CAMERA LACERATING MY URETHRA, and inside the pyramid it looks like a *khaniqah* with animal skins for mats but the walls are adorned with portraits of the black gods—Noble Drew Ali, Master Fard Muhammad, the Honorable Elijah Muhammad, Malcolm X, Minister Farrakhan, Allah the former Clarence 13X—and Nubian Islamic Hebrew paintings of black Ali with his double-bladed sword and black Fatima in white *niqab* with their Nubian babies Hasan and Husayn. Maybe a pair of crossed axes and the Universal Flag.

The doctor studies what he sees, the parts of me that I can't see, adjusting the brightness, contrast, and resolution of the picture. He can push a button and make the camera on the tip move independently of the tube. I can't feel if it's moving or not. My fists are still clenched, ankles still locked. I want to cry, and I really want to jump up off the table, but that could make things worse— should I beg the doctor to pull out? Would he? At this moment, am I capable of speech? He says words with a reassuring tone, but they're not registering as words. What is he doing? How long can this take? Back to Patmos. They've almost completed the pyramid, reverently kissing each holy log as they place it. When the pyramid's done, they'll drape it in a black-and-gold veil just like the Ka'ba, very Nuwaubian, but I see that there's still one log missing—and that's when I turn sideways in midair and gravitate horizontally toward the empty spot, all of these phallocentric Orientalists coming around and putting their hands on my body to make sure it fits right, because the missing log is *me* . . .

### . THE SEAL OF MUSLIM PSEUDO .

"The worst is over," the doctor says. "Just twenty seconds or so." I can't tell the worst from any other part of this experience, but at least twenty seconds is measurable. He pulls out and I can feel that he's out, but I still ask anyway. "I'm out," he says. "You did great."

"Should I go to the bathroom?" He has left his water inside me.

"Sure, you *have* to. Just to warn you, it's gonna hurt for a while, and you might see a little blood, but it'll get back to normal."

Hunched over, the Seal of Muslim Pseudo dips into the adjacent bathroom and closes the door. The Seal of Muslim Pseudo's genitals and surrounding area are covered in yellowish-brownish gunk. You know those commercials about the mistreated animals, where the sad abused dogs and cats look straight into the camera and break your heart? My penis looks at me that way. I lift the seat and lean over the toilet, bracing myself against the wall. The initial burst feels like I'm pissing thumbtacks, but then it flows without my feeling anything at all—I wouldn't even know unless I was watching. It comes in starts and stops and each time it starts again, it hurts. There's also a gob of clear gel that oozes out like post-ejaculate; I squeeze it from myself like I'm a tube of toothpaste.

The Seal of Muslim Pseudo goes back and sits on the table and the doctor returns to say that nothing's wrong, no stricture of the urethra. "Your path is open," he tells me. It must be a small bladder and whatever psychological hang-ups I've piled onto myself, like I was told years earlier: *All that piss is in your head.* Just know that caffeine and alcohol aren't your friends, he says, and then I'm good to go.

The rain's coming hard outside and I try to hold my broken penis without looking like I'm holding it. The stargate hurts and the rest is numb. Because of the downpour, it feels like I could be pissing my pants as I head down the street, but there's no way to tell. Even if doused in urine, the Seal of Muslim Pseudo is still better off than a lot of the guys on Patmos, because I'm not wearing a tinfoil fez and I can always walk away from the island and swim home. Allah says to be among the thankful.

# Acknowledgments

Peace to Denise Oswald and Anne Horowitz at Soft Skull Press, and Laura Mazer, Luke Gerwe, Kelly Winton, and everyone at Counterpoint. Peace to Phyllis Wender, Susan Cohen, Allison Cohen, and everyone at Gersh Agency.

Peace to Mahdi Tourage, author of *Rumi and the Hermeneutics of Eroticism.*

Peace to the Five Percenters, the Moorish Orthodox Church, the Nimatullahi Sufi Order, and the Moorish Gonzo Cipher. Peace to my friends who were with me through some strange times.

Peace to Azreal.

Peace to Peter Lamborn Wilson.

Peace to my father, Wesley Calvin Unger (1938–2010), and my aunt, Naomi Ruth Stewart (1939–2010).

## About the Author

**Michael Muhammad Knight** is a novelist, essayist, and journalist. He converted to Islam at 16 after reading *The Autobiography of Malcolm X*, and traveled to Islamabad at age 17 to study at a madrasah. His books include *The Taqwacores, Blue-Eyed Devil, Impossible Man, Osama Van Halen, and Journey to the End of Islam.*

Printed in the United States
by Baker & Taylor Publisher Services